THE ALASKA BUSH PILOT CHRONICLES

More adventures and misadventures from the Big Empty

THE ALASKA BUSH PILOT CHRONICLES

More adventures and misadventures from the Big Empty

by Mort D. Mason

Voyageur Press

First published in 2009 by Voyageur Press, an imprint of MBI Publishing Company, 400 First Avenue North, Suite 300, Minneapolis, MN 55401 USA

Editor: Kari Cornell
Designer: Elly Rochester
Cover Design: Brian Cornell
Printed in the United States of America

Library of Congress Cataloging-in-Publication Data

Mason, Mort D., 1931–
The Alaska bush pilot chronicles : more adventures and misadventures from the Big Empty / Mort Mason.
p. cm.
ISBN 978-0-7603-3433-1 (hb w/ jkt)
1. Mason, Mort D., 1931– 2. Bush flying—Alaska. 3. Bush pilots—Alaska. 4. Alaska—Description and travel. I. Title.
TL540.M36737A3 2009
629.13092—dc22

2008025388

On the front cover:

Main image: Author takes off in his Cessna 206 floatplane from Shadow Lake, high in the Talkeetna Mountains, about one hundred miles north of Anchorage. *Photo by John Erskine, Anchorage, Alaska*

Inset image, left: A De Havilland Beaver with an outlandish external load. These loads are commonplace in the Alaska bush, though certainly not legal according to the Federal Aviation Administration regulations.

Inset image, center: The author holds the world's largest moose trophy to be taken with a handgun up to that time. Al Goerg took this photo on a volcanic lava cinder bed above Meshik River near Port Heiden. See "The Al Goerg Story" in *Outdoor Life Magazine*, May 1968. *Photo by Al Goerg*

Inset image, right: A Rust's Flying Service float-equipped De Havilland Beaver flies over a flowing river of ice in the rugged Alaska Range. *Photo courtesy of Todd Rusk, Rusk's Air Service, Lake Hood, Anchorage, Alaska*

Acknowledgments

I happily acknowledge my wife's unfailing support, encouragement, and inexhaustible proofreading efforts, often carried to the point that her gorgeous blue eyes were about to fall out.

I would be remiss if I didn't acknowledge the ministrations and guidance of Michael Dregni, my publisher's Number One, who encouraged this sequel to *Flying the Alaska Wild* even before pencil was first put to paper on it; and to my forever patient, encouraging, and most helpful favorite editor, Kari Cornell, without whom I would truly be lost.

I want to give special thanks to Jules Tepper, incredible outback pilot in New Zealand, for having allowed me to include two of his white-knuckle flights between the covers of this book. Thanks, too, must go to Eric Dorondo, for letting me include in this book the tale of his very, very short flight in a loaded Cessna 150. My profound gratitude for his contribution to this book has to go to Phil, whose last name must forever remain unspoken, as he wishes to avoid the ribbing of his fellow pilots.

Finally, my sincere thanks go to Todd Rust, who carries on the fine Alaska outback flying tradition of his father, Hank, for allowing our use of some of his great color photographs.

Dedication

To the memory of my parents, Donald and Irene Mason, who successfully ushered me through my childhood and teenage years, probably with no little exasperation—and to my wife, Peggy, who has successfully ushered me through the last few decades of my adult life, clearly with a plethora of justified exasperation. To my children, who suffered through decades of their father's flying. With great sadness, to the memory of Andrew J. "Bear" Piekarski, rugged outdoorsman, lodge owner, and frequent flying companion, taken in his prime by one careless moment and Alaska's unforgiving elements. Finally, to all the superb pilots of the QB, those gone west as well as those still with us, almost all of whom were, and are, better pilots than I—Burro.

Table of Contents

The author carefully cleans the windshield of his Bigfoot Super Cub. A special cleaning agent is used to prevent scratching of the soft Plexiglas windshield—a scratched windshield would make landing on tight bush strips and into the morning or afternoon sun extremely hazardous. *Photo by John Erskine, Anchorage, Alaska*

Introduction

If you're not living on the edge, you're taking up too much room.

I should admit to you here and now that I never was a real crackerjack airplane driver. I did pay a lot of attention to preventive maintenance, though. You might say that I was very careful about it. On the other hand, you *could* say I was scared to death that something bad might happen while I was way up there off the ground. Either way, I paid close attention to the maintenance part of flying on the edge. And while it cost me a few bucks along the way, I've never cried over money spent for good maintenance. Notice that I said *good* maintenance.

I wasn't a natural pilot, either, and there weren't a lot of good flying instruction books around in those days. At the time that I took the written portion of the private pilot's exam, there were only about fifty simple questions—primarily having to do with stuff like light-gun signals from the control tower, or those flashing beacons once used for nighttime cross-country flying that are, for the most part, no longer available. I took my written exam during a short lunch break from my daytime job at Chugach Electric, the local Rural Electrification Association (REA), in Anchorage, Alaska.

The flight portion of that test was a different bucket of worms in those days, too. For example, full stalls, spins, and serious forward- and side-slips were required back then. The budding pilot could be a little sloppy and get away with it, though. A two-turn spin in each direction was required, but the aspiring airman had only to come out within ten degrees of a predetermined heading in order to pass his or her private pilot flight exam with flying colors. We knew that spins to the left were more easily accomplished, and more accurately stopped, than were spins to the right, but most of us had practiced enough of them to be at least ten-degrees accurate in either direction. And, most of us thought spins were fun—they were and they still are.

To give you an example of how far my own ground training and book study went, I had only started my first climbing turn after takeoff during my private pilot flight test when my examiner asked what I thought the rudder was used for, and I replied that it helped to turn the airplane. His response was, "Take me back!"

He was patient, though, and he must have taken some pity on me, for he allowed me to complete the test. He did, however, hasten to tell me that the rudder was put back there to overcome the drag created by the ailerons when the pilot raised or lowered a wing to begin a turn. Or at any other time a pilot changed the position of an aileron, for that matter.

I had some trouble, too, in trying to understand that power controlled altitude rather than air speed, and that the stick controlled air speed rather than altitude. Hell, I could see that someone had it all backward: the power controlled air speed and the elevators controlled altitude, clearly.

My touch-and-go's were satisfactory to him, but my stalls just about scared him shitless! I had determined that the best way to pass this flight test was to be positive with all my control inputs. So, when the examiner finally asked me for a power-on stall, I just pulled the nose up—w-a-a-a-y up—and waited for the coming shudder and falloff.

He took the airplane away from me and shouted that I had just scared him out of ten years' growth! "Gimme the airplane," he said. By then I was shuddering like skis on rough ice.

He pulled the little beast up into a full hammerhead stall, which scared the hell out of me! He proceeded to enlighten me about the joys of tail slides and their guaranteed come-apart results on little fabric-covered airplanes such as the 65-horsepower Aeronca Champion in which we were then staggering and flapping along. By the time he was finished with that little explanation, I was shaking like a sled dog passing peach pits.

My forward slips and side-slips helped save my bacon that day, I think. I could ace those maneuvers all day long, regardless of aircraft type, load, or wind conditions. And I had practiced so many spins by that time that I could easily stop one—in either direction—within five degrees of a predetermined heading, and in almost any kind of light aircraft, with or without turbulence or heavy winds.

My emergency landing techniques were pretty good, too. I have to say, though, that these techniques were carried to the extreme in those days in Alaska, and almost any kid with more than four hours' dual instruction could safely dead-stick a light aircraft to a safe landing almost anywhere he or she wanted to put it. We didn't know anything at all about radio procedures, but we could sure as hell fly airplanes! Anyway, I got my ticket that day, and by the time I had completed that check ride, I had learned more about flying than in all my previous hours of dual and solo flight put together.

You should probably know that things were much different in many ways, in those interim days of flying. We weren't far beyond the days of the rugged airmail pilots and their barnstorming brethren. This was especially true of flying in Alaska. There were almost no tricycle-geared airplanes there, probably because there were so very few airports or airstrips. We sort of grew up on sandbars, beaches, and gravel bars. The bolder ones among us also used mountain ridges or slopes, glaciers, and, if the tires were big enough, even the tundra. Except for the more expensive light aircraft, radios were a rarity. For that reason, most light aircraft in Alaska didn't have generators and, as a result, few had starters. Most were "hand-propped," an art that seems pretty much lost today. A few aircraft boasted exterior wind-driven generators, but these were considered by many to be too dangerous to be worth the risk. Should the rapidly spinning little propeller ever get loose, it could cut through the cockpit of a small airplane like a knife through hot butter. Almost everything we knew about light aircraft flying was different, I guess.

We didn't have to ask for the tower's permission to taxi out from the tiedown areas in those early days, but we all knew where we were supposed to go in order to warm up our little ships. When we were ready, we knew just to spin the plane around in a tight little circle, finish at a position of forty-five degrees to the tower, and await the light signal that would clear our aircraft to the active runway. We could tell from the wind tetrahedron or windsock which runway was in use.

If we got a steady green light from the tower, we would bang the ailerons up and down a few times to acknowledge receipt of the signal, then taxi to the active. If the tower hadn't seen us yet, we'd spin around in that angry little circle again, hoping to attract someone's attention.

Light signals were the fashion in landing operations, too, and even though Merrill Field in Anchorage, Alaska, was at that time busier than LaGuardia in New York, all went well in those days. Light signals had neither language nor dialect, so the tower could be clearly understood no matter what the pilot's background. Even with ten or twelve small aircraft in the traffic pattern—which was only six-hundred feet above the runway—everyone paid close attention. There were no air-to-air problems, and virtually none on the runway. Some days, though, waiting for a runway for takeoff was an exercise in patience. It really was a busy airport. And it still is.

We all knew to leave the pattern at forty-five degrees from the downwind leg and in a climb. And we knew to enter on a forty-five to the downwind and at pattern altitude. We all knew how to get our little planes into and out of the pattern safely. And properly!

We knew, too, how to hit a precise spot during our landings so no one seemed to take more than his share of runway time. Since spot landings were taught from the very first hour of flight, almost every Alaska pilot in those days could plop his plane's tail wheel atop a hat placed on the runway. Hell, we thought every pilot could do that! I've since learned that's not the case.

I've watched Citabrias and two-place Cessna trainers take up better than four thousand feet of a five-thousand-foot runway. Today's pilots seem just to get close to the runway and then let the airplane carry them along until it finally just quits flying. It doesn't surprise me that so few seem to survive the most routine of off-airport landings these days.

In Florida, where I live now, it isn't at all unusual to read about a Cessna or a Piper single-engine model that "crash-landed" on a golf course, killing three or four. My goodness! In Alaska, we'd have given most of our dogs and half our kids for something as wonderful as a golf course to use as an emergency landing area! We were stuck with beaches, trees, mountain ridges, creek beds, cold swamps, glaciers, and river sandbars or gravel bars. Here in Florida, with its uninterrupted sand beach, broad north-south highways, and no less than a gazillion golf courses, we still have our share of airplane crashes and terminated lives. Alaska pilots just don't understand this, and we never will.

The local paper from three days ago featured a Piper six-place Cherokee that was forced to abandon flight and look for a place to land. The pilot, a long-time Florida pilot, elected to try to stretch his glide to make a local airport. He didn't quite make it. In spite of the fact that he was within gliding distance of several golf courses, Florida's Turnpike, the beach at the Atlantic Ocean, and Interstate Highway 95, he put the little tin Piper into the only patch of standing trees within gliding distance. Both he and his wife of many years perished in the crash. On today's TV news, I watched some footage of a Cessna 206 that was forced to make a dead-stick landing beside a baseball park in Anchorage, Alaska. With an available landing distance of less than five hundred feet, the pilot of the loaded, 4,000-pound airplane—which carried the pilot and three passengers—elected to land and ground-loop the plane in this little back yard. No one aboard was injured. Faced with the same situation, I doubt that most stateside pilots would have done such a good job of it. I suspect that most stateside pilots wouldn't have considered trying to land on a spot only five hundred feet long in the first place!

Some of Alaska's pilots routinely operate on floats while flying daily to and from the snowfields of high mountain glaciers. Others use wintertime skis to operate off mud flats somewhere along the coastal regions. Of course it's not impossible to operate from water when flying on skis, though, when landing, the pilot is well advised to be in no more than six or eight inches of water before his forward momentum comes to a halt. It is certainly possible to operate on floats from Alaska's many snow-covered glaciers, and it is routinely done by some Alaska pilots.

All this shouldn't lead you to believe that Alaska's wilderness pilots walk on water or leap tall buildings at a single bound. Only a very few are up to that. Most of us just learned to do it a little differently than those pilots from the Lower 48. And not all our flights turned out to be what we were expecting when we left the ground earlier in the day.

Like its predecessor, this book tries to bring some little understanding of what it's like to fly on the other side of the tracks. Alaska's outback pilots aren't really fascinated with flying the "big iron" of our scheduled airlines. Many of them see the life of an airline pilot as just one long bus run. It isn't, of course, but neither is it expected to put the pilot on the edge of the seat during almost every flight. This book, then, tries to take the reader off the beaten path just a little, sharing some of my experiences as well as those of a few others.

What you read in this book is just a mirror held before some of my own past flights. Along the way, I've also included a few stories of flights performed by others. I've tried to keep things in chronological order so you can see that, while I gained experience along the way, I guess I sometimes didn't profit enough from it.

Well, perhaps I'll get a little smarter as I go along.

Flying itself is not inherently dangerous,

but, like the sea, it can be terribly unforgiving.

As can the Alaska wilderness.

Combined—the two can boggle the mind.

Chapter 1

Your First Alaska Bush Flight

THE ONLY TIME YOU HAVE TOO MUCH FUEL ABOARD IS WHEN THE AIRPLANE IS ON FIRE.

There is more truth than fiction to the following brief description of Alaska bush flights. While this short, and hopefully humorous, chapter was admittedly written with tongue planted firmly in cheek, it is nonetheless disturbingly close to the bone. For those of you looking forward to your first such flight, I suggest you fasten your seat belts before reading any further.

Prior to leaping happily into the passenger seat of that little airplane for your first Alaska bush flight to one of the state's more remote areas—and before your keen-eyed bush pilot carries you aloft for this exhilarating experience—there are a few things you really should know. For example, it is very likely that you have been contaminated by a previous environment. Your idea of flight might include shiny new airplanes and squeaky-clean general aviation air terminal facilities. Maybe even parking ramp attendants. Or somebody else to put gas in the little thing for the pilot. Probably a coffee shop with cute little long-haired waitresses. You won't find any of that up here.

I presume by your enthusiasm that this will be your first bush flight, since almost no one that I know ever got very excited about being a repeat bush passenger. The human psyche can only tolerate so much of a good thing, and one bush flight usually provides enough exhilaration and excitement to last a lifetime.

A De Havilland Beaver with an outlandish external load. These loads are commonplace in the Alaska bush, though certainly not legal according to the Federal Aviation Administration regulations.

A word should be said here about the appearance of that very special heavier-than-air-machine that will carry you to your Alaska wilderness destination. It will certainly be like no other light aircraft you have ever seen.

First of all, it won't be sparkling clean and brightly waxed. It probably won't have a front wheel either. That third roller will very likely be a little bitty devil way back there under the rock-dented tail section. That's where your bush pilot thinks it should be, contemporary three-legged aircraft design notwithstanding. If he should land in a really soft place, he doesn't want to break off an expensive nose gear assembly just before the airplane flops over onto its back. He has very likely performed this particular maneuver several times by now and no doubt considers himself something of an expert in the matter of inverted parking techniques.

The exterior paint will probably be faded, chipped, or flaked—perhaps even missing entirely—but do not be put off by the plane's shoddy appearance. To your pilot, paint only means added weight. He really wishes the rest of it would hurry up and fall off anyway. That would increase his available payload by several pounds. Famed bush pilot Don Sheldon thought the increase might be by as much as eighty pounds. Remember, an increased payload capability is the bush pilot's Holy Grail.

Unless the airplane is mounted on floats or skis, you will notice that the tires are much too big for the small plane that wears them. Your pilot is not accustomed to operating from smooth gravel airstrips, paved runways, or other such hard surfaces. That knowledge, in turn, should prepare you for what's to come.

No doubt you will also notice things hanging from, or otherwise affixed to, the exterior of this small airship—things like moose horns, snowshoes, or building materials. If the aircraft is or ever has been mounted on pontoons (your pilot will refer to them as "floats," and you should, too; pontoons are for bridges), you will find strings or ropes—called "lines" in the aeronautical environment—either suspended from the outboard wing struts, lashed to the front float davits, or hanging somehow from the tail end of the airplane. Don't ask your pilot what these lines are for, since you certainly won't get a straight answer from him. He would probably try to convince you that these appendages are (a) static discharge wicks, (b) hang lines for sky divers, (c) air speed indicators, or (d) any number of other things. Actually, they are used only for ground handling and tiedown purposes. It's just too much trouble for your pilot to remove them before each flight. He will probably need one or more of them at his next landing anyway. He places his faith in their assignment to keep his spirited little ship from wandering away while it is tied down during his absence.

Do not be alarmed if these lines flop and flap loudly about as you later fly along. The thumping and banging will bring a certain calming rhythm to your flight and keep your pilot alert (or at least keep him awake).

In the event you have heard the term "Alaska Mods" (modifications to the airplane), for Pete's sake don't question your pilot about such things! His response would only alarm you needlessly. These airframe modifications are designed to strengthen one part or another of an airplane for the sole purpose of somehow holding it together during that period between rough takeoffs and subsequent rough landings. This is the "flight phase," for those of you who insist upon accuracy in the little details. The old adage that an airplane is nothing more than a collection of spare parts flying in close formation is certainly true of the Alaska bush plane. To learn that your pilot nonchalantly anticipates this airframe abuse may leave you a little unsettled. Up to this point, you were expecting your Alaska bush takeoffs and landings to be feather light and petroleum smooth. Your pilot knows better, of course. So should you.

Even the carefully paved runways of larger airports will not be smooth for the Alaska bush pilot. He is so accustomed to landing on any surface that appears to him as even slightly out of plumb—that is, less than perfectly vertical—that he sees no challenge whatsoever in paved runway operations. His inattention to approaches and landings at controlled airports will be so complete as to leave you believing that each of his airport landings has been only slightly more successful than a controlled crash.

Alaska modifications, beyond oversized tires and wheels, may include beefed up landing gears, beefed up horizontal stabilizers, oversized and beefed up tail wheel assemblies, and so forth. Notice all that beefing up? There is a message there, too.

A favorite Alaska mod is the extended baggage compartment. This only means that the baggage compartment has been increased in length by moving the headliner (the back wall, you know?) rearward to provide a greater storage area. In a Piper Cub, for example, a placard marks this baggage area, proclaiming MAXIMUM BAGGAGE 50 POUNDS. Most Alaska pilots agree that Mr. Piper somehow dropped a digit in this number. They know from experience that this fifty-pound limit is not to be trusted, and so they routinely ignore the little placard's advice in a universally accepted support of their flying activities.

Your pilot may be a skilled airplane driver, but he probably is not a skilled mathematician. Certainly he does not understand the niceties of calculating from percentages and decimals. He has read FAR (Federal Aviation Regulations) 91.38(2) but believes the number "115" found therein should be multiplied against the fifty-pound figure from the baggage area placard to determine the correct baggage weight limit. When he got an answer of 5,750 pounds, and in the certain knowledge that a "zero" doesn't mean anything anyway, he simply dropped the last digit. Without a doubt he will try to load 575 pounds into that baggage compartment at every opportunity. He knows that the government formulated this Federal Aviation Regulation in a shocking display of exasperated surrender when it finally dawned on them that Alaska pilots, in spite of everything, were going to load into their little airplanes anything that wasn't already rooted in the ground, bolted down, welded in place, or actively aflame.

Besides, the experienced bush pilot will occasionally cram an additional passenger or two back there, and the smaller original baggage compartment did not allow stowage of such bulk. An extended baggage area, however, will. Your pilot favors that modification for this reason if for no other. Your pilot finds no need for seat belts in this rear compartment, since passengers or freight crammed into that small space will be so tightly packed that nothing can bounce around much back there anyhow.

He also thinks it's no trick at all to put one moose or two full caribou bulls inside a Super Cub. The horns, because of their bulk, are usually tied outside to the wing struts or float braces, where they are pretty much out of the pilot's way. Of course these horns interfere dramatically with the aerodynamics of this small flying machine, but that doesn't seem to bother the pilot at all.

If your vacation trip includes a bush flight in one of Alaska's many floatplanes, you are really in for a thrill. Don't be alarmed if you notice your pilot forcing sixty pounds of gear into each twenty-pound-limit float storage locker, by the way. These specially modified float compartments are designed to carry a little of the stuff that the pilot can't otherwise cram inside his small craft. The pilot has every confidence that the float manufacturer, whether it was Edo, P-K, Wipline, or another, has surely miscalculated the load-carrying capabilities of the product, and he puts everything in there that will fit. The gear stowed in a floatplane's float lockers will all get wet, by the way, so make sure your pilot doesn't load any expensive camera equipment here.

When taxiing away from the dock or beach, note how your pilot looks very casually aft over his left shoulder. Recall that he didn't involve himself in any complicated weight-and-balance calculations before leaving the docking or beach area? It isn't that he overlooked that little chore. It's more likely that long ago he forgot how to perform such complex and advanced mathematical calculations. He has by now set the throttle at 1,000 rpm and is checking the heel of his left float. If it is not completely submerged, which would be an indication that the airplane may even then be sinking in place, your pilot knows that the aircraft will probably take off. If it doesn't become airborne after two or three serious takeoff attempts, the pilot will simply stop, offload a six-pack of your favorite beverage, and then try it again. Usually, removing the six-pack sufficiently reduces the weight, and you will soon be winging your way to your first Alaska bush adventure.

Do not be too eager to help your pilot load his airplane before takeoff, by the way. While he long ago dispensed with any formal weight-and-balance calculations, he is still most particular about what goes where in and on his little aircraft. He can pretty closely estimate the relative weight of any given piece of freight or baggage that he puts into his little ship. Although he won't know exactly how many pounds anything really weighs, he will know which items are heaviest. He will always want these loaded toward the front, even though the recesses of his mind hold the vague recollection that this may, in some cases, move the center of gravity forward so far as to place things outside the gravity envelope of his little aircraft. Unlike so many teamsters today, he is more than happy to load his own vehicle.

If this is to be your very first floatplane ride, the takeoff will most likely scare the hell out of you. At your pilot's first application of full power, your forward view will immediately change to reveal only a picture of the sky above. The pilot has also pulled the control stick or wheel fully back, and the float bows have risen dramatically. Don't be alarmed at this turn of events. Your pilot can't see anything either. Still, if he succeeded in pointing his aircraft more or less in the right direction before he added that takeoff power, chances are pretty good that he won't bump into anything big right away. If all has gone well up to this point, the aircraft will soon tip forward and settle down to a more or less level attitude. You are now skimming smoothly across the water at about forty miles an hour. On a calm day, that is. On a windy day, you will now be bouncing and banging along fit to fracture your dentures. In this planing attitude, which your pilot refers to as "being on the step," your forward visibility will once again be somewhere between fair to good, depending upon where you are seated within the airplane. You won't see much at all if you're stashed back there with the suitcases and sleeping bags.

I won't go into the maneuver known as the "step turn." To do so would mean trying to explain centrifugal force, horizontal wind loads, the tendency of the outside float to dig in, general overturning tendencies, and what will happen to you if one wingtip should ever hit the water at this speed. You wouldn't get within five miles of a floatplane after reading all that.

Almost every Alaska flying adventure will take you into, over, or through a mountain range of some sort. You will hear such names as Merrill, Windy, Rainy, Portage, Lake Clark, and Chickaloon. These are mountain passes—low altitude routes through all those big rocks you know are piled up pretty high just ahead of you somewhere. You may have formed a mental picture of these mountain passes already. You know: wide, green valleys dotted with standing spruce, dainty white birch, majestic cottonwoods, lush alders, sparkling blue lakes . . . ? Well, I must tell you, that picture is all wrong. Most of these passes will be narrow, scary little devils. Several of Alaska's more frequently used passes—Lake Clark or Merrill, for example—have at least one ninety-degree turn hidden somewhere inside. Others, such as an unnamed pass leading to Purkeypile, have more, of course. Certainly places like Shellabarger or Mystic Pass couldn't be called scenic.

To the new passenger, many of these passes will not appear to be wide enough to accommodate both of the airplane's wings at the same time. But, not to worry! Air is just air, whether your left wingtip is ten miles or only ten feet from the face of solid rock, and usually your pilot will not abuse you by bumping into anything while flying. Remember, too, that he is always in the front seat. He knows full well that he is destined to be the first at the scene of any mishap. He will try to avoid that at any cost.

If you are an amateur photographer or a sightseer, you will very likely not experience real bush landings. Hunters and fishermen, on the other hand, certainly will. Unless your first bush landing in a wheel-equipped airplane occurs on a long, broad, sandy stretch of quiet beach, you may find yourself growing somewhat apprehensive during the final approach phase of this first landing.

To begin with, you will be unable to see anything that in any way resembles a landing strip capable of accepting your hurtling little airplane. No blacktop runway, no control tower, no windsock, no other airplanes—not even tire tracks. Sometimes, in fact, not even much of a clearing between the trees. You will simply have to trust your pilot's choice of landing areas. After the second such landing, your faith and confidence in him will be paramount and virtually unshakable. You will swear that he can safely land in—and take off again from—the top of a tall cottonwood tree. I should tell you that he cannot, so please do not encourage this maneuver.

Since outback landings are frequently confusing to the new bush passenger, it is not unusual that such maneuvers are accompanied by a greater or lesser degree of passenger disorientation. It is for this reason that your pilot does not want you to exit the airplane until it has come to a complete stop, he has shut down the engine, and the propeller has stopped turning. Please follow this sound advice. Alaska pilots will only rarely ask a passenger to deplane while the airplane is in cruise flight.

The propeller, by the way, is referred to by some of Alaska's bush pilots as the "fan." It is this important implement that keeps your pilot cool, although this is not its only function. Still, as long as it keeps turning around and around really fast, the cooling effect upon your pilot cannot be denied. It is said that a pilot may tend to "lose his cool" if this fan should stop going around and around during flight.

The departure from your remote bush location will be even more enlightening to you than was the landing. Just remember that unless your aircraft is mounted on floats, your takeoff will be more easily accomplished than was the landing, since a longer ground roll is usually required to land. Keeping this in mind would be a good idea as you peer nervously through the windshield prior to takeoff. Your perspective will convince you that you are already at the far end of the takeoff area, even though your pilot has not yet started the engine. Certainly your "airport" will be a small one.

It would be a good idea for you to ask your pilot how long he has lived and flown in Alaska before you entrust your care, custody, and control to his flying and navigational skills. If he is just up from California for the summer season, you might want to recall a previously scheduled appointment that you dare not break before climbing aboard the plane.

Stateside pilots seem to favor good flying weather, while dyed-in-the-wool Alaska bush pilots prefer something less sunny and bright. It's easier on the eyes, I suppose. Don't be put off if your Alaska pilot is ready to take you aloft even though the ducks and geese are walking. On the other hand, there are definitely some practical weather limitations to safe bush flight. If you've observed small groups of ducks and geese standing huddled together on a street corner, obviously waiting for the next bus, you might want to reschedule your flight for another day.

While your pilot certainly has a good pair of sunglasses—usually a pair of Bausch & Lomb Ray-Bans strapped to his belt in a leather case that is so worn the metal lining is showing through in several places—he tries to avoid really sunny days. He isn't used to flying in good weather. You have only to remember that government offices in Juneau, Alaska, the state capital, have been known to close when sunny weather has been forecast for two consecutive days.

First of all, the air is often bumpier on clear days. Your pilot knows all about adiabatic lapse rates and unstable air masses, of course, and he can certainly handle all those little bumps. But more importantly, clear weather makes his passengers want to fly a little higher than those altitudes at which the bush pilot is most comfortable. His world loses a lot of its familiarity at two thousand or six thousand or ten thousand feet. It is quite possible for him to (a) get caught up in the panoramic grandeur of it all and lose his concentration, (b) get a nosebleed, thereby distracting his passengers, or (c) become noticeably disoriented, seriously confused, or even completely lost, with the disappearance of his familiar low-level landmarks. His world from up there looks entirely different than it does from down there between sixty and two hundred feet. If you convince him to fly above these altitudes, you would do well to follow along, on your own map, with the plane's progress over the ground. Your pilot may even turn to you for directional assistance at these rarified altitudes.

Your bush pilot is a dedicated and hard-working professional. Each and every one of his efforts is made with your personal comfort, safety, convenience, and enjoyment in mind. His legal responsibilities are for your health, safety, and welfare, but this phrase may paint a rather grim picture for the first-time bush passenger (which is why I have avoided using it up to this point).

Your pilot's work days frequently begin before sunup and often extend well into the hours of darkness. It is only natural to expect him to sit back, prop his feet atop a comfortable footstool, and relax during the slower winter months. He will doubtless even enjoy a warm brandy or two on those evenings when winter storms hurl themselves against his snug but modest Alaska home.

And, while a few of Alaska's professional backcountry pilots will occasionally take a sip or two during the ice-out months, I can say in all honesty that I have seen very few dedicated Alaska bush pilots tippling on short final. You will find them safe and conscientious pilots, dedicated to making your first Alaska bush flight as memorable as possible. And I can assure you that it will be.

Chapter 2

Who Are These Guys?

Learn from the mistakes of others. You won't live long enough to make them all yourself.

Who are those guys who elect to spend their working days—and lots of their working nights—banging around up there in the murk, flirting with unfriendly mountains, crevasse-loaded glaciers, squirrelly winds, the world's absolute worst visibility, and an almost endless string of don't-go-there landing spots?

I mean, to talk with any of them, you wouldn't walk away thinking they were necessarily mentally deficient. They speak clearly—well, most of them do, anyway—and most seem to have at least a modicum of intelligence. No matter his or her appearance. (And, yes, Alaska does have some pretty foxy chicks flying the backcountry, too.) Some of these outback pilots seem to be unable, with any noticeable frequency, to visit suitable bathing facilities. And there are some who, for the most part, must be actively provoked into anything resembling true and meaningful conversation.

Since a large part of Alaska bush flying is done with floatplanes, most of the outback pilots wear hip boots and, more often than not, their favorite articles of raingear. You should understand that, while many bush flights are conducted with dry-land-type, wheeled aircraft, the ground out there in the wilderness is almost always wet. And I mean wet to the knees, not just downtown Chicago sidewalk damp. So, floatplane or not, hip boots are the predominant footwear.

Remember back when you were in high school? Then you will certainly recall your school's football and basketball teams. Well, your handsome high school jocks were involved in "team sports" when playing basketball or football. Baseball, too, unless the guy happened to be either the pitcher or the catcher.

Those two positions left their occupants with a feeling of the Alpha male, not an accepted feeling for those who were actually part of the "team." That is to say, the infielders and outfielders. The pitcher and the catcher were really pretty much on their own, sort of solo performers, even though each was a part of the overall team, and each had to interface with the others.

The same is true of the track team, I suppose. The high jumper or broad jumper and pole vaulter or shot putter—in fact almost every member of the track and field "team"—were little more than solo performers within a gaggle of solo performers. So it was, too, with the swimmers and springboard and platform divers. Solo performers. They preferred it that way, though they probably didn't realize it at the time. My guess is that it was simply their nature to be "loners" in their athletic pursuits.

What they may have been doing, if my guess is correct, was setting themselves up in positions that would clearly give them credit for their individual accomplishments and would punish them individually for their failures. Every performance was a personal test, and every accomplishment was a personal win.

None of these "solo" performance athletes, of course, was really a lone wolf. Each had a support team somewhere behind him. The coaches, the trainers—the very uniforms these solo performers wore—were included in the support "teams" behind them. But they were very likely, for the most part anyway, just lukewarm about other student organizations. They weren't really antisocial: they just didn't care all that much about the social side of things at that stage of their lives.

If they grew up west of the Ohio River outside any of the larger cities found there, they were no doubt also experienced hunters, trappers, and fishermen by the time their academic pursuits welcomed them into the higher grades. And neither hunting, trapping, nor fishing requires a "team" effort. Quite the contrary, in fact. If you see a "team" of hunters, you are probably looking at a dedicated group of hard-drinking poker players.

Surely, some of these "loner" characteristics are to be found in those who fly the remote outback, whether in Alaska, Canada, Africa, Switzerland, South America, Australia, or New Zealand. And, believe me, there is still plenty of "outback" left on the surface of our globe. Areas just too remote and too tough to be tamed and cultivated or successfully built upon. I think it will be many more decades before roads are built into most of those low- or no-population wilderness areas.

There are other "loners," though, who choose to live in these remote areas—for all intents and purposes, living off the land. And, for the most part, even these hardy folks need at least a dab of support in order to make it at all out there. It's another "loner," the bush pilot, who provides a lot of this necessary support.

Let's see just what a "loner" is in this instance. As an example, presume the pilot has flown the bush in Alaska for something like ten thousand hours. Not really a whole lot, to some of these longtime outback pilots.

The clear majority of these hours represent time spent flying supplies, medicines, or grub and building materials from some city or town to the remote wilderness dweller, and most often flying back with an empty airplane. Either way, the driver was most likely the only living person in the airplane.

The Alaska bush pilot doesn't usually bother with picking up much in the way of altitude for his routine flights, even in the state's incredibly mountainous geography. Most of his flights occur down there between two hundred and two thousand feet. Radio reception is not at its best down there, so much of his time is spent with only the roar of his airplane's engine for company. But, not to worry: he prefers it that way.

As to his personal comfort, not many light aircraft are really all that luxurious. The Cessna 206 and 185 models are somewhat more comfortable, as is the Cessna 180. De Havilland's Beaver isn't bad, either. But a whole lot of those hours will be racked up from the front seat of something like Piper's little Super Cub. With its widest part—at the very front of the pilot's seat—measuring only twenty-four inches, his world is indeed a small and very personal one.

Now, take those ten thousand flying hours and convert it to work time for the typical American office worker. Roughly speaking, the ten-thousand-hour pilot has spent the equivalent of very nearly five years of forty-hour work weeks strapped down to the small and uncomfortable seat in his tiny and very noisy office. On top of that, he has no doubt loved about every minute of it! For my own part, and after almost twenty thousand of those hours, I came to dread only the smooth and sunny days that most weekend pilots seem to pray for. Speak of absolute boredom, that's it! Reduced visibility, a smattering of turbulence, and no current weather forecast for my destination—aaahhhh! That's better!

Now ask the office worker, whether secretary or upper management, how he or she would like to spend the next five years strapped into the chair they now occupy. No coffee or kitchen breaks, no telephone calls to or from friends, no water cooler chats, and no potty runs. Even in a chair that is certainly more comfortable than a light airplane's front office seat, that scenario would appear terrible to most. Takes something of a "loner" to actually enjoy—indeed thrive on—this sort of self-applied abuse.

Alaska's outback pilots aren't much for social interaction, but if another pilot is reported to be in some sort of trouble out there somewhere, almost all of us will drop everything to pitch in and help. And, although most such "emergencies" have been the result of some small pilot error—something left undone, an error in judgment, a bad estimate as to fuel quantity required, a blown tire or a damaged float—we're all ready to go to the limit in order to help in some way. Hell, we may never even have met the guy before, but he's "one of us," he's in trouble, and that's reason enough.

We don't make much of it, and we certainly don't spread the news that it might have been a mistake on the other pilot's part in the first place.

I remember way back in the mid-sixties when another pilot and guide flipped his Super Cub over onto its back when trying a short landing in the wrong place. The accident happened near Meshik Bay at Port Heiden, way down there on the Alaska Peninsula and right next door to the remote Aleutian Islands. The incident occurred somewhere around six hundred miles from Anchorage.

The biggest damage was to the greenhouse skylight above the pilot's seat. Well, a Super Cub doesn't perform all that well with its little green skylight smashed out and missing. All that breeze tends to head right back into the fuselage where it slows things down quite a bit. The pilot needed another skylight right away. He had bear hunting clients waiting for him there in Port Heiden, and the world wasn't going to stop turning just because he had been a little careless or sadly unlucky.

I just loaded him aboard my four-place Cessna and flew him the nearly six hundred miles back to Anchorage, where he could buy another lid for his damaged little Cub. Charge him for the flight? Certainly not. It's all just part of the job. Unfortunately, this same pilot later slid backward from a steep snowfield while trying to hold his wheel/ski-mounted Cessna 185 in position with engine power. He was holding so that his last passenger could get out of the powerful airplane. Gravity overcame the power of his Continental 300-horsepower engine, and the airplane finally just slipped backward over a snowy lip and into a crevasse. The pilot was left hanging upside down in his harness—

with a badly broken back—for more than eight hours, it was said. It was the end of both his flying and his guiding career.

To my knowledge, though, there are no social nor fraternal organizations dedicated to a membership of Alaska outback pilots. Certainly there's the Alaska Airmen's Association, a worthwhile group that I heartily support, even though I'm not a member at this time. Alaska's Registered Guides have their Alaska Professional Hunters Association, which I supported as a professional member for many years. But even the wilderness guide is frequently in the company of others. More so, at least, than is the bush pilot. This flier may spend ten hours a day in that cramped little front office, and he may do so for many, many days on end. During the hunting and fishing seasons, he may spend as many as twelve or fourteen hours a day locked into his little flying machine. It's not really legal, according to the Federal Aviation Regulations, but who's to see him out there in all that wilderness and bad weather? Besides, if he won't fly that much, his clients will just find another pilot who will.

Unlike the office worker, he can't just stand up and walk around his desk to relieve either his boredom or his cramped legs and swelling feet. He's bloody well trapped in place. His only relief is his David Clark headset, through which he is no doubt listening to country western music, if the danged radio station isn't too far away. But, would he trade his uncomfortable little prison for any other place on earth? He is quick to tell you that he would, but, in truth, he certainly would not!

His attitude can't be given to a limited intelligence. To get his commercial pilot license, usually with instrument and seaplane (float) ratings tacked on, he had to show more than a little in the way of mathematical skills. He had to learn about weather, navigation, and radio procedures and to master a completely new vocabulary. New phrases like "adiabatic lapse rates," or "standing waves," or "rime ice." "Upslope" and "convection fog," "thermoclines," and "haloclines," too. He had to learn to read the complex and never-ending series of weather maps and charts that he encounters almost daily, and frequently several times a day. He certainly has memorized myriad cloud formations and knows intimately what each formation means to him. When the ATIS (Automated Terminal Information Service) broadcast tells him that "towering Q" is reported "all quads," he has to appreciate what that will mean in the way of turbulence—very likely quite severe near thunderstorms and probably accompanied by heavy rains, lightning, and, possibly, damaging hail. These "thunderheads" can also provide his day with no end of dangerous thermals (updrafts, if you will) if he decides to approach them too closely.

He must know at least enough about his airplane, its powerplant, its systems, and its structures to evaluate any problems he may encounter and to then make temporary bush repairs if something goes south for him while he's far from his mechanic.

And, while he may look pretty casual about loading his airplane with passengers and baggage or freight, he certainly has a firm grasp of the airplane's gravity envelope, of stations fore and aft of datum, and of resultant moments. So, while he or she sometimes appears as part of the great unwashed, neither really is.

Bush pilots are also almost fanatically dedicated to their flying responsibilities. If one of these stalwart characters tells you that he'll meet you at the bend in the Stony River one-quarter mile upstream from the big midriver rock just below the big bend near Lime Village—and to be there at ten o'clock on the morning of August 3—it would be well if you were there to meet his flight. Although he may have made this commitment several months ago, he will nonetheless be there. Weather permitting, of course. And perhaps there's the rub.

The weather system on one side of that mountain ridge over there is very likely different from the weather on the opposite side. So, have a little patience when dealing with one of these guys. He certainly didn't just forget about you. Lots of these pilots will fly in weather that discourages ducks and geese, but there are still limits to what the bush pilot can do. In a no-instrument environment like the Alaska outback, he simply must see *something* to conduct his otherwise seemingly roughshod, casual, and almost limitless flying chores.

***

The Alaska bush pilot prefers to load his own airplane, too, whether the load is groceries, moose meat, caribou horns, an injured hunter, or a dead body, he will be most particular about what goes where in his airplane.

I've said before that these guys appear to throw the light stuff in the back, and the heavier stuff up front. In reality, they are trying to get the loads as near as possible to the center of gravity of their high-performance airplanes.

This isn't always true, since there's little that's quite as disconcerting as a Cessna 206 with only the pilot as an interior load. The aircraft wants to be carrying something, workhorse that it is, and an empty Stationair seems a little nose-heavy in that configuration. An empty Cessna 206 is slightly beyond the plane's trim range, at seriously low air speeds. And the pilot is probably a little on the lazy side, after all is said and done, so he sort of resents having to hold back pressure on the control yoke of this four-thousand-pound (when loaded) airplane during the final approach and landing phases. Once the pilot is seated and strapped in with the engine running, he prefers to ride along with a minimum of outside influences. An empty Stationair is truly an outside influence.

So, who are these guys? They're the pilots who, when the phone rings in the middle of the night, are ready to go. If the caller says, in a weepy and shaky voice, that her husband hasn't returned from his fall moose hunt and is now more than two days overdue, the pilot only asks, "Where did he go?"

Frequently, the answer is, "He said you'd know where he'll be." And the tired pilot agrees that he probably knows where the missing hunter is. Nighttime? Rainy with low clouds? The hunter is camped high in the Talkeetna Mountains? Ah, well. Strap on the hip boots and light out.

Or the wife who calls at midnight to report her husband is overdue on a river float trip from Skwentna. Planned to bring the big river boat across Cook Inlet, with its frigid, silty water and its thirty-nine-foot tides, he did. And to do that in the dark! Sure, I'll go. Strap on the hip boots, fire up the ol' Cessna 206 floatplane, and beat it across Pt. McKenzie, over the Little Susitna River, to begin tracking the Big Su upstream. And then to find the missing husband and his companions were only having a warming drink at the Lake Creek Lodge, comfortable and completely unconcerned over the fact that none of them had tried to contact his wife, ... who is now nearly hysterical with worry.

These are the guys. Drop everything and strap themselves into their tough little flying machines and light out, summer or winter, night or day. They always go. And they almost always come back. *Almost* always . . .

They're the guys who can—and do—build a new vertical stabilizer from old five-gallon avgas cans. And who will patch up torn fabric on a faithful ol' Super Cub with duct tape or wet newspapers just so they can maneuver their little ships back to a maintenance facility.

They're the guys the outback homesteader, trapper, or lodge owner depends upon when the fit hits the shan, as they say. Because they're the guys who can—and who will—make the flight at almost a moment's notice. No schedules, and no excuses.

They're the "bush pilots," whether in Alaska or New Zealand, Canada or South America. Next to Alaska crab fishing, this profession is said to be the second most dangerous in the world. Did we really think so? Naw, but it was good press. Hell, it was just another usually boring job. Admittedly, with a few surprising moments tossed in.

Chapter 3

The Earliest Years

If you push the stick forward, the houses get bigger. If you pull it back, they get smaller. If you pull it all the way back, they will get bigger again.

We have all heard it said that "There are old pilots and there are bold pilots, but there are no old, bold pilots." My own experience has convinced me that this isn't true at all. Especially in Alaska. Unless a pilot carries about him a solid belief in himself and his equipment, and is steady when flying on the edge of performance, he should certainly avoid flying Alaska's backcountry. Except, of course, if the pilot is at altitude, is on airways, is on a filed Instrument Flight Rules (IFR) flight plan, and is comfortably situated between two or more wing-mounted engines. If he is flying behind a single spinning propeller in deteriorating weather far from towns or villages, he is better equipped if he wears a confident personality that borders on the nonchalant (some would even say idiotic or insane). A pilot who is easily distracted does not belong in the Alaska bush. He should also be comfortable in an environment that others see as disarmingly—maybe even distressingly—lonely. The Alaskan outback is surely not lonely, but those lacking intimate association with its limitless wonder may see it as such.

We didn't have much in the way of radio communications in the Territory of Alaska back in the early and mid-fifties when I first began to fly. Some would say that there isn't much even today, what with Alaska's seemingly endless mountain ranges and distances that strain the eyes just to think about them. More than that was the fact that there wasn't much civilization between Point A and Point B, no matter where you were or where you had decided to go.

Even at that, Alaska pilots come to think of their small aircraft as little more than extensions of themselves. Kind of like a rancher and his pickup truck, or yesterday's American cowboy and his horse. We came to be pretty casual about flight through the vast emptiness known then as the Territory of Alaska.

I remember one Sunday morning when my wife told me that we were out of bread, so there wouldn't be any toast for our eggs, bacon, and coffee that morning. Are you kidding me? No toast with bacon and eggs?

I dashed to the airport, hand-propped the little yellow N9459E, our 65-horsepower Aeronca Chief, and headed quickly away to the town of Kenai (about forty miles south) to hit a grocery store that I knew was open early on Sunday morning. Neither my wife nor I thought that was the least bit strange. Looking back on it, and from a much more conservative environment here in southern Florida, I guess it was pretty goofy. But we did a lot of goofy things in those days. Besides, what would bacon and eggs be without toast, for cryin' out loud?

On the 26th of January in 1957, I was flying an Aeronca Champion from Merrill Field to Lake Louise, about 170 miles to the north-northeast. It was in the dead of winter, and the little Champ was mounted on fixed skis. The flight would take me fifty miles north to the town of Palmer. Then, after a right forty-five-degree turn, it would take me up the Matanuska River toward the moraine of the Matanuska Glacier, thence past Sheep Mountain to the high plateau country around Lake Louise and Mendeltna. The reason for the trip was a wintertime snowshoe hunt for rabbits (the snowshoe rabbit, more accurately, Alaska's varying hare) and willow ptarmigan, those gorgeous little far-north birds that turn a beautiful white during the winter months.

I was flying low up the Matanuska River, after having passed Palmer, when I noticed a low cloud deck up ahead. I could see that it met the face of the glacier farther along, so I figured I would have to climb and fly over it. When I leveled off above that layer, though, I discovered that I was now flying between layers. With a total of only thirty-one flying hours, something whispered to me that this sort of foolishness might be just a tad beyond my skill level. I probably couldn't climb to get above the higher layers because of airframe icing—and even if I was successful at that, how the hell was I going to get back down? Or even know where I was? This was serious mountain country, after all, and definitely not a place for blind letdowns. You have to remember that these were the days when every student pilot could safely spin down through an overcast, if he were certain that there was room enough beneath it to come out of the spin. In this case, though, I just did a smooth and intelligent 180-degree turn and got the hell out of there, dropping down later and turning again to try it once more below the lowest cloud deck.

After a while, I noticed that I was looking up at the road, where cars were passing me in both directions every now and again. I had the Champ's vertical stabilizer stuck hard up against the overcast and was hoping that the layer would let me scoot around that radio tower I knew from the charts was just a little farther up ahead. If I could make it around that antenna—which was propped up on a pretty hard little pile of rocks even higher than the road now above me—I knew I could drop in at Sheep Mountain Lodge for pie and coffee. That would give me a chance to absorb a little of the adrenaline that had about half-filled my venous system by then and to gather my wits for the rest of the flight into completely unknown and still unseen territory.

I was banging along at about 1,000 feet above sea level, with 6,800-foot peaks within two miles of my left wingtip. Off my right wing, mountains climbed quickly to above 12,000 feet, but this valley was probably three miles across, so there would always be space enough to turn around and go back, if it came to that. I still had the three options I had started out with: find a place to land, proceed straight ahead, or turn around and go home.

The valley tightened up to slightly less than one mile across at that radio station. At my present altitude, I would have to scoot hard around to the left and then hang a sharp right in order to get where I was going. I guess all you Southern fliers simply call that a "dawgleg turn"?

Well, I could have gone to the right, but that would have put me over the tongue of the Matanuska Glacier, and I didn't yet know one danged thing about glaciers, except that I wouldn't be able to land on one given my airplane, my lack of experience, and my high level of trepidation and uncertainty about that sort of thing. Besides, if I had been forced to fly straight ahead after having made that right turn, I'd pretty quickly have to climb to over thirteen thousand feet just to stay above the ground! The glacier would rise pretty fast in that direction.

I did make it around that pile of rocks, though, and I was able to settle down onto the Sheep Mountain Lodge strip. The pie and coffee were delicious, as always. Later, though, when wrestling the little Champ around to align it for takeoff, I lost a perfectly good Zippo cigarette lighter somewhere in the deep snow. I hope the guy who found it knows, at long last, where it came from.

***

Charlie Hubbard was an architect, and a good one. He was a friend of mine, and we slaved together in Anchorage for a time with Ed Crittenden, Fellow of the American Institute of Architecture, one of the founding fathers of architecture in Alaska. Some of Charlie's architectural designs are still earning accolades in Connecticut and in other areas near his northeast home.

Charlie and I flew several times into places where a sane man wouldn't poke an old umbrella or sling a dead rat. I stretched Civil Aeronautics Administration (CAA, forerunner of our current Federal Aeronuatics Administration) regulations until they were thinner than golf slices. We sneaked in and out of Coastal Air Defense Identification Zones down on the Alaska Peninsula as though they weren't even there, acts that could easily have seen us forced down—or shot down, maybe—by USAF F-94 or F-89D Scorpions in those early Cold War days. This was definitely a warm period in that Cold War, remember. Except for the fact that we stayed well below radar coverage—always below fifty feet, and most often below twenty—the skies along the Alaska Peninsula might well have been black with F-94s and F-89Ds searching for our little asses. At those low altitudes, we wouldn't be sending a radar echo to some young USAF radar operator in King Salmon. I knew that because I had once been one of them. And they certainly had plenty of them at the USAF Radar detachment, part of Alaska's 10th Air Division (Defense) in King Salmon, where we had to stop, both coming and going, for fuel and eats.

On one particular return trip from the Alaska Peninsula wilderness, we flew through light, melting snow and had to deal with a leaky main-shaft seal that loosed a fine spray of oil across the windshield. Visibility could have been better, what with this combination of snow and oil, but we could still see through the windshield. I knew we weren't losing enough oil to risk the engine seizing, but the leaky oil made it a bit of a pain when trying to find the best route through some narrow slot or other in the mountains.

For almost fifty years, I've been both embarrassed and very sorry for having stuck Charlie's neck out on that trip.

And I've never, ever done something like that again!

Several weeks later, though, Charlie asked if I would fly him to the Matanuska Valley—a great agricultural area about fifty miles north of Anchorage—to photograph some of the farms and fields from the air. Charlie was either a very slow learner or a brute for punishment. I told him I'd be tickled to do that, and we took off the following Saturday for the short trip.

Charlie had been snapping shots from about thirty-five hundred feet and asked if we could descend for some pictures from a lower altitude. Well, gliding and spiraling both take a little time. They tend to super-cool the engine, too. Besides, a spiral winds up a few g's and is sometimes uncomfortable for passengers. It can pull about three g's, and I don't like to call upon the wings and airframes of older airplanes for the required structural response if I can avoid it.

I asked Charlie if it would bother him if I would just spin down to a lower altitude. He said no, so I moved the carburetor heat control full out, throttled back to idle, and pulled the nose up toward a stall. Right at the top, and just before the elevators stalled out, I kicked in full left rudder, pulled the stick back firmly against its stop, and let the little Aeronca Champ go over the top just the way it was supposed to do.

The left wing stalled, the right wing came over our heads, the nose broke through the horizon on its way down, and we were spinning to the left, losing about five hundred feet with every revolution.

Just as we broke over the top, though, Charlie, sitting behind me, had grabbed the window sills on either side of the narrow cabin to brace himself. When he did, he pushed the rear seat throttle forward against its stop, shooting a burst of prop wash across the tail feathers. That goosed the rudder, of course, and our rate of spin increased in a way I hadn't expected. Spins in the little Aeronca were usually quite docile, even somewhat relaxing. This spin, though, was really wrapping up, and it took a moment for me to realize that my throttle control had disappeared and the engine was approaching redline, now the obvious cause of all this head-spinning rotation.

I glanced down at the left-side windowsill and, sure enough, there was the little throttle knob, pressed fully forward to its high rpm setting.

I throttled back, pressed the right rudder pedal to stop the rotation, and then pushed the stick forward to unlock the stalled elevators. Our air speed picked up quickly, and, once I had full command of all the control surfaces, I pulled the stick back again to stop the dive we had now entered. As the nose climbed through the horizon again, I held it there bleeding off a little excess air speed, and then we settled back down to comfortable cruise flight.

In those days flight instruction in Alaska included spins and spirals. I was taught within four hours of beginning my flying lessons to execute spins in an airplane safely. I was pretty good at emergency landings by the sixth hour and had complete control through any number of spirals at twenty hours. It was a spiral that killed young John Kennedy Jr. one drizzly evening while flying a high-performance Piper Malibu off the east coast, you'll remember.

That spiral, though, was entered quite by accident. It wasn't a controlled maneuver from the very beginning, and the end could have been predicted by almost any licensed pilot, including young John himself. I suspect that John was a bit confused when he noticed his compass course drifting for some mysterious reason. And even more confused when he noticed that his air speed was increasing. He may have let reflex action sneak out to pull back on the control wheel, which only tightened the turn. The altitude continued to unwind, and he very likely pulled back even more on the wheel to stop the insidious descent. By that time, though, the "graveyard spiral" was pretty much in control. Unless and until he leveled wings and then began to pull back a bit to stop what would then become a dive, the spiral was going to win. And it did.

But back to the story at hand. Charlie got his pictures, and I had learned a little something more. If nothing else, I came to realize that passengers, even those in the back seat, can grab something they shouldn't be grabbing. Staying alert would help, but staying really alert would be even better. We weren't finished for the day, though.

We had taxied through a little mud and water prior to takeoff from Merrill that morning. I hadn't thought much about it, but if I had, I wouldn't have been surprised to find one or both of the brakes mud-packed and subsequently frozen. I was reminded of that possibility immediately after the main gear touched down at Merrill again. I had decided to make a smooth, main-gear-first "power" landing—usually the smoothest of landings—but when the frozen right wheel touched the asphalt runway, my spirited little steed headed for the barn! A dance between throttle, brake, and rudder saved our bacon for those few split seconds it took for the right wheel to catch up with the rest of the cantankerous little flying machine.

All in all, Charlie took the high-speed spin quite well. Charlie always was a gentleman, though. As for the close call of our near ground loop on account of a frozen brake, he did later admit that he was ready for another cup of that strong, black, Alaska coffee.

News recently reached me that Charlie has now gone west. Not long after our flights, Charlie took his collection of bow ties and returned to the northeastern United States where, for many years, he ran a successful architectural practice. A silent toast to you, Charlie. You were indeed a piece of work.

***

In June 1957, I arrived back at Anchorage one dark night—I had logged one hour and ten minutes of nighttime flight by then—to find Merrill Field flat on its face with a measured ceiling of 500 feet overcast and 1,500 feet broken. I could see that the low stratus was flat on top but that it sloped on the bottom. I could also see that Anchorage International Airport across the city from Merrill was wide open. Since my approach to the city was over open water, I had no qualms about setting up a glide and slipping down into the dark, wet cloud layer in order to descend through the thick fog. I knew enough by that time to keep both the needle and the ball in the middle, and also to watch that the air speed didn't begin to build up. When I slid out beneath the overcast at 500 feet, the city was a sea of lights, and Merrill Field was only a few minutes away.

Since almost none of us had radios in those days, and since a lot of us seemed to fly with something akin to an absolute confidence that bordered on complete and wild abandon, I'm surprised we weren't running into one another at every turn in the sky. But, we weren't, though it did happen twice to folks that I knew.

***

It was June of 1957 when Dave Stanley, perhaps the best instructor I've ever had, introduced me to seaplane flying. In Alaska, we call them "floatplanes" rather than "seaplanes," and we don't practice for a "seaplane" rating. Up here, it will always be a "float rate," I guess. Alaskans can be pretty set in their ways. Some of us still, for instance, refuse to call Mt. McKinley by its new name, "Mt. Denali." I'm told that the native Alaskans had originally named the mountain Denali, but my own experience was that the Indians named rivers, lakes, and valleys, but they seldom named hills, ridges, or mountains. So, like many of us ol' hard-heads, I'll just refer to it as Mt. McKinley in this book, if it's all right with you.

Anyway, Dave taught me the usual things like docking and sailing and step turns and glassy water landings and rough water landings and all that stuff. We were using an Aeronca Champion on Edo floats, N84669. I've always thought the little dude was a 65-horsepower model, but my logbooks say it was 75-horsepower, so I'll go with that.

At sea level and with no load inside (or hanging on the outside, a typical Alaskan addition), it was an honest enough airplane. With an adult in the rear passenger seat, or for any serious outback flying, it became something of a slug. Oh, it would stagger off the water and flop around up there, all right. But as a real airplane it always seemed to be just a wee bit lacking. Most pilots would simply say it was "underpowered," though in an academic sense it was not. In all fairness, I have to admit it was a fun airplane to fly for the relaxation of it, and many pilots loved the forgiving little ship. On August 18 of that year, with 120 flight hours in my logbooks—only 18 of which were on floats—I made another monumentally questionable decision: I would airdrop supplies to a sheep hunting camp in the Kenai Mountains, a mildly rocky spine running the length of the Kenai Peninsula. For those of you with an Alaska map of any good sort, the sheep camp was on Surprise Mountain (some old timers call it Russian Mountain), which lies just north of Skilak Lake and hard up against the Skilak Glacier.

The high point of Surprise Mountain is only 4,350 feet above sea level, and a meager 3,850 feet above Lower Russian Lake, from which I would be operating with the little float-equipped Aeronca Champ. At the south end of the mountain, which isn't the highest end, is a bump of rock with sheer faces overlooking Skilak Lake. It was here that, two years earlier, Jack "Smilin' Jack" Wade, flying a Cordova Airlines Aero Commander 580-E, came to the end of his flying career while trying to abort a mail delivery flight to Seward, only a few miles farther south.

Merle K. "Mudhole" Smith, one of Alaska's famous and accomplished Pioneer Bush Pilots, operated the small airline. It flew primarily into and out of Anchorage, Cordova, and Valdez. The airline also had a mail route to Seward and was being paid by the pound-mile for the mail it delivered by air to that town of 1,600 citizens. When the weather was really too crappy to get the mail through by air, Smitty would have someone drive it to Seward in his station wagon. He wasn't supposed to be paid for that sort of delivery, though, and his pilots tried very hard to make the Seward trip by air whenever they could. Still, Smitty always got the mail through, one way or another. Well—almost always.

Jack Wade, a friend of mine and a crackerjack pilot, just couldn't get through Resurrection Pass that windy and overcast day. Seward usually closed its small field when the winds got above sixteen knots, and they had been reported as gusting to fifty that morning. Jack had turned around over Upper Russian Lake while trying to sneak through Resurrection Pass and had begun an instrument climbout using the Kenai Visual OmniRange (VOR) for directional reference. He almost made it, too. That is, until the strong south winds slammed him into the north face of Surprise Mountain—only twenty lousy feet from the top.

I had been in the operations office that morning and had asked Jack if he was going to try the mail flight. With his Joe Stalin mustache and deeply curved pipe, Jack had allowed that he'd "go have a look at 'er, ennaway." An hour later—and while Morgan in the Cordova Airlines operations office was still trying desperately to raise him on the company frequency—Jack had already cashed in his chips and gone west like so many other Alaska pilots before him. And like the many who were yet to follow him through the intervening years.

There's a small saddle in the southern part of Surprise Mountain. It provides something of a high pass between the Lower Russian Lake and Skilak Lake. It was in this pass that the sheep camp was to be set up, and it was here that my target for the proposed airdrop was located.

I had assembled on the north end of Lower Russian Lake all that stuff I planned later to drop at the camp location up above. I would tie it atop the left float deck and slide it off from there. Trouble was, I knew everything would be soaked—including stuff like the sleeping bags—when I tried to get the little floatplane up on the step for takeoff. My answer to that was to tie an old G.I. rain poncho over the pile of supplies, carefully tucking it in all the way around. That should keep things relatively dry for the few moments that the bow spray would be at its worst during a takeoff run. The bundle was securely tied and finished with a handy-dandy slipknot. The bitter end of this line was passed through the left-side window where I could yank it loose when the time came for the drop.

The little Champ was game enough, but its small engine just wasn't up to effective climb rates. I had to circle the lake several times in order to climb the 2,500 vertical feet required to get me up to that saddle for the drop.

Once up there with the first of my two loads, I lined things up as best I could and made my pass for the initial drop. Just as I scooted low over the drop zone, I yanked the slipknotted rope and watched for the bundle to pitch off the float deck. Absolutely nothing happened. The bundle just sat out there, staring back at me. I descended back down to land again on Lower Russian and revise my thinking a little.

This time, I would take a length of alder branch to poke the bundle loose after yanking the knot. That ought to work, right?

Another seemingly half-day of circling and climbing found the weak little ship and me back over the drop zone once again, this time ready with a faultlessly engineered release system.

I had lined up perfectly for this pass, and I knew that success was only moments away. I had already poked my custom-built, green alder release prod out the open left window—fighting the slipstream that threatened to tear it from my hand—and was ready to shove the bundle off the float deck the moment I yanked loose my carefully tied slipknot. It had begun to feel a little busy in the small cockpit by then, what with the stick, the wind, a dangerously low air speed, and just a pinch of concern over what now seemed perhaps something of an ill-conceived exercise. One hand was busy with the window ledge–mounted throttle, while the other was occupied with maintaining control of that damned alder pole, now waving madly around in the slipstream outside. That left the control stick pretty much on its own, and I was now flopping around using only rudder and throttle, unable to speak to the ailerons or elevator at all.

I was trying to hold a minimum air speed without losing the last ten feet of altitude that I was carrying when the moment of truth finally arrived. I yanked the knot and pushed mightily with my ingenious little alder release pole. Nothing! That is, nothing of any positive value.

What did happen was that the poncho instantly became a parachute, a drag chute billowing full of air but still firmly attached to the float. It was, for all practical purposes, the world's largest air brake, hanging out there on my left float and threatening either to turn the airplane completely around or else to slow it so drastically that my choices would be limited to (a) hitting the mountain or (b) hitting the mountain.

I had been flying east during this aviation fiasco, and it was my good fortune that the east side of Surprise Mountain is rather steep. When I passed over the edge—barely—the gods slid open the door to my safe escape. I say safe escape because just before the little Champ slipped over the edge, my altitude had to have been no more than five feet, the air speed indicator had been sticking its tongue out, and the little ship had been traveling more sideways than straight ahead. If there had been any time for it, I probably would have been scared to death.

After a landing back on the lake, where I succeeded in soaking everything in that ill-conceived little airdrop package, I decided that most of that stuff should really be packed 2,500 feet uphill on my back anyway.

Later, though, I did get my wits together and made a safe and successful airdrop.

Some have said that we don't gain much experience through success. We are sentenced to gain the most through our failures. I think I have to agree with that. On the other hand, if I admit to a lot of experience, I probably have to admit to having made a bunch of poor choices over the years, don't I? Well, it's true that we don't gain much in the way of valuable experience through someone else's failures, isn't it?

It was during the subsequent Dall (probably more accurately Dahl) sheep hunt with outdoor writer Al Goerg, for which that airdrop had been made, that my daughter, Tanya, was born back in Anchorage. The one thousandth patient in the new Methodist Hospital on Ninth Avenue and L Street—directly across the street from the old Providence Hospital—she was making headlines in the local newspapers while her pilot of a father was making an ass of himself in the Alaska bush.

***

It was in the dark of night during the middle of April 1958 when Anchorage Approach Control gave me a radio call. I was returning from the town of Kenai, halfway down the Kenai Peninsula, in a Cessna 172, one of those models before Cessna swept back the tails of their little airplanes. This one, N5043A, was a dandy little airplane, and I had enjoyed several hours of flying her.

The call from approach had come from out of the blue, and they were requesting practice surveillance approaches to Anchorage International Airport to aid in training new operators to the system. I agreed without thinking, and approach came back with the command, "Check and set your gyros. Make no more transmissions on this frequency."

Truthfully—since I had been caught virtually daydreaming my way along up there—I had no idea what the guy was talking about. I reached up and rotated the gyroscopic compass control, just to be doing something, but setting who knew what heading under the lubber line. I had responded with the expected, "Roger," and the approach controller came back now with "Turn right to zero-four-five for identification."

Now I was stuck, and I knew it. The original radio call had so unnerved me that I was now about three jumps behind the power curve. No matter what other instructions he might give me, I knew I couldn't comply with them. Surely they would be changes in direction because he was trying to direct me to a place in the sky where my flight path would intercept an imaginary line that extended from the centerline of Anchorage International Airport's Runway 5 to the nose wheel of the little Cessna.

What's even worse, in those days I still thought the CAA represented God, and that all their instructions carried at least the same weight as did the Ten Commandments. I could see my young license already slipping away somewhere in the fading light. I fully expected the CAA to have a representative meet this little airplane right smack dab in the middle of the runway, if I ever again put it on the ground.

God only knows what I had set the gyrocompass to, but I dutifully turned right until 045 degrees came up under the lubber line. It was already clear to me that I hadn't set the gyro correctly, since I was bright enough to know I surely wasn't headed any 045 degrees, but now the instructions were coming so fast that I seemed constantly turning in one direction or the other. This didn't give the magnetic compass enough time to stop swinging wildly around in its little liquid-filled case. There was now absolutely no time for me to correct the gyrocompass, and it didn't take the approach guy much longer to figure that out.

After some pretty esoteric radio exchanges between us, he finally allowed me time enough to properly set the compass, and from there on out I think we both had a pretty productive evening of it. The moral to this story? Don't do anything in a hurry when you're in the front office of a moving airplane, regardless of its size. Ever.

***

On June 29 of that year, Al Kirsch, a sales rep for Xerox, asked me if I could show him some bears within easy flight distance from Anchorage. Al was from the Lower 48—the term Alaskans still use for the 48 contiguous states—and I suppose had never seen a wild animal outside a zoo.

I told him I was confident we could see a black bear or two along the Yentna River, only fifteen or twenty minutes flying time from Merrill Field, and we agreed to do that at the end of the business day.

Flying my little two-place Aeronca Chief, N9459E, we did see several black bears along the gravel bars of the Yentna. Having spotted a particularly large one, he asked if we could get closer. I told him we could simply land on the gravel bar and sneak up on the bear, if he wanted a really close look. He seemed thrilled at that idea, so I lined the little Aeronca up on the bar and plopped it down there. I shut down the little engine, and we crawled out to begin a quiet stalk on the blackie.

The closer we got, the closer Al wanted to get, until we had sneaked up to within about thirty yards of the approaching bear. Since we were tiptoeing upstream while the bear was ambling downstream, we were destined to meet if one or the other of us didn't decide pretty quick to reverse his course.

It was a big, fat ol' blackie. The spring had been a good one for the bears along the Yentna, I had my .270 Winchester-Cook by my side, and I could use the meat for our larder. Without much more thought than that, I squeezed off a handloaded round of a 130-grain Nosler partitioned bullet ahead of 59-grains of my favorite powder. Hit in the neck, the bear simply dropped in his tracks, and that was the end of that.

Al wanted some more pictures, this time of the mighty hunter and his dangerous bear. It wasn't long before I had the carcass opened up, its innards safely out and away, and the bear spread open on a built-up pile of brush. I figured it would be safe there until I could return the following morning to fly it out to my meat cutter, who would then hang it for three weeks at slightly under fifty degrees Fahrenheit, butcher it, wrap and mark it, and then slip it into a freezer for me.

In those early days in Alaska, by the way, it was still quite legal to fly and shoot the same day. In fact, there was still a bounty on such wildlife as foxes, coyotes, wolves, wolverines, harbor seals, and bald eagles. Yep, you read that right, bald eagles. But I'm getting off the path here.

***

Later in 1958—the last day of moose season, in fact—Eugene P. "Bud" Graves and I were crammed into the little Chief for a final shot at a moose hunt. We were flying upstream, again along the Yentna River, cruising at a comfortable two hundred feet, when the engine—without a burble or a hiccup—became silent as a tomb. The little powerplant had abandoned its assigned task without so much as a cough or a backfire. Still, warning or no, the silence was deafening. And most demanding of immediate attention.

After all, two hundred feet isn't all that much when you have to hang your hat on it. Twenty stories seems pretty high, unless you happen to be flying a rag-bag airplane sixty miles from the nearest human being, repair station, telephone booth, or coffee shop.

I would later learn that the sediment bowl had dropped loose and fallen from the engine compartment. In that little normally aspirated engine, raw fuel was even then exhausting itself out the bottom of the cowling, and the engine was as silent and unresponsive as a stone. The two hundred feet of altitude now didn't seem as comfortable as it had a few moments earlier, and I was looking all over the place for a suitable spot to park the stricken little thing. At the same time, I was scanning across the meager panel and searching my addled brain for a possible reason for this outrageous behavior on the part of an otherwise stalwart and dependable little flying machine.

Bud asked what we were going to do now. He was as cool as a cucumber, by George, I'll give him that. Well, I told him, I guessed we'd just land 'er and see what the trouble might be. I also told him that it might be a wise idea to tighten up on our seat belts, just in case.

I thought for a moment that I might glide to a little dab of a sandbar dead ahead of us, but we were gliding downwind, and I knew almost instantly that we wouldn't remain in the air long enough to make that spot.

Dead ahead, too, were two large spruce trees, conspicuous in a world of stunted willows. The thought flashed through my head that I could fly between the two and wipe both wings off. That should slow us down a bit. I instantly pitched out that idea, since I'd rather be flying a silent and powerless airplane than riding a wingless arrow. I thought, too, that I should maybe use the primer, since it appeared to be a case of fuel exhaustion for some unknown reason. I passed that idea up, too, though years later I would wonder whether I should have tried that. A friend and former high school classmate—who, along with his wife, now owns and operates a flying service back in Ohio where we were raised—has since convinced me that the primer idea wouldn't have worked either.

I decided that it might be better to make the emergency landing into the wind rather than with it and, with the help of the Aeronca's incredible wing span, had enough time to make the shallowest of turns to swing us around 180 degrees for the landing. Throughout that turn, my mind was running through the lessons I had learned about such times. Like the one that cautions against these near-the-ground turns, for instance.

I settled the little yellow Chief into the eight-foot willows. The forward movement couldn't have been more than two feet! The landing gears broke apart and slammed straight up on either side against the doors, effectively locking us both inside the tiny cabin. The Ruger Blackhawk .357 Magnum I had laid atop the baggage compartment lid behind me went sailing past my left ear and right on out through the plexiglass side window. Bud's left knee broke off the ignition key with the jolt. And that was the end of it. Except for the terribly sad sound of dry willow leaves settling down across the huge expanse of the little Chief's motionless wings. I would make my last bank payment against that little ship the following Monday. The airplane wasn't insured, either, so you know where that left me: like a cowboy without a horse, I was walking again.

The pilot of an ancient Curtis Robin floatplane had watched our landing. He circled us to make sure we were all right, then settled down onto the Yentna River and waited for us to stroll through the swamp and dry willows to meet him. He would fly us back to Anchorage.

He already had a full load, but he was kind enough to load us aboard anyway. Bud and I sat on the plywood floor and watched his air speed indicator bobble around as the pilot roared his aging red floatplane downstream for mile after mile, trying valiantly to get up on the step and then away from the earth. When finally airborne, we watched the air speed indicator bounce between sixty and ninety knots at cruise speed. Not the fastest of airplanes, but what the hell. After all, he was saving us one long, lonely stay in the Alaska outback.

***

I was in Florida during most of 1959. On July 22 of that year, I was flying a Cessna 172 (N4248F) from Ft. Lauderdale to Daytona Beach to pick up a passenger, Tanya Graef, and her little pink poodle and return them to Ft. Lauderdale. Shortly after takeoff from Ft. Lauderdale, and as I was approaching Palm Beach from the south, I heard a radio call from a pilot stating that he was flying a Piper Tri-Pacer northbound and had encountered a severe rainstorm. At that time, he reported that he could only see straight down but could not see ahead at all. He was only able to hold his airplane level by his dim view of the earth directly below.

I have to admit that both he and I were at that time flying through the heaviest rainstorm I had, until that time, ever seen. Officially, my logs show the weather report as "500-ft sky obscured in rain showers, 1/4-mile visibility with winds from the southeast at 35-knots." Not at all a nice day, really. And the heavy rain sounded for all the world as though all seven of Snow White's little pals were hammering on the windshield, each with a ball-peen hammer in both hands. The truth is, I thought the windshield would probably just break, and I wasn't the least bit comfortable with that thought. I was thinking that, when it finally happened, I would just dump the Cessna in the Intracoastal Waterway, explaining it all later as best I could. After I had swum back to the Ft. Lauderdale airport, of course. I was better off than the Tri-Pacer driver, though, since poor visibility had been my almost constant companion during the last few years of flying Alaska's backcountry.

It was only moments later that I broke out into blinding sunshine, and I immediately made a radio call asking Palm Beach Approach to relay the fact that the Tri-Pacer pilot was less than one minute from CAVU (ceiling and visibility unlimited) weather. I heard my transmission repeated by approach, but the Tri-Pacer pilot didn't respond. I was later told that the Tri-Pacer had crashed into the Intracoastal Waterway only scant seconds before the pilot would have seen blue skies and sunshine. The pilot didn't survive the crash landing, I was told. It made me glad, once again, that I had learned to fly in Alaska rather than in one of the southern forty-eight states.

On the return flight to Ft. Lauderdale with Tanya and her little dog, we soon found ourselves passing the landmark Jupiter Lighthouse. As we approached the singularly wealthy and notably snooty Palm Beach area—under a gorgeous and cloudless blue sky—we were following the surf line along the beach. We were flying below three hundred feet, but with the entire southeast Florida beach as an emergency landing field, we were risking neither life nor property at that altitude.

Ahead, we could see someone wading in the clear, warm ocean, just a few yards offshore. The guy was about waist-deep and was completely unaware of a large shark swimming figure eights some thirty or forty yards beyond him and in slightly deeper water. After passing the wader, I turned out over the ocean to fly a 360-degree left turn, arranging to fly the airplane's shadow across the sandy bottom just ahead of the lazily cruising shark. When the shadow shot across the sand ahead of the big predator, he whirled with a surprised rush and headed for deeper water. It's doubtful that the wader ever figured out what we were up to with that tight 360-degree turn. It was that tight turn, though, that pushed the little pink poodle beyond the realm of doggie comfort. When he had lost his breakfast all over the back seat, it was really my fault, not his. Or was it a her? I never knew whether the little fella was a him or a her. Ms. Graef, though, was most certainly a her.

***

On March 3, 1961, I found I had to fly my friend, Chic Lane—whom I've always considered to be one of the world's finest and most design-sensible architects—to the small city of Kenai, about forty air miles south of Anchorage. I had selected a Piper Commanche for the trip. This high-performance, retractable-landing-gear, low-wing airplane is a nifty little piece of machinery. At 250 horsepower—in those days—it goes like the wind. Unless you have become acquainted with it, you'll find such a plane a little hard to slow down once you approach your selected landing airport or strip. It's a really clean little plane, and it doesn't want to slow down so that you can lower the gear or flaps. Beyond that transition concern for pilots new to it, it's a dandy little airplane.

We departed Merrill Field on schedule, and I got the clearance to cross Anchorage International Airport in the climb to the south toward Point Campbell, Turnagain Arm, and, on the other side, Point Possession. I had had precious little sleep that day, and there was a blanket of fresh, blinding snow beneath a cloudless and startlingly sunny sky. And—wouldn't you know it!—my sunglasses were at home.

I climbed to 3,500 feet and leveled out N6823P for the cruise, squinting against the awesomely bright day. Not excited about staying glued to the controls for the short flight, I engaged the autopilot just after having leveled off at cruise altitude. The gyroscopic compass apparently hadn't enjoyed much of a maintenance program, I guess, and it tumbled at just about that precise moment. The two-axis autopilot was slaved to that compass, and just as I settled back for a comfortable, if lazy, flight, the nose dove for the waters of Turnagain Arm, and I came up against the seat belt.

I stabbed the autopilot switch to the "off" position, grabbed the control yoke again, and pulled us back into level and controlled flight. For the rest of the trip, I rode the controls as I always had and simply left the autopilot to its snoozing. Except for the occasional, and rare, instrument bush climbouts, I've avoided autopilots for the past forty-some years. Thousands of pilots will not agree with me, but I figure that if someone really wanted to be a pilot, it meant that he or she really wanted to fly airplanes. So I do that and leave the autopilots to the big iron and to those pilots that seem much more weary of flying chores than I.

***

It was on the eighth day of February 1961 that I first went under the hood for instrument flight training. Until you've been there for the very first time, you very likely can't appreciate what a feeling it gives you. One thing is certain: no one in his right mind would close his eyes while flying an airplane! And to fly when you can't see out? Fuggedaboudut!

Later, I would become comfortable in the instrument environment, as have many before me. Making approaches down to minimums no longer leaves me white-knuckled and perched tensely on the front edge of the driver's seat. Still—especially during cruise flight at night and on solid instruments—I don't like to think of losing my instruments and having to go to the standby of needle-ball-and-air-speed basics. And, for that reason, I have practiced the technique for years. Those three instruments are solid, they are dependable, and they are always there. But, more than that—and even with those three attitude instruments solidly directing you—there is the haunting possibility of electronics failure. The pucker meter would surely go to somewhere between eight and nine—on a scale of one to ten—while you were trying to figure out (a) where you really are, (b) where you really are going, and (c) how are you going to know when you get there? By the clock? Well, okay. Maybe so. But how are you going to get down and land after you've arrived? Unless he is in a radar environment, the pilot truly has to believe in himself. And in his instruments and their maintenance, as well.

***

On September 2 of that year, I flew a Cessna 170A (the model with metal wings and Cessna's small, newly designed flaps) to Nugget Bench for our winter's moose supply. There were four of us in the plane, which boasted a flat prop and a 165-horsepower, heavy-case Franklin engine, a definite improvement over the factory-installed 145-horsepower Continental engine and cruise prop.

The strip at Nugget Bench had been bulldozed out of the tundra and was a mud-with-gravel little thing. Plenty wide enough and long enough for the experienced pilot. The charts showed it to be 1,600 feet

The author holds the world's largest moose trophy to be taken with a handgun up to that time. Al Goerg took this photo on a volcanic lava cinder bed above Meshik River near Port Heiden. See "The Al Goerg Story" in Outdoor Life Magazine, May 1968. *Photo by Al Goerg*

in length, though I could only get 1,200 feet when I measured it. The strip sloped upward toward Mt. McKinley and downward to Anchorage, about one hundred miles away. At its upper end lay a huge hole in the earth, the result of a placer mining operation that had taken over six million dollars in nuggets and flower gold from the stream, Nugget Creek, in years past. And that, remember, was when gold was sixteen dollars per fine ounce.

If a pilot were to take off uphill, which was often the case because of the usual prevailing winds, a falter would place him, and his unhappy little airplane, at the bottom of that hole in the ground, which was at least eight stories deep.

We took two nice moose on that trip. I bagged one with my .270 Winchester-Cook, a custom rifle made by a friend back in Marietta, Ohio. The other was taken by Bob Farmer, who actually owned the airplane at that time, but who couldn't fly a lick. His moose was taken with a .45-caliber Colt Single Action Army, the piece all cowboys carry in the movies and which was originally called the "Peacemaker" for obvious reasons.

I was a little nervous about Bob trying to sneak up on a full-grown bull moose with only a dirty old Stetson hat and that little single-action Colt handgun of his. I covered him from the hillside above, though I don't think he knew I was there. Just as well. He didn't need me, and my being there might have been poorly received. Bob really was a cowboy, and I got the notion that cowboys, by and large, don't need much help with much of anything.

***

An interesting series of flights occurred in September of 1961. A very good friend of mine, Captain Joe Crowley, who was still in the United States Air Force, asked me to give him a few clues regarding his planned transition from heavier military aircraft to Alaska's lighter bush-type flying machines. He would later go for his civilian privileges as a commercial pilot. I told him I thought that my forgiving Cessna 170-Special, with its heavy-case, 165-horsepower Franklin engine, was a reasonable machine for that transition.

Joe was so smooth on the controls that I was almost embarrassed to fly with him. His background ranged from the old F-86 Saber—and later the 100-series jet fighters—through the huge supertankers. Joe eventually got the hang of it all, but he had a big problem with landings for a time. He just couldn't get behind the technique of closing the throttle down on short final. To finish an approach to the earth without power was beyond his ken, and what should have taken about six hundred feet of runway would sometimes take several thousand. Still, he was one smooth pilot! His wife, Pat, was as gorgeous a Southern gal as you've ever seen. These were my bachelor days, and, looking back, I guess I had something of a crush on her. She was stunning, but I was a gentleman, so I just bit my tongue and behaved myself.

***

On October 12 of that year, I flew Chic Lane up to the Denali River country for caribou. We stopped for pie and coffee at Eureka, a roadhouse lodge and eatery a little way up the road from Sheep Mountain. As usual with Alaska strips, this one sloped generously. Located at 3,289 feet above sea level, it boasted a hard-packed earth strip of 2,600 feet in length. It's plenty long enough for just about anything that flies up in that direction.

Pie and coffee stops like this one are sort of typical for Alaska outback fliers. The cooking, especially the baking, is out of this world. And the coffee is made the way only Alaskans can make it. It's usual, too, to ask about the local hunting or fishing. The pilot always expects to get something a little short of the truth, but that's an anticipated part of these conversations. If you're not going to talk hunting and fishing, what the hell would you be doing flying around in the Alaska outback anyway?

As expected, the pie and coffee were both excellent. The news of the Nelchina Herd of caribou was also just about what we expected.

"Well now, we ain't seen much of them fellers yet this season. I guess they're still pretty much fu'ther north and east of us yet. Maybe you'd do better to look around the highway at Tanacross, I don't wonder."

Well, I was born at night, maybe, but it wasn't last night. After paying our lunch tab, we climbed aboard the Cessna 170-Special and lit out for the country right behind the lodge. We'd just mosey up toward Susitna Lodge and Denali Strip, then hang a left and scoot down the Monahan Flats. Most likely, we'd come across a good bull or two along the Upper Susitna River.

Well, we did that, and we did that. That is, we did fly that direction, and we did find some suitable bulls for the larder. I should tell you here that, in those days, the Alaska game regulations allowed the same-day fly-and-shoot.

Besides, the Nelchina Herd boasted about 77,000 caribou that year, and we wouldn't thin the herd by much with our plans.

We spotted the two bulls that we thought we should take, and I figured where I thought they might cross a small ridge and head down to the river. We just landed on a sandbar a mile or two ahead of the spot I thought was most likely, stepped out, and cooled our heels over some good, black, thermos-jug coffee to wait them out.

Sure enough, in about thirty minutes, they came loping over the crest of the hill, handsome as could be in the bright October sunlight. We waited until they were within easy packing distance and then put them in the bag. Chic's Winchester .308 and my own .270 Winchester-Cook were both loaded with Nosler's famous partition bullets, and on game the size of Alaska's caribou, one well-placed shot was sufficient for each of the bulls.

We weren't horn hunting, so we left both the horns and the beautiful fall-color hides for the wolves, foxes, and porcupines to quarrel over. We bagged and loaded all the meat, and, in short order, we were flying directly toward Mt. McKinley. Soon we would turn south and slide smoothly along the last one hundred miles or so to Merrill Field. This time with a whole lot of meat-cutting and freezer-packing to get behind us. It looked like another Alaskan, high-protein winter diet for the both of us.

Chapter 4

The Other Guys

Flying isn't really dangerous, but crashing sure as hell is.

Before I get into this little tale, let me repeat my firm belief that a pilot who doesn't fly almost every day—four or five days a week, that is—will find it difficult if not impossible to maintain the sharp edge of flying proficiency. That doesn't mean, though, that a pilot who flies less than that will be an unsafe pilot. It does mean, in my estimation, that he can't be comfortable at the razor's edge of the flight envelope. Which, I also believe, isn't for just everybody in the first place. I hasten to assure you that I'm not criticizing those who don't live and fly on the edge. The truth of the matter is that I bow to their superior intellect. So, I'm sure, would my wife, who sometimes was less than ecstatic over a few of my flying escapades.

Some of the "Other Guys" were the real giants of Alaska outback flying. To read of their flying experiences is to paint the mental picture that they all stood somewhere between seven and nine feet tall, remained bundled up in caribou furs and sealskin mukluks year in and year out, and flew only to new and exciting places. The latter, of course, almost always during incredibly cold temperatures, blinding nighttime snowstorms, or chilling daytime "whiteout" conditions.

For those of you who might not know what a real Alaska "whiteout" is, just imagine yourself trapped inside a suddenly noisy box of cotton. Of course, you won't notice the noise. Except for gravity—which you may have both the equipment and the skills to overcome—you, and certainly your passengers, will have no idea which direction is up and which direction is down. There is no horizon to look at, no color on the ground, nor any in your sky—nothing but white. Stark white. Scary white. And, unless you are instrument rated and flying on an instrument flight plan, whiteout conditions can be completely unnerving to any pilot who hasn't experienced the phenomenon before. It's worse than ice fog, but only because it lasts much, much longer and is much, much deeper. If a pilot should descend into a layer of ice fog, usually not found at temperatures much above about minus twenty-five degrees Fahrenheit, he will often find it less than one hundred feet thick, and sometimes as little as ten or twenty feet thick. He will also find that he can't see his hand in front of his face in it.

When reading about some of the early Alaska pilots' more dramatic flights, one can't help but feel a little worm of unease crawling insidiously along somewhere deep inside. The real truth is, though, that hundreds of dull hours may pass for the pilot between those few moments of almost sheer dread. Then, as today, the real problem faced by most Alaska bush pilots is one of woodcraft and has little if anything to do with worrying about surviving an emergency landing. Hell, we all believed we would survive the landing. We still do—and a lot us have, of course. Sort of goes with the territory. Our real concern was how we'd repair any minor airplane damage (we were certainly confident that there wouldn't be any major airplane damage!) and then take off again from the lousy place we'd had to pick for our emergency landing spot to begin with.

Like Joe Reddington, father of the 1,100-mile Alaska Idatarod Sled Dog Race from Anchorage to Nome. Older than dirt and as purposeful as a mountain grizzly, Joe lit out one winter day for a flight in his own rag-bag little Super Cub. As I recall it, he had to make a flight through—or at least to the neighborhood of—Rainy Pass. Maybe he had business in McGrath or Farewell or something, I don't remember.

Anyway, on his return trip home, he encountered a bit of engine trouble and elected to land somewhere out there in the deep and silent snow. He did that, and then he performed a little dab of engine maintenance, putting things back in proper working order. Or, so he thought.

On the next leg, though, Joe had to do it all over again. And then still again! Soon, it seemed to him that he was being forced to dribble his little Super Cub like a basketball across the frozen expanse of Alaska's great outback.

In the meantime, many Alaskans—certainly most of his close friends—feared that Joe had enjoyed his last Alaska winter sunrise. After all, it was bitter cold out there in the bush, and he was no longer a spring chicken. Dog mushing, not flying, was his real forté. If he had cracked up somewhere, who knew how badly he might have been hurt? Worst of all, they thought he might have survived the crash, been seriously injured, and faced the lingering wilderness death that so many Alaskans have confronted throughout the years, that of simply freezing to death.

In the long run, it took quite a few days for Joe to finally limp home in his reluctant little Cub. Remember, here was a man accustomed to running behind his sled dogs, almost nonstop, for more than 1,100 miles across the remote and empty Alaska wilderness. And he did that in the darkest and coldest of months. And he did it repeatedly! Moreover, he did it mostly for fun! Worrying about Joe Reddington having to spend a cold night in the bush was a lot like worrying about Alaska running out of empty. It just wasn't really a thing to worry all that much about.

***

Max Shellabarger, on the other hand, was a whole 'nother matter. There's now a scary little pass in the Alaska Range named after Max. It's kinda the northern approach to Farewell, in case Rainy Pass is closed. If a pilot takes the wrong turn when trying to enter Shellabarger Pass from the east, he'll end up at Purkeypile Mine, most likely. And that private strip isn't for the timid or inexperienced pilot, either. I can name a hundred pilots who won't try to sneak through Shellabarger Pass—or its next-door neighbor, Mystic Pass, either, for that matter.

Well, Max returned to his log home with a winter hunting client one day a number of years ago. His Super Cub had been running a little rough, and, after landing with skis on the lake a half-mile or so from his home, Max told the client just to mosey on up to the cabin—where Max's wife surely had baked some fresh cookies to go with the strong Alaska coffee that was bound to be set near the back of the old wood stove—and to put away a cup or two while he finished up with the Cub.

Max shut the engine down, opened the cowling, and tinkered inside the engine compartment for a short while. Then he started the engine to check it out. Still wasn't quite up to Max's standards, so he went through the process yet again. And then, maybe once or twice more.

To lighten his Super Cub for bush flight, Max had removed the battery, as did many Alaska outback pilots. He had no one to talk to while flying anyway, so the radios weren't needed. And—hells bells!—a pilot who couldn't hand-prop his own Super Cub wasn't much of a pilot at any rate! This time, though, it was going to be a little different.

The lake ice was a little slicker than Max had thought, and when he swung the prop through for the last time in his life, his feet slipped out from under him. He was immediately pulled through the spinning propeller. He lay dead on the ice where his wife and the client later found him when they walked down to see what was taking him so long. The ignominious end to a truly great Alaska guide and airplane driver. That seems to be the way of things in Robert W. Service country, "A land where the mountains are nameless and the rivers all run God knows where. Lives that are erring and aimless, and death that hangs just by a hair."

***

The equipment with which the pioneer bush pilot had to contend wasn't as reliable as the equipment we have today. In something just shy of twenty thousand flying hours, I've had less than a small handful of engine problems, power failures, and emergency landings. And many of those could probably have been prevented with a little more care on my part.

Not too many years ago, however, that wasn't necessarily the case. And a lot of today's troubles in outback flying come simply—and I believe understandably—from faulted judgment. I didn't say "faulty," because a lot of it isn't that. Sometimes, for instance, the pilot doesn't have all the information he really needs, so his judgment is faulted by that lack. A good example might be a weather report that paints a less than accurate picture of what's really happening on the far side of that mountain range. PIREPS (Pilot Reports) made by inexperienced pilots, perhaps, will sometimes cloud judgment. All pilots appreciate hearing PIREPS, from whatever source. They can always evaluate what they've heard, tempering it with their own past experiences.

But, maybe the most frequent cause for faulted judgment is information provided by inexperienced nonpilots, including clients and customers in the form of an honest—though dreadfully erroneous—appraisal of landing conditions:

"Hey, I've got a clearing more than a thousand feet long about a quarter-mile north of my place. Got plenty of airplane gas, too. You can just fly in and land my grub in that clearing and I'll pick it up there." How many times have I heard that sort of invitation?

Sometimes, as was the case back in 1984, some guy will say, "Why, Charlie didn't have any trouble getting in and out of that little gravel bar. I know you can make it!" I heard that encouraging speech from J. W. Smith, manager for Painter Creek Lodge. He was talking about a little dab of a rough and narrow gravel bar at the mouth of Marguerita Creek, where it rushes into the King Salmon River.

Trouble is, ol' Charlie had been flying a lightweight Super Cub, and my friend wanted me to drop in there with a loaded Cessna 206 Stationair amphibian, for Pete's sake! The Stationair POH (Pilot Operating Handbook) notes that this beast requires 970 feet for a takeoff roll, all things considered. I did later use the little gravel bar many times with a Cessna 180, though. The bar measured just over five hundred feet. The big Cessna 206 would have been there until it could later have been dismantled and flown out, piece by piece, in a Super Cub. Or floated down the river to some distant—and considerably larger—gravel bar.

Bill Shirley—William S. "Sugarfoot" Shirley, though as I recall it the "S" was really for "Stanley"—was a very good friend of mine. Still is, for that matter. He now owns cattle ranches in South America as well as a big chunk of the Marshall Islands, I hear. Bill, looking for all the world like a taller, slimmer Clark Gable, could sell electric freezers to Eskimos living without power in temperatures below minus fifty degrees Fahrenheit. It was in the late 1950s when Bill found some reason or other for flying into Soldotna in a Cessna 170B. You know, the one with the metal wing and the big, barn-door flaps?

So, on a sunny midday way back on March 7, 1957, Bill lit out of Anchorage in N1470D and headed south for Soldotna, down on the Kenai Peninsula about thirty flying minutes out of Anchorage. With Bill that day was Charles "Charlie" Burnett, owner of the fine little Cessna airplane.

It was about one o'clock in the afternoon when the two of them departed Anchorage's Merrill Field. They must have moseyed around a bit up there because they didn't reach Soldotna until around a quarter to three that afternoon. The weather was still holding severe clear, as they say, and the immediate future was looking good to the two fliers.

Soldotna, aligned roughly east-and-west, lies close along the south side of the Kenai River, which also runs east to west here on its way to the Cook

Inlet. The Kenai (pronounced "Keen-eye") is Alaska's premier king salmon stream, where these sea-run, heavy-fighting brutes average fifty pounds and frequently go to well over ninety.

Anyway, Bill had a dab of business to conduct there that afternoon and was no doubt looking forward to the successful closing of a deal of some sort. Bill always had a deal going, and still does even today, more than fifty years downstream. Anyway, with Soldotna now in view up ahead, Bill began making his plans for the approach and landing.

The *Alaska Airport Directory* for that period listed the Soldotna strip as 2,500 feet long, gravel, with a note that states, "trees 50 feet high surround area." More recently, Jeppesen's instrument approach plates for Soldotna show both landing and takeoff procedures for instrument flight from an airport that now even boasts pilot-controlled lighting for night operations. The instrument pilot can select from the NDB DME Runway 7 approach, the VOR-A approach, and even the RNAV Runway 7 approach. Back in 1957 when Bill made his fated trip, he couldn't have dreamed of such improvements. Nor could I, back in those days.

Now, ol' Bill had only around one hundred flying hours at that time, and he was probably looking closely at the small strip, which no doubt looked even smaller to him than it really was. Surrounded by trees five stories tall, though, the strip wasn't made with a whole lot of slack for the casual pilot. I'm only guessing, but my own experience tells me that he was very intent on the limited size of the strip he was seeing from a moving airplane, and he may have overlooked a small thing or two in the cockpit.

Operation of the flaps, for example.

At any rate, Bill first made a low pass along the length of the strip as he checked for wind direction and general field conditions. He circled the field once more before he finally lined up for the landing and gave it a try. He was a bit too high and too fast for it, so he circled the field once again.

This time, he thought it looked good, so he went for the landing. It's my supposition that Bill had overlooked pulling down the Cessna's barn-door flaps, since he wasn't really familiar with this model, and he probably came over the fence at around sixty-five or seventy miles an hour. Maybe a bit fast for the four-place Cessna with its high-lift wing. His wheels touched the runway smoothly enough, but after about fifty feet, the wheels struck what Bill believes was a frost heave, which pitched the Cessna back into the air. He left the power reduced to almost nothing, and once again the airplane touched the gravel strip's uneven surface.

Bill could see that what was left of the little strip ahead of the rolling Cessna wasn't going to be enough. He verified that the carburetor heat control was in the "cold" position and then pushed the throttle to the full forward position, applying takeoff power for the go-around. Without flaps to increase lift on the slow-moving wings, the added power wasn't going to be enough, though.

With the trees at the end of the strip seeming to grow ever higher—and at an alarming rate as well—Bill just plain ran out of air speed, and the stalwart Cessna entered a power-on stall, a very quick-acting stall, indeed. Bill immediately lowered the nose in an attempt to pick up a little more air speed, but it was too little and too late. He was about 170 feet beyond the end of the strip when the landing gear impacted a rock about half the size of Texas. And the airplane stopped for good.

Bill's written report of the accident, as shown on the U.S. Department of Commerce, Civil Aeronautics Administration Form ACA-2400 (ll-55) is a masterpiece of understatement: "I then pushed the Carburetor heat to the cold position and applied full power to go around. In an effort to clear the trees which was [sic] on the end of the runway I stalled the airplane. I then dropped the nose to pick up air speed and at that time I must have dropped the nose low enough to hit the rock which was at the South bank of the slough located approximately 175 feet from the end of the runway."

I especially like the part where Bill says he "must have dropped the nose low enough to hit the rock."

It wasn't really all that smooth, one has to think. Under the section that says, "Describe Aircraft Damage," Bill had written: "Right wing tip, Right landing gear pulled out of fuselage, Propeller beyond repair, Engine stopped with full power applied, Extensive damage inside fuselage, Engine mount and cowling badly damaged, Fuselage twisted, Windshield broken." The truth of the matter is, good ol' 1470D must have hit that rock like a hot cow pie.

That sort of thing can ruin a guy's whole day, of course, and I suppose it ruined both Charlie's and Bill's. Bill was pretty badly banged up, what with broken legs, lots of cuts and bruises, and contusions and the like. But then, Bill's always been a survivor. Charlie ended up with several fractured ribs, a busted kneecap, and a soberingly impressive list of cuts, bruises, bumps, and abrasions.

I'm glad Bill did survive that little episode, since he's still a good friend of mine, now more than fifty years down the road. In fact, Bill was the best man at my second wedding, a long, long time ago. And, though that marriage went away a long, long time ago, too, I can't hold that against Bill, can I?

***

The story of Dyton Gilliland, though, is a sadder one. You may remember Dyton, who was at one time holder of the world record for Alaska moose horns. Dyton lived down there beside Kenai Lake, just up from where it becomes the famous Kenai River, a fast-running, world-class fishing stream. Dyton lived there year round, and at times the weather got so bad—and hung on so long during the winter months—that some of the locals began carving perpetual motion machines from green spruce wood just to keep from going completely squirrelly.

One crisp fall day back in the mid-fifties, Dyton picked up his favorite rifle and moseyed out to find some winter moose meat for his screened meat house, a staple against the coming winter. He bagged a real monster, too, but since he wasn't a "horn hunter," he left the big rack of horns lying in the woods out there behind his place. That set of horns probably weighed more than 160 pounds anyway, so why bother with all the work of packing it back home?

The next spring, though, he thought about those huge horns, and once again he traipsed into the woods behind his place. Locating the horns—surprisingly still not porcupine-chewed—he lugged the huge things back to lie underfoot on his front porch for several more years. I can't tell you how many times we cursed as we walked around those big things. One of his more skookum friends finally told him he should have the horns measured for the next edition of the *North American Book of Big Game Animals*, as recorded by the Boone & Crockett Club. After stumbling over the damned horns for several years—he had left them on the porch right beside his front door—he finally decided to take them to Anchorage to have them measured and scored. Lo and behold, they were the new world record moose antlers!

It was only a few years later that Dyton decided on a little Sitka deer hunting trip to Montague Island, out there in Prince William Sound. Flying his own Super Cub, he was. Got a little careless with a very low ceiling, some said, and just plain flew into the face of solid rock. Another incredible Alaskan gone quietly west.

That wasn't the case with Pat Kelly, though. Pat and his wife lived near us in Bootleggers Cove, part of "old" Anchorage. Pat flew as chief pilot for Bob Reeve's Reeve Aleutian Airways for something like twenty-eight years. Two things stand out as pretty remarkable about those twenty-eight years: Reeve Aleutian could boast of a perfect safety record, and the airline flew the Aleutian Island chain, a series of islands that extends more than one thousand miles out into the cold and lonely north Pacific Ocean. The worst weather in the world is born there, and it is a bastard child born with a howling vengeance. It is there, too, that the United States was invaded during World War II. Many folks seem to have forgotten that the Japanese stormed ashore there in the Aleutian Islands, and it later took a powerful lot of bad-weather flying, and no small amount of shooting, to dislodge them. The Army Air Corps lost a batch of planes during that far-away little war.

Pat Kelly flew the long, cold, and lonely schedule—and did it both cheerfully and safely—for each of those twenty-eight foggy, windy, rainy, snowy, and generally miserable years. His reward for all that? He was hit and killed by a little red pickup truck as he walked along the highway near Talkeetna, Alaska, a little town about one hundred air miles north of his home in Anchorage.

As for the airline's founder, Bob Reeve, he certainly had his fair share of luck, both good and bad. Of course, he flew to places where most of us wouldn't throw a dead skunk. He sometimes pointed out that the weather had been so bad the year he was born that not a single flight got off the ground! Of course, he was born in 1902, a couple years *before* the Ohio bicycle mechanics, Wilbur and Orville, made their historic first-flight contribution at Kitty Hawk.

Bob Reeve arrived in Alaska after cutting his teeth on the Andes Mountains in South America. When he smacked up a little Lockheed at Santiago, Chilé, after hitting a rock on a newly graded runway, he knew that Pan American Airways management might be a little testy about it. Rather than get the sack, he jumped the gun on them and headed home to Wisconsin for a short visit. While there, though, he fell through some winter ice and had to walk four or five miles home, still wet and nearly frozen. He lay flat on his back in bed for a month after that episode. He was alarmed one day to find that his right leg seemed to be shrinking. And it was, though it would only be years later that he would learn that he had actually suffered an attack of polio. That was back in 1932. He headed for Alaska as soon as he was able to travel.

When I first met Bob, his airline was already something of a legend. The line's home office was just behind the old Kennedy Hardware, which sat on the corner of Fourth Avenue and E Street in downtown Anchorage. Bob was never without his cane or his snap-brim fedora. And he always had a bright twinkle in his blue eyes.

To see him—indeed, even to talk with him—one would never guess at his incredible background. During the early part of World War II, he supplied building materials and equipment to most of the Army Air Corps fields that were being so hurriedly constructed in remote parts of Alaska. He relied heavily upon a big, yellow Boeing 80-A that Morrison-Knudsen had ordered for him. It was a huge and ugly old thing, a big yellow devil with three engines. It was perfect, though, for the work ahead. It wasn't at all unusual to see the big tin bird stagger off the ground with an overload measured in tons rather than pounds. Rated at about four thousand pounds, Bob would often double that load. And he did it with the casual air that he seemed to carry with him wherever he went. By the time Bob had flown this yellow beast for two or three days, he felt comfortable in loading six or seven thousand pounds inside it for almost every flight. And though one of the three engines usually gave up on takeoff, Bob found the ship flew just about as well on two as on three. If the plane came off the ground, Bob would fly it away.

During the construction of the runway facility at Northway, Bob and his "Yellow Peril" flew in with a boiler that weighed eleven thousand pounds! Alaska's seeming penchant for overloading its airplanes didn't start with Bob Reeve, but it didn't stop with him, either. The same attitude, and the same overloads, are still seen throughout the state even today. I think the FAA gave up on that state when they slipped in a short exception to their restrictive regulations: Alaska bush pilots are allowed a 15 percent overload in their special little airplanes. Since the 15 percent doesn't really amount to much, Alaska's pilots don't pay much attention to those numbers, either. They just throw the heaviest stuff up front and the lighter stuff in the back. If it comes off the ground, or off the water, they figure it'll fly.

Bob had cut his teeth on the Andes Mountains of South America back in the days when he flew the mail for Pan American. When he first arrived in Alaska, he was impressed with a territory that looked for all the world as though it was made entirely of mountains. After looking over several spots in his search for a place to begin his cold northern flying career, he settled on Valdez. If nothing else, Valdez can rightfully claim to be "mountainous." It was here that Bob Reeve perfected his technique of flying on skis all year round. He could hit the glaciers and high gold mine strips on skis, then land on the mud flats when he got back to town. The trick was that he had to stop on the mud—or in some pretty shallow water—when the plane finally ground to a halt. When he was ready to depart, the upturned skis would climb to the surface, if underwater, then slide along smoothly until liftoff. This technique is still used in Alaska today, and I suppose it's used in lots of other places, too. It's a bit like using floats to land on snow, mud, or grass. The only real problem is that, when the airplane finally stops, the pilot must already have it headed in the direction he intends to go when he takes off again.

Bob's first glacier landing went much like the "firsts" of so many other bush pilots, both yesterday's and today's. He was asked to fly supplies, equipment, and men to The Big Four, thirty or forty miles from Valdez and somewhere up on Brevier Glacier. Jack Cook, owner of the mine, told Bob that there was a perfect landing spot right at the mine. Said it was a thousand feet long, flat as a stone, and as smooth as silk.

When clear weather allowed Bob to have a look at the mine, Jack Cook went along as a passenger. From the air, Bob could get a true picture of the "perfect" landing spot. It was really a steep, hollowed-out snow shelf hanging off the side of the world. It might have been six hundred feet long but certainly looked less than that. And it sloped uphill at something like twenty-five degrees, with a big curled ridge along the outside.

There were no trees and no brush growing there, so depth perception would be a matter of pure guesswork. It was a stark white world, and Bob knew he was in a tight spot. He decided to do a "low-and-slow" over the proposed landing area. But, when he came in on his look-see run, he fell a little behind the power curve. The slope ran uphill faster than his plane could climb, and he ended up smashing into the mountain at the top of the incline. The snow was so deep, though, that there was no damage done to the plane, and he and Jack were able to stomp out a flat spot, turn the plane around, and take off downhill again without much trouble. Later, Bob would hire another pioneer bush pilot, Harold Gillam, to fly him over the strip so he could drop out a bunch of gunnysacks to mark the landing area and to give the pilot a little depth perception.

Glaciers are a very special sort of environment. There is no argument about their being dangerous. They just are. An experienced former U.S. Marine pilot discovered that a few years ago. What should have been nothing more than a routine aircraft delivery flight for him turned out to be tragic.

It seems that this very experienced pilot was delivering a Cessna Agcat to Anchorage. For some reason—and I have no idea what that reason was—our pilot elected to fly west toward Merrill Pass and Mt. Spurr, a semiactive volcano. While in that vicinity, he decided to set the agricultural model—*at least it was a taildragger!*—down on a great snowfield near its top. Big mistake number one. The view from there, however, was magnificent!

Upon landing, of course, the plane sank up to its wings in the snow, and the ex-Marine was now afoot. He was in radio contact with Anchorage, which he could plainly see as he looked eastward and down across Cook Inlet toward the Chugach Mountains that formed the city's backdrop. Approach Control told the pilot to stick with his airplane and wait for a rescue helicopter to pick him up. One would be there shortly, he was told.

"Naw," he replied. "I'll just walk on down the glacier. They can pick me up at the bottom. Wouldn't want them to put down in this deep snow up here." Big mistakes numbers two and three. I expect he calculated that a helicopter liftoff from his present position might be a bit hazardous. Perhaps so, but the USAF air-sea-rescue wallahs do it all the time. As I said, big mistakes numbers two and three.

Had he stayed with the aircraft, which wasn't hurt in any meaningful way, he would have (a) been protected from the wind, (b) possibly had some semblance of survival gear he could use, perhaps a sleeping bag, tent, rations, and the like, and (c) still had radio communications with the outside world. Given the disarmingly mild and sunny day, and with visibility out beyond two hundred miles, I'm sure the pilot's perspective was a little out of whack. He clearly thought the stroll down the snowfield and off the mountain would be a piece of cake. And, of course, it *was* a beautiful day.

When he released the microphone button after that last transmission, he had effectively severed all connection with his fellow man. As far as I know, he was never heard from again, nor has his body ever been found. Alaska: the big, the beautiful . . . and the terribly unforgiving.

***

Merrill Field, which lies along East Fifth Avenue in Anchorage, used to be, and mostly still is, something of a shabby little thing. Oh, it now has paved runways, a better control tower than the old World War II model that finally disappeared during the 1964 Good Friday earthquake, and a few more flight schools than it used to have, but it's still a little shabby by modern standards. Anyway, the airport was named after Russ Merrill.

Russell Merrill came to Alaska after flying for the U.S. Navy. He started a little air service out of Anchorage, back when the "airport" was just an empty stretch of cleared land that later became the "Park Strip," located between Ninth and Tenth Avenues and stretching west from C Street to L Street. Sometime during the afternoon of September 16, 1929, Russ lifted his little Whirlwind Travel Air off at Anchorage, this time carrying a compressor that had been ordered for a gold mine operation. He never got where he was going, and the wreckage of his airplane was never found. A small piece of fabric later washed up along Cook Inlet, and it was identified by Merrill's mechanics as belonging to his little Travel Air.

***

A very large percentage of Alaska's earliest pioneer bush pilots were destined to fly out but to not fly back. One of the very greatest was Carl Ben Eielson. Eielson Air Force Base in Fairbanks, Alaska, was named for this great flier.

By early 1929, Eielson had already flown Captain George Wilkins, the crusty Australian pilot-explorer, from Alaska to Spitzbergen, Norway. Later that same year, they flew toward the other pole, this time finding new land masses from the air, the first time this had ever been done. That same year Eielson was given the Distinguished Flying Cross. President Herbert Hoover also presented him with the Harmon Trophy, the highest civilian award this country can grant, and he was already planning another Antarctic expedition. The trip was later cancelled, by the way. It was in the fall of 1929 when Eielson's string finally ran out.

In October of that year, the trading motor ship *Nanuk* found itself hopelessly icebound just north of the Siberian village of North Cape. Along with the crew, the ship carried fifteen passengers and more than one million dollars in furs. Officials of Seattle's Swenson Fur and Trading Corporation feared a market collapse. They wanted those furs offloaded as quickly as possible for shipment to Seattle and New York. The passengers had to be rescued, certainly. Toward this end, they offered Eielson the handsome sum of five thousand dollars to rescue the passengers and remove the furs, taking both back to Alaska.

Eielson accepted the contract, and, along with mechanic Earl Borland, flew to Teller, Alaska, the village that most agreed was the best place from which to stage the operation.

In late October, Eielson and Borland flew Eielson's all-metal Hamilton on the first trip to the icebound *Nanuk*. Pilot Frank Dorbrandt and mechanic Bud Basset, flying a Stinson, also made that first trip. Headed home to Teller, though, they were caught in a blizzard and were forced to land on the Siberian coast. They were weathered in for five more days before their return flight was possible. After their safe return, bad weather kept them on the ground for nearly another week.

Dorbrandt, a flier not all that put off by the terrible weather, wondered when Eielson was going to get back into the air, openly accusing him of being cowardly in the face of some less-than-sunny weather.

On the morning of November 9, Dorbrandt could take no more of this lazing around. "You can sit around here all you like, but I'm leaving!"

Reports have it that at 10:45 that morning, people in the roadhouse heard Dorbrandt's Stinson lift off. Eielson and Borland shucked into their parkas, and at about 11:15 that same morning, their Hamilton lifted off and headed west.

Later that morning, stopped by dense fog in the Bering Strait, Dorbrandt and Bassett returned. Eielson and Borland did not.

The sun had by now dropped below the horizon, providing only a few meager hours of hazy daylight at midday. The sun wouldn't rise again for some time. Moreover, the winter of 1929 would be a real brute. The temperature dropped to minus forty, and winds up to seventy miles per hour buffeted the area with discouraging regularity but certainly without mercy.

Radio messages from the icebound *Nanuk* continued to pour in, but they always said the same thing: "Ceiling and visibility nil—high winds."

Every morning, bone-cold mechanics would stumble to their aircraft carrying the oil that had been drained the night before. Placed near the roadhouse stove, it was warm each morning, but even when one of the bold pilots took off into the frigid darkness, he would return in only a few minutes. The Bering Strait was impassable.

Appeals to Russia for their help seemed to fall on deaf ears. There were no official relations between the United States and the Union of Soviet Socialist Republics, and our own state department refused to act.

Eielson, though, was considered something of an Arctic hero in Russia, too, and Moscow posted a one-thousand-dollar reward to Siberians for any word of the Arctic flier. Soviet planes were ordered to proceed to North Cape as soon as weather would permit.

The whole story of this agonizing search effort would itself make a whale of a book. The end result, though, wouldn't change: the remains of Eielson's plane would be found on the ice almost a month after it had slipped into the air back at Teller. It wouldn't be until February 13 that mechanic Borland's body would be found. The body of Carl Ben Eielson would be found on the morning of February 18. Canadian and American pilots banded together to complete Eielson's contract with the Swenson Fur and Trading Corporation, even replacing the fuel that had been provided on the Soviet side of the Bering Strait.

A complete, and truly moving, account of the Carl Ben Eielson search can be found in Jean Potter's great book, *The Flying North*.

***

Among the pioneer Alaska bush pilots there were the great, the not-so-great, and a few that defied any category at all—such as Archie Ferguson.

Now, Archie started the farthest-north airline on this continent. Based out of Kotzebue, hard against the Arctic Sea, Archie's airline did just fine. And although his little airline seldom flew north of Barrow, he advertised that he would fly "ANYWHERE—ANYTIME." Archie was truly a whole gaggle of geese. Once, when returning to Nome, the radios there blurted out, "Nome Radio, Nome Radio, this is Cessna two zero seven six six. Christ, it's startin' ta rain up here! Looks like some awful dirty stuff ahead. I'm comin' in! I'm comin' in!"

"Cessna two zero seven six six," came back Nome Radio, "are you declaring an emergency?"

"Yer damn right, it's an emergency," Archie shouted. "Christ, any time I'm in the air it's an emergency!" Yep, that was Archie.

Like the time he flew a small polar bear back to Kotzebue from Point Hope. Had the little white bear trussed up like a Christmas pig, but during some heavy turbulence, the ropes somehow came loose. Next thing Archie knew, the bear was loose in the cockpit with him.

"Ya hear that noise?" he asked of Nome Radio. "That ain't static; that's a bear! Oh, Jeezus . . . he's tryin' ta eat up the fuselage!"

When Archie finally landed, observers thought it was the smoothest landing he had ever made. Many insisted that the bear was most likely at the controls, since Archie wasn't known for making smooth landings. One has to wonder how many times the Alaska outback has heard Archie's enthusiastic, "Christ, I love ta fly!"

***

Alaska pilot Johnny Littley was another who sometimes faced odds calculated to exasperate a saint. He was carrying several passengers, including a little Scotch terrier (known all over Alaska as a Scotty dog), all destined for some sort of medical treatment or other when they arrived at Flat, another not-much village in the Interior.

One of the passengers, Big Hans, had a rupture. Another, Gus Wilson, was traveling with a leg crushed by a collapsing wind dam. The leg was now as big as a large ham. Prospector Walter Culver was aboard, too, along with the little Scotty, who had been rather badly mauled by a handful of malamute sled dogs.

During the takeoff, Littley's right wheel hit a large grass-covered hump, breaking the lower strut. With no way to shout above the engine's roar, pilot Littley passed a note to Big Hans. In spite of Big Hans' rupture, Littley wanted him to crawl out the window, tie a rope around the lower strut, and pull it up so that the wheel would be in position to land. He told Big Hans that Walt Culver would hold his legs so he wouldn't just slip on off and disappear into the big Alaska wilderness.

Now, Big Hans was a two-hundred-pound Dane. He also wasn't feeling all that well because of his rupture. Still, he was game if Walt Culver was. Walt simply grabbed Big Hans' big feet and poked him headfirst out the open window.

Well, Big Hans finally roped the broken strut, hauled for all he was worth, and finally got it tied into place. He had lost his glasses, his fountain pen, and his wallet in the process, but he figured that was a small price to pay. At least he hadn't slipped off the wing!

With all the strength Walt Culver could dredge up, he hauled Big Hans back through the open window. Pilot Littley thanked them both but admitted that he didn't believe one rope was going to be enough. So, back out the window went Big Hans, with prospector Culver once again hangin' on for dear life.

When they finally arrived at Flat, Littley circled the field several times to let everyone know that there was a bit of a problem with the aircraft. Then he lined 'er up and settled on down for the landing.

One of the men on the ground saw what the trouble was and immediately started his old stake-bed truck, driving it out onto the runway. As Littley landed, the ropes holding the landing gear broke, but the airplane settled only a few inches. The truck driver had pulled his vehicle beneath the airplane and matched its speed as he drove along under the wing. Quite a show, really, and Littley was able to land the little airplane without further damage. Local miners helped Littley mend the broken strut and, in no time at all, he was on his way again.

***

Patching up a bush airplane isn't much of a challenge to many of Alaska's outback pilots. Floats have been patched with five-gallon aviation fuel cans. I once patched a Super Cub float with two lengths of a hunting cabin smokestack and yellow duct tape. I've heard of bed sheets being used as fabric, painted onto the airplane with sourdough pancake mix and then allowed to freeze in place. I've used wet newspapers as fabric patches, allowing them to dry in place before flying away. Once when I had done that, and had returned the following morning to change out the torn horizontal stabilizer, I found a red tag applied by the old CAA along with a note telling me the government didn't consider newspaper a suitable patching material and that the airplane was no longer "airworthy." This was one of those times when I had to agree with the government.

I've used angle iron to fortify a wing strut, and several of us have used the five-gallon avgas cans for such things as rebuilding a vertical stabilizer in the bush. A flying dentist, Doc LaRue, once used the side rail of a baby's crib for the same purpose. Someone said old Lon Cope broke a tail ski and replaced it with a coal shovel. Artie Brauetigam and I once tried to repair a broken Super Cub tail spring by wrapping it with a nylon strap. It held just long enough to get us off a little bitty crooked and bumpy gravel bar at the foot of the Tokositna Glacier and then to make one more very cautious landing back at Anchorage.

Come to think of it, I guess that's pretty much why all of us flew the vast and empty Alaska backcountry: we all wanted to make just one more landing.

Those pilots who flew, and still fly, to rough landing spots in the Alaska bush—and those who fly in the aid and comfort of those hard and hardy folks who struggle to live there—will never be content to taxi along the blacktop and concrete of major airports. And those who have mastered the techniques of flying year in and year out over the Big Empty could never be happy when chained to those routes above roads, railroads, and cities heavy with people. These are the pilots who learned early on the various options available to the quick and the skilled when it came to emergency landings. Knocking off the landing gear to soften a landing, for instance. Side slipping to the landing so that one wing might absorb much of the impact. The records are a testament to the skills of these outback airplane drivers: in the ten years preceding World War II, Alaska pilots flew more than thirty million air miles under the world's worst weather conditions. In all those backcountry miles, only sixty-three pilots and passengers lost their lives. All this in wilderness areas so remote that the government had yet to establish itself in the effort to "help" the bush fliers in their awesome undertaking. As if these guys wanted any help from the government in the first place.

These were the guys who flew in such terrible weather that, when forced down by fog while flying floats along coastal areas, they might shut 'er off, climb down onto a float, and taste the water to see if it was salt or fresh! That would give the pilot some idea of where he might be.

Listen to one of the old-timers telling one of the new pilots how to get through Rainy Pass: "To get through the pass, ya gotta start where the Rhon River meets the south fork of the Kuskokwim. There's a cache on the mouth of the creek right there. Turn left and take the first canyon to your right. You'll see a canyon on your left that looks pretty good, but don't take it—it makes a lazy turn to the left, then a hard to the right. If you can crawl under the fog that far, you'll make it through okay. You'll jist go by a little green lake and come on out on Ptarmigan Valley and start down the Happy River past Stillman Lake and then go into Happy River canyon." If you're not comfortable with instructions like that, it might be best not to look toward making a career of flying the Alaska wilderness country.

***

I guess my own hero has always been the legendary pioneer bush pilot, Harold Gillam. "Thrill-em, chill-em, no kill-um Gillam," as some said of his bad-weather flying abilities. He was known throughout the territory for his contempt of bad weather. Since many of my contemporaries sometimes found fault with my flying in bad weather, I've thought quite a lot about it. I've decided that, in my case anyway, it wasn't really a death wish. I found that I just had better vision than some of the other guys. It has made me wonder whether Harold Gillam might have been plagued—or blessed, as the case may be—with the same hyper-sensitive vision.

In my own case, I had 20/5 vision, which meant that I could see clearly at twenty feet what others expect to see at only five feet. Beyond that, my eyes could detect motion at twenty images per second. That means that my eyes could perceive twenty separate pictures per second. Most people's seem to top out below sixteen, I have been told.

That may be why I found flying in "blinding" snow not all that difficult. The curse is that I can see a flickering in all fluorescent fixtures, and working under their light source gives me a headache after about one hour. In today's world, that truly is a curse and more than makes up for the blessing of being able to fly while the ducks and geese are walking. I'm glad to remember that there were precious few fluorescent lights in Harold Gillam's day!

Chapter 5

Eric and the Spruce Tree

It's always better to be down here wishing you were up there, than up there wishing you were down here.

I'm certainly not the only Alaska pilot who sometimes fell behind the power curve. Witness what happened to a friend of mine, Eric Dorondo, now of Aloha, Oregon.

Eric Dorondo began his flying career in 1969. In the next two years of flying out of Anchorage, Alaska, he managed to build up some thirty-five flying hours as a student pilot.

In the spring of 1971, he rented a two-place Cessna 150 (N5786G) from Flight Proficiency, a flight school based at Anchorage International Airport, the big airport that borders Lake Hood and the world's largest seaplane base.

Eric had a good relationship with Flight Proficiency and was almost one of the family there. He had spent a lot of time with them as a gas boy, line boy, aircraft detailer, maintenance helper, and general gofer for the company. You know—go fer a san'wich, go fer some parts, go fer some coffee . . .

Anyway, on to Eric and his sharp little Cessna 150. The ship had been fitted with long-range fuel tanks, and Eric saw to it that these were topped off to the filler necks that morning.

Then he loaded in a duffel bag with all those goodies he thought he might need in case of an emergency. Among that gear was at least one sleeping bag, a bunch of dried food and other stuff, along with his father's .22-caliber pistol and extra ammunition. (At that time, a firearm and ammunition were among those articles required as part of a pilot's emergency gear under Alaska law.)

Eric's plan was to scoot across Turnagain Arm and head on down to Kenai and Homer.

He had lifted off in a light drizzle that morning, weather more typical than not in this part of Alaska. He would fly over to meet his father at a small airstrip, Siefker Airstrip, just south of Anchorage and directly in line with his planned route to the Kenai Peninsula. The little strip is officially named "Sky Harbor," but not many of the locals call it that.

The tiny strip is not recommended for low-time pilots. Like so very many Alaska strips, it was whacked out of the woods in a locale not especially friendly to light aircraft in the first place. Heavy winds often buffet that area as they come roaring out of Prince William Sound, pour through restrictive Portage Pass, howl up Turnagain Arm, and bend with determination around the edge of the Chugach Range near Rabbit Creek to generally abuse large parts of Anchorage, this part included.

Eric found the small dirt-and-gravel strip without trouble, but it didn't look very large from his perspective. It did look suitable, though, and Eric set up for his approach and landing. It should be noted that the little dab of clearing is listed on the charts as a meager 1,200 feet in length and that it slopes uphill. Eric's little C-150 would need 1,385 feet of runway to clear those trees at the far end, though, even on a hard-surfaced runway. And the charts label this field as "soft," even in *dry* weather. It's the kind of airstrip that most pilots from the Lower 48 will pass up as much, *much* too small. Alaskans, though, learn to fly off these little buggers, and I doubt that Eric gave it much more than a brief second thought that drizzly morning. After all, it was an airstrip, wasn't it?

Eric had never flown into Sky Harbor before, and he wasn't aware that the strip sloped slightly upward toward the nearby Chugach Mountains. With only thirty-five hours under his seat belt, he probably wasn't as equipped to read the strip as some of the local bush pilots. The strip was surrounded tightly by tall trees, too, both birch and spruce, leaving the clearing even harder to interpret, especially since it was raining that typical precipitation that haunts coastal Alaskan cities like Anchorage.

The persistent drizzle had made the runway pretty mushy. Eric thought that it looked as though it might have been recently graded. Most of the families nearby had cut and graded their own access roads to begin with, and maintenance of this little clearing was pretty much left to the local residents.

Well, Eric set everything up for the landing and then descended smoothly onto the little strip without incident. In fact, it had been a damned good landing he figured, everything considered. Eric felt pretty good about it, since the strip carried that cautionary note about low-time pilots. He didn't know that he had just rolled the dice—and lost.

He taxied over to his father's car, which was then parked alongside the strip. After a few moments spent in just passing the time and chatting, Eric decided it was time to get moving. Looking around the wet and muddy little strip, he judged the wind direction and velocity—as near as he could, that is, from his position on the protected little homemade airstrip buried deep beneath the crowding trees—and decided it pointed to an uphill takeoff.

Now, remember that Eric wasn't all that impressed with the slight uphill pitch in the strip's surface at this point and may, in fact, not even have noticed it. Neither was he concerned with the wet softness of the ground here. Perhaps the very last thing he was concerned with was the heavy load of aviation fuel in those long-range wing tanks—still filled to the tops of their filler necks—or even with the extra weight he carried in emergency gear that morning. In any event, Eric's little Cessna N5786G was plenty heavy. It was now poised for takeoff on a wet, muddy, and no doubt soft, raw earth strip—and one that was not only surrounded tightly by adult trees but that pitched up toward the six-thousand-foot-high mountains, just a stone's throw away. Eric was right where so many of his flying fraternity brothers have been over the years: balanced precariously on the razor's edge of disaster.

The little Continental engine was still warm, so Eric didn't have to tarry long after he had made the decision to leave. He taxied to the end of the strip, where he surely did a magneto check and verified that he could get full fuel flow for the takeoff. Then, lined up and standing on the brakes for a moment in order to get a quicker start with his takeoff run, Eric looked once more down the length of that muddy little strip. When he released the brakes for the takeoff, Eric Dorondo's immediate future was sharply chiseled in stone.

One can only imagine Eric's takeoff run along that marginal little strip. The muddy surface grabbing at the Cessna's skinny 6.00x6.00 tires. The mud, squirted up by the wheels and dispersed by the spinning propeller, painting large red-brown stripes along the underside of the little Cessna's wings. The horizontal stabilizer was by now coated with the thick red stuff, too.

The little Cessna skittered from side to side a bit, though the small nose wheel helped to keep the hurtling little plane pretty much aligned with the mud and gravel strip as it dashed boldly along. Eric was by now quite busy on the rudder pedals.

With the throttle jammed against its stop, it began to dawn on Eric that he was only limping toward an air speed sufficient for liftoff. By then, though, he figured that he had passed the point of no return and was now fully committed to the takeoff.

By the time Eric's busy thought processes grasped the fact that he was now in hot water clear up to his belt buckle, it was already too late. The trees at the far end were no longer far at all. More than that, they now seemed much taller than before!

At this point, a more experienced pilot might have elected to ground-loop the little ship. The thought of purposefully inflicting damage upon someone else's airplane, however, very likely didn't dawn on Eric. There was only time now to pull firmly back on the control wheel and hope for the best. And, with the pedal to the metal, as they say, that's exactly what Eric did.

The stalwart little craft wobbled and struggled reluctantly free of the muddy strip, encouraged by ground effect—a condition wherein certain aerodynamic anomalies would keep the aircraft flying even though it might be struggling along below its known stall speed. The trees at the strip's end filled the windshield as Eric raised the nose, asking now that both air speed and altitude join him in his decision to rotate and fly away to safety. Neither was listening to him, though.

Almost before he knew it, the shrubs and small spruce at the field's end were passing in a blur beneath the belly of Eric's struggling little airplane. And, for a moment at least, Eric believed that he had made it. Probably his father, watching from the safety of his car, saw all too clearly that gravity had more influence on Eric's flight at that point than did lift and power. He wasn't at all sure that Eric was going to succeed. He turned the ignition key and started his car.

Back in the cockpit, things seemed to be happening with blinding speed. Eric had the wheel as far back as prudence would allow. The stall warning light was flashing before his eyes, and the alarm buzzer was now screaming with all the strength its irritating and piercing electronic voice could muster. Eric was in a pickle.

Both Eric's eyes and his mind had developed tunnel vision by now, his breathing had become so shallow that it might as well have stopped altogether, and the thought of any possible option at this point lay concealed

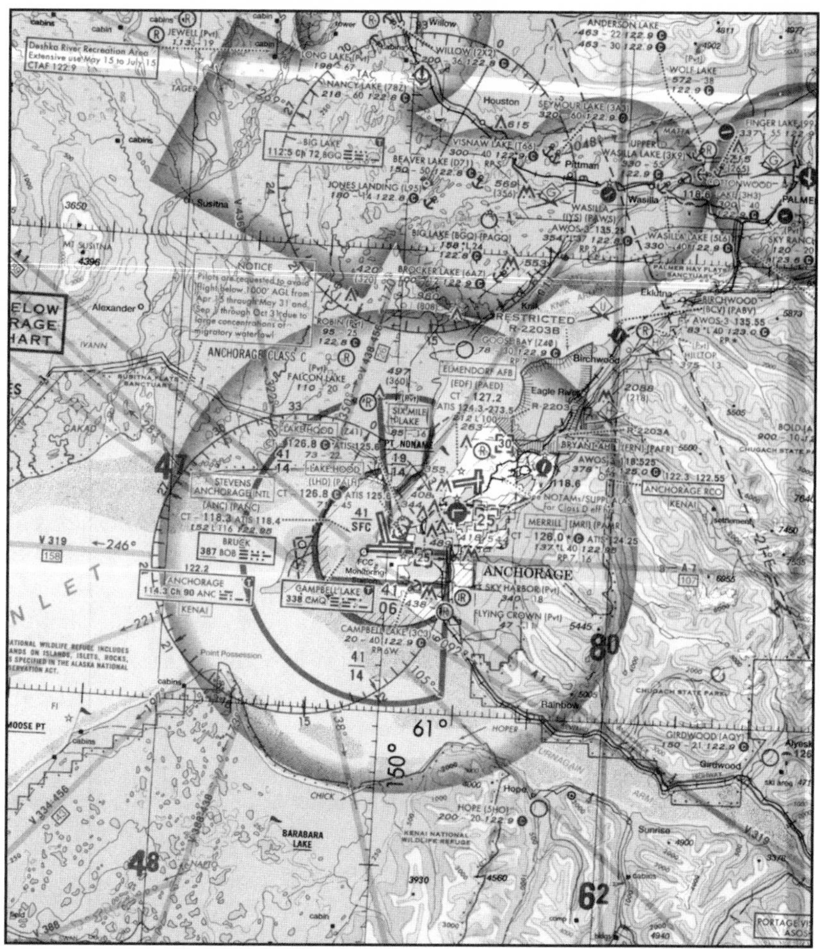

The busy skies at Anchorage see aircraft from as many as nine local airports, strips, and lakes. It was at one of these small local fields that Eric misjudged his airplane's performance and landed in a spruce tree.

somewhere deep inside his brain. If he had yanked the flap handle to the full down position—even though it certainly isn't recommended—perhaps the increased lift would have overcome the added drag and reduced his stall speed by a couple of knots, giving him the miracle he now so desperately needed. At any rate, Eric was now an accident that had finally found a place to happen.

The ground ahead was rising faster than the airplane could climb. The little two-place Cessna was struggling valiantly for altitude, and Eric thought for a brief moment that he might have passed the critical point in this takeoff. Not so.

With an air speed bordering on the danger point already, Eric knew he couldn't begin any sort of turn to avoid the rising ground ahead. To do so at that air speed was to enter a climbing turn stall, often a spectacularly violent maneuver even in the mild-mannered Cessna 150. He could only wobble straight ahead and hope his climb outpaced the growing hill dead ahead, which he now felt he could almost reach out and touch. Eric's legs would begin to cramp in a few more moments, but that didn't matter now. He no longer had a few more moments.

In only seconds more, he noticed some of the treetops beyond his wingtips were higher than the windows through which he glanced. Oh, man—*now they're higher than the wings!*

Still pushing against the throttle control, Eric glanced at the air speed indicator. With the red stall warning light, the screaming stall buzzer, and the shaky air speed needle now hovering dangerously shy of forty miles per hour, Eric knew he couldn't pull the yoke back another millimeter. He was clearly at the mercy of those gods who watch over fliers.

With the last of the trees—clearly the very tallest ones—smack dab in the center of the windshield, Eric gritted his teeth and ordered his white-knuckled grip to pull back just a wee bit more on the control yoke. The faithful little Cessna, though, had already given all it had.

When the landing gear hit the first of the trees, Eric felt his plane yaw first one way and then the other. He knew the airplane was slowing from each encounter. And then it happened.

Eric hit the trees with a solid impact, and the prop dug in to whack off a few of the smaller top branches. Eric didn't hear the noise. Nose high, the engine still roaring to answer Eric's need, the plane hit the next big spruce with a solid WHUMP! The prop sheared off a few more branches before it, too, stopped.

The plane nosed over and slid slowly down the tree trunk until it was only ten or fifteen feet above the earth, where it finally came to rest. Fuel was now running from the tanks buried inside the battered metal wings. In the heat of the moment, Eric forgot to turn off the master switch, so the Cessna's electrical system was still fully energized. The fuel racing toward the earth now focused on the hot engine and its live electrical connections. As it flowed over the hot exhaust stacks, it gave off a smoky mist that Eric recognized. He was sure that an explosion was only seconds away. Still, he did not think of the master switch. He did, however, look to another immediate problem: getting himself the hell down out of that tree!

As quickly as the shock of the situation had worn off, Eric loosened his seat harness and opened the door. With the airplane now in a nose-down attitude in the tree, the door flopped forward, fully open, allowing Eric to stand on the instrument panel, now where the floor should be, and step out to grab a substantial tree branch. Using those rough and sticky Sitka spruce branches as handholds, Eric made it to the ground in only a minute.

Just then, Eric heard a loud "WHOOSH" from above. Looking up, he saw the cockpit already burning. The flames were trying to crawl up the tall spruce, but the tree was too wet to start burning. None of the other trees caught either, and what might have been a number one forest fire later in the year was now only a black smoke signal to other fliers.

The FAA later conducted an investigation of the accident, of course. Eric offered that he thought the Cessna wasn't delivering the power it should have. The FAA responded by reminding him of the soggy strip, standard aircraft performance, the fully loaded airplane—including the long-range fuel tanks—and the inclined runway. In typical governmental speak, they noted: "Failed to obtain/maintain flying speed."

Eric continued to fly for another thirty or forty hours, but, as with many of us, the financial impact of flying finally caught up with him. He hasn't flown for many years now. Still, at a modest fifty years old, he looks forward to sitting in the left seat again one day. While a long layoff will surely have dulled the sharp edge for him, it's still much like riding a bicycle: you just never forget how. And, once there, the flying bug never leaves your blood.

Phil makes still another emergency beach landing with Dan Graves' recently purchased Stinson. *Photo used courtesy of Phil*

Chapter 6

Stinson Fever

When in doubt, hold your altitude.
No one has ever collided with the sky.

Phil grew up in Juneau, Alaska. He had owned a Stinson since the age of eighteen and had learned to fly in that slightly aging but inarguably comfortable and capable airplane. Roomy and truly a four-place airplane, the Stinson has found—and has certainly kept—an honored place in Alaska aviation.

Phil's buddy, Dan Graves, had flown with Phil many times over the last few years, almost always in Phil's Stinson. The plane had safely and comfortably hauled them and their gear through many hunting, fishing, and camping trips over the years. The airplane's comfort and reliability had convinced Dan that he wanted one of the same models, and he had been saving his money toward that goal for several years by now. And at last he was ready.

Phil, of course, had flown the Alaska outback for a long time. Dan was relying upon his friend's experience and advice when it finally came to buying his first airplane, which sort of put Dan in a pretty good position. He could simply have gone ahead and bought the first Stinson that cropped up, but with Phil's certainly qualified help, he was pretty well assured of getting his money's worth. The two of them began poring over the newest "Trade-A-Plane" and other newspaper sources as soon as these publications hit the stands.

One of the first that Dan had stumbled upon had been located in Florida. Photos of the plane showed a really well maintained Stinson, and both Phil and Dan were excited over the possibilities. After several telephone conversations with the owner, they decided they'd better fly on down there and look the airplane over. But, a couple days before they were scheduled to lift off for Florida, Dan told the seller that he wanted to make sure that all the airplane's logs were intact and available.

"Didn't I tell you?" the owner asked. "There ain't no logbooks with it."

Phil had reminded Dan that the logbooks are the airplane. They had to pass this one up and continue the search for another, and much more suitable, airplane. If the search had been for a Super Cub or a Maule or a Cessna of some kind, it would have been much easier. They still make those airplanes. The Stinson, though, is something of a dinosaur, and good ones are kind of hard to find. Still, Dan knew that, if he could find the Stinson he wanted, it would all be well worth the time and effort. Not to mention the money.

The next Stinson that seemed to fill the bill for Dan was located in Texas. This one, too, seemed just about right, and after several phone calls spent listening to the owner insisting that his particular Stinson was in the peak of health, they were both quite interested. The owner also hinted that he was fielding a lot of calls from other interested buyers, too. Dan got the name and telephone number of the mechanic who had been servicing the airplane for several years, and that guy proclaimed, "It's a sweet little plane. I just wish the owner would have had me fix the small leak in the right fuel tank!" Dan called the owner back and asked about that leak.

"I've put the last dollar into that airplane that I'm gonna. And the price is firm!" was the owner's response. Needless to say, the search went on.

The next Stinson they found was located in Fairbanks, not so far away as Texas or Florida. It was low time, too, and well within Dan's price range. This one was owned by a used car salesman, and he knew how to market his product. The pictures he sent showed a showplace Stinson, gleaming and bright in the sunlight. Phil and Dan decided that a trip to Fairbanks was more than worth it, so off they went to check this little jewel out. When they arrived, the seller took them directly to the tiedown area where the little beauty was parked. It turned out that the pictures they had seen were of the only three views that could possibly appeal to a serious buyer. From any other angle, the poor little craft looked like a serious pile of used and abused spare parts!

The headliner had several rips in it, as did the upholstery. The carpet looked as though someone had knifed it out of the floor of his boat, which had probably been the case. It smelled pretty heavily of past salmon catches, and who knows how many salmon had been hauled in this rag-bag Stinson. It looked as though there were three inches of dead bugs on the instrument panel, and the rear carpet was supporting an unhealthy crop of mold.

In spite of all this, the owner fully expected first to wrestle thirty thousand dollars from Dan and then to take them for a short flight in this less than charming bucket of bolts. When it had finally soaked in on the seller that these two weren't interested in a rebuild project, he became downright snotty. In fact, he wouldn't even drive them back to the terminal building where he'd picked them up! So much for contemporary Alaska manners, it seems.

Phil and Dan caught a cab back to the main terminal, and by the time they had boarded a flight for home, they learned that they would only arrive in time to take the late flight out of Anchorage to Juneau. That at least gave them another opportunity to see what the local airports might have to offer in the way of a suitable Stinson.

With a rented car to solve the logistics problem, they visited all the airports they could reach in the six hours of slack time they had between flights. They hit Merrill Field (in Anchorage), Birchwood Field, and finally both Palmer and Wasilla airports, which at last found them more than sixty miles north of Anchorage. Almost desperate now, they were looking at any suitable used four-place airplane that they could find, Stinson or not. While in Wasilla—a pretty small town that measured its residents in the hundreds, they finally spotted a little Stinson tied down right beside the Alaska National Guard hangar.

They drove the rental car over to have a closer look and—lo and behold!—this was the best-looking Stinson either of them had ever seen! This little ship was a real beauty! When Dan mentioned that there was no "For Sale" sign on the plane, Phil said he was going to find out the story behind it anyway.

"Ya never know," Phil said.

Behind the National Guard hangar were two guys sitting in lounge chairs and, as usual, drinking strong Alaska coffee. Phil asked if either of them knew anything about the little Stinson.

"Sure," replied one of the men. "Owner lives in Anchorage. A gal owns it, by the way. Said just last week that she was thinkin' of sellin' the thing. She don't fly it much anyway."

Trying not to show his elation at this revelation, Phil wandered over to where Dan was kicking the tires and generally looking over the pristine little Stinson. Phil told Dan that this might be the one, since the owner reportedly was ready to sell her. They ambled back over to the coffee drinkers and were able to get a telephone number for the owner. Fact is, they got both a home and an office number for the owner. They dashed to a telephone and called her immediately.

"Why, yes," she had said, she would consider selling the airplane, if the price were right. She agreed to meet the two of them at seven o'clock the following morning at a restaurant right there in Wasilla. Phil and Dan cancelled their reservations on the flight to Juneau and found a hotel room for the night. Neither found it easy to get to sleep. After the long search for the right Stinson—and after all the disappointments that had already befallen them—who could blame them for being a little too excited to sleep?

Over a good Alaska breakfast, Dan and the seller finally agreed on a sale price. As is usual, the price included a fresh annual inspection, which would make the aircraft officially "airworthy" for another calendar year.

The owner arranged with a local aircraft mechanic to perform the annual, which was done right there in the National Guard hangar. Phil and Dan did what they could do to assist with the inspection, which gave Dan an opportunity to get a little hands-on time with his "new" airplane and its engine. Little did Dan know that, before he would finally sell the little airplane, he would have learned enough about Franklin engines that he could have taught a class at Alaska University in their particulars. Or at any other university, for that matter! He was destined to have lots and lots of experience maintaining and repairing that engine before the episode was finally over.

After the annual inspection, which was a really thorough one, Phil took the Stinson out on the tarmac and ran the engine up to check it out. When he had warmed the engine and had checked its systems out as thoroughly as possible without actually flying the fabric-covered four-place Stinson, he taxied to the active runway to perform three stop-and-go landings to see how it handled. Turns out that it was truly a jewel among Stinsons, and Phil brought her back to tie her down for the night. They would spend one more night in Wasilla, then light out early the following morning for the long flight to Juneau, the state capital, only reachable by sea or air. There is still no land access to the state capital in Alaska. Probably won't ever be, since the capital city clings precariously to the side of a pretty impressive mountain. That mountain plunges steeply almost directly into salt water, so there's not much flat land around Juneau.

They were both excited about the coming day. Neither of them could possibly have anticipated what that day would bring for them.

They were both up and ready to go before their alarm clock rang at five o'clock the following morning. Quick showers and a short taxi ride to the airport found them ready to preflight Dan's new Stinson, eager to lift off into the smooth morning sky. Phil had planned the first leg of the flight to be nonstop to Cordova for fuel. They saw no need to stop in Anchorage just to waste a part of their flying day.

With one more coastal pit stop in Yakutat, another Alaska town tightly surrounded by some pretty impressive mountains, they would be down to their final leg. This would be a two-and-a-half hour hop on into Juneau. Yakutat would interrupt their trip long enough to allow for a quick lunch break. Didn't work out that way, though.

They had stopped for avgas in Cordova, right on schedule, and then had taxied to the active for departure. It wouldn't be a run-of-the-mill takeoff, though. As the handsome little Stinson lifted off the Cordova runway, the main seal at the forward end of the crankshaft let loose. Oil spray almost covered the windshield, and Phil had to open the pilot's side window and stick his head half out into the slipstream in order to follow the twelve-mile paved road straight back into Cordova. Meanwhile, Dan was keeping one eye on the oil pressure gauge. If that needle went to zero, the engine would seize in a matter of seconds.

Phil finally lined up on the Eyak Airstrip in downtown Cordova, finishing this short but troublesome flight with a smooth landing. Though backed up with many thousands of Alaska flying hours, Phil was no doubt a little like most of us when he knows full well that everything can go south in a hurry. I reckon his focus was pretty well narrowed to flying the ailing little airplane.

In typical Alaska fashion, a mechanic from Cordova Air Service jumped right in to help them sop up the oil spill.

By the way, don't confuse Cordova Air Service with the old Cordova Airlines. This latter was the airline built by Merle K. "Mudhole" Smith, one of Alaska's pioneer bush pilots. His portrait still hangs in Anchorage International Airport's terminal building. I worked with Mudhole's airline back in the mid-fifties. The airline was built of Cessna 180s, a couple of old DC-3s (actually DC-3Cs, having been converted from old U.S. Army C-47 Dakotas), and one Aero Commander 580-E. That one would claim the life of Jack "Smilin' Jack" Wade near the very top of Surprise Mountain, down there on the Kenai Peninsula. But to get back to the Stinson's problem . . .

The mechanic then pulled off the prop—a necessary preamble to removing the cowling—so that he could see what was going on in there. It only took the mechanic a moment to see the leftover bits and pieces of the ruptured seal. It seems the airplane had undergone an engine rebuild six years previously but had been flown precious little since then. As most of us know, seals tend to dry out when not used, and this one certainly had. A new seal was flown in from Anchorage the next morning.

After the new seal had been installed, Phil ran the engine up and then flew it around the traffic pattern a few times. All seemed to go well—everything was in the green, as they say—and it looked as though the little Stinson's problem had been solved. With that encouragement, Phil and Dan boarded the plane and once again lit out for their hometown of Juneau. If not for the spirit of the guys at Cordova Air Service, I suppose Phil and Dan could still be walking the streets there, looking for a steamer that was headed south.

It was still a beautiful sunny morning when they lifted off, but it soon turned typically Alaska coastal. Though the ceiling had dropped to about 1,500 feet, forward visibility was still virtually unlimited. By Alaska standards, it was nonetheless a gorgeous flying day. It was very likely quite smooth, too.

An hour later, they were in cruise flight about a hundred miles on down the Alaska coast from Cordova when the engine suddenly made a popping sound. Phil suspected a few drops of water in the fuel and expected that they had passed on through the normally aspirated carburetor and were now gone. He applied carburetor heat right away just in case it was a bit of carburetor ice, and the popping didn't occur again. For a moment or two, that is . . .

Alaska pilots always have an emergency landing spot in mind as they ply the often unfriendly skies of that huge and virtually empty state. So it was with Phil, of course, and when the engine started popping in earnest, he told Dan that they might have to put it down on the beach. He also told Dan to tighten up his seat belt, just in case.

Although they were flying right above the sandy beach, they were miles and *miles* from any meaningful assistance. Still, Phil thought he had spotted the wings of an airplane on the ground and just inland a short way. With the engine now popping and sputtering in a seriously dedicated fashion, Phil decided to head up a small river that was running down to the sea and just ahead of them. He was pretty sure that he had spotted an airplane just upstream a short way, and it was entirely possible that some sort of help might be available there.

Almost immediately Phil could see some cabins and a small grass strip ahead. It looked to be about eight hundred feet long, plenty good enough for the Stinson, he knew. It's very likely that this small miracle had popped up just in the nick of time.

Phil coaxed the little Stinson to a smooth landing and then taxied over to the airplane he saw tied down at the strip's far end. From one of the cabins there immediately appeared a man they would come to know as Ed Dierick.

Phil apologized for having dropped in unannounced this way but said he'd had precious few choices just then. Being an outback pilot himself, Ed Dierick certainly understood emergencies and right away offered to help troubleshoot the burping and gagging Stinson.

Together, they drained the fuel tanks, drained the carburetor, and checked the magneto wiring and everything else that they thought might cause the little Stinson to hiccup in such an unfriendly fashion. Having satisfied themselves that they had done all they could do for the moment, Phil climbed aboard and did a few engine run-ups. Everything was once again in the green, and the engine was once again purring like a satisfied kitten. Phil strapped himself down and once more lifted off for a short checkout flight around the pattern and, after having checked the fuel flow and both magnetos in flight, decided that everything once again seemed just fine.

After Phil had returned to the little strip, Dierick pulled out a local Sectional Aeronautical Chart and, using a ballpoint pen, circled maybe twenty little strips that he used in his operations as the owner of Dierick's Tsiu River Lodge near Yakutat. He said that he would be flying back to Yakutat in a few hours and that, if he spotted the Stinson on the beach anywhere along the way, he'd drop in and give them whatever help he could. As it turned out, Phil wouldn't be able to nurse the ailing Stinson very much farther along the coast at all.

The two intrepid fliers continued on down the coast, finally approaching a place called Cape Yakataga. Just after Cape Yakataga lies the three-mile-wide Icy Bay. And just beyond that lies Yakutat Bay, this one seven miles wide. They would have to pass this last bay just before arriving at Yakutat.

The ceiling had crept on down to about 1,200 feet by the time they reached Cape Yakataga. It is here that the Cape Yakataga strip is located, about 4,350 feet long and sporting a no-frills gravel surface. The strip also boasts a generator building, along with some other buildings that might have been used when commercially fished salmon were flown from this airstrip many decades ago.

As usual, Phil operated the carburetor heat control to check for carburetor icing just before heading out over open water. When he did it this time, he thought the little engine was going to abandon its motor mounts! Talk about your shake, rattle, and roll—that engine was doing it all. It banged and backfired as though it had just thrown a rod.

Phil made a quick 180-degree turn and scooted back the mile or so toward the Cape Yakataga airstrip. When he was confident that he could make that strip in the event that everything went south, he overflew the strip to get to the far end, which allowed him to land into the wind.

It occurred to Phil that to anyone observing this series of short and irritating hops from afar, it would appear as though they were dribbling the Stinson along like a basketball rather than flying it from planned stop to planned stop.

After taxiing back, Phil turned the ship around and blasted off again. He came around for another landing and then did it all again. The engine once again performed flawlessly. At the third takeoff, however, the engine began banging and popping worse than ever. Since this takeoff had thus far only used up about two-thirds of the runway, he aborted the takeoff and landed straight ahead on the little strip.

Phil taxied up to the generator building and shut the balking engine down. Both climbed tiredly down to tie the aircraft securely before doing anything else.

"You know, Phil," Dan observed, "I've landed with you only four times in this crazy airplane, and three of those landings have been *emergency* landings. This ain't lookin' all that good, ya know!"

They headed up to the generator building and, wonder of wonders, found a room there with a telephone in it. They quickly used the phone to cancel their flight plan and to call their respective wives. It was a little hard to explain, without upsetting their wives, exactly why they were going to be a "little late." About an hour later, Ed Dierick flew over, saw the balky Stinson, and landed. After some brief conversation, during which they explained to

Ed the most recent series of discouraging events, Dierick gave them a lift into Yakutat.

Phil and Dan met with Lee Hartley, owner of Alsek Air Service, a local fixed-base operator and charter outfit. Lee agreed to take his mechanic back up the coast to have a look at the erstwhile Stinson. Lee and his mechanic had agreed that it sounded to them like a magneto problem, so they rounded one up and prepared to dash back up the coast a little way. Another old Alaskan hanging around the hangar had overheard all this conversation and couldn't help but add his two cents' worth.

"Sure hope that little ol' airplane of yours makes it through the night okay," he said.

"Aw," offered Phil, "she's tied down pretty well, and we got 'er facing into the prevailing winds up there. She should be all right."

"Nah, it ain't that," came the reply. "It's the danged bears! They like the crunch that them Stinson tail feathers add to their diet."

Well, thanks a lot! Dan's flagging spirits couldn't have been bolstered much by that comment.

Lee Hartley, after giving it some thought, had ended up taking two new Slick magnetos for the Stinson, rather than just one. After these were installed and tested, the mechanic flew the plane on down to Yakutat with no further problems.

In typical Alaska fashion, both Ed Dierick and Lee Hartley went beyond the call of duty, so to speak, in helping Phil, Dan, and the reluctant little Stinson. Without this sort of extra effort by folks who could just as easily have turned their backs and walked away from someone else's problem, Phil and Dan would have been in a world of hurt. Truly, both Ed and Lee are real Alaskans.

In the overall scheme of things, N97421, Dan's good-looking Stinson, hadn't turned in a really sterling performance so far.

During a subsequent telephone conversation, the mechanic reported that everything now seemed just fine. He also said that he had some business in Juneau pretty quick, and would Dan like him to just fly the Stinson on down there and deliver it for him? Jeez, yeah, Dan had said, he sure would! The little ship was soon delivered to the proud new owner, two weeks later than was originally expected, but things now began, at last, to look more on track with Dan's new purchase.

Phil and Dan took several sightseeing flights around the Juneau area in the now humming little Stinson, and it performed for all the world like a brand-new airplane. Having satisfied himself that his purchase had been a good one after all, Dan lined up an instructor and began the climb that would take him to his private pilot certificate.

The little airplane continued to perform like a champion, and Dan was beginning to rack up some serious hours in it. It was now easy for him to see why so many are devoted to the Stinson. Until he had added about twenty hours of dual instruction, that is.

One sunny afternoon while Dan and his instructor were flying up a river valley near Juneau, one of the spark plugs blew right out of its cylinder. Yet another emergency was declared, and N97421 was coaxed back to its home base at the Juneau Airport. All the emergency trucks were rolling and flashing their attention-getting red lights for the occasion. The landing went without incident, and Dan was left to order another cylinder for his new little Stinson. After he had installed the new jug, things seemed to go smoothly with the ship, and it looked as though the surprises had finally come to an end.

While Dan found an opportunity to take his lovely wife on a Caribbean vacation, Phil put another dozen or so hours on the Stinson. Though Phil about half expected something else to happen during those hours, the Stinson performed flawlessly. Couldn't have been better, in fact.

When Dan and his wife returned from the islands, he put a few more hours on the ship he had finally come to really enjoy. His wife, still with both feet on the ground, had informed him that if one more emergency—of any kind—happened with that airplane, they were going to sell it. Period.

It was another sunny day—admittedly not all that common along Alaska's southeast coastline—when Dan decided to take a short flight over to the nearby town of Gustavus to practice a few touch-and-go's. On the way to Gustavus though, and while flying through a pass near Funter Bay, the engine cowling broke free at its piano hinge connection and blew away. Well, it didn't really blow away. It wrapped itself around the right wing root and stayed there, banging around like a banshee in a hurricane.

Once again Dan had to declare an emergency. He reversed his course and headed back to Juneau. The cowling wasn't all that aerodynamically clean, what with all its banging and flapping around out there in the breeze. All that parasite drag was causing the Stinson to crab rather dramatically to the right.

In true Alaska fashion, Dan slipped across to the right seat so he could grab the offending hitchhiker and wrestle it off the wing. Opening the window next to the flapping piece of aluminum, he yanked, wrestled, pulled, and tugged until it finally broke free. Rather than just flying aft to wrap itself around the tail feathers of the stricken airplane, it thoughtfully fell free and sailed away without fanfare into the Stinson's wake. With a relatively clean airplane now under his control, Dan slipped on into Juneau for the landing.

After turning off the active runway, Dan taxied directly up to the maintenance shop that had been servicing his pride and joy. After switching off, shutting 'er down, and climbing out, Dan walked directly over to the mechanic and said, "See that gorgeous little Stinson over there? Maybe the best danged Stinson in the whole dern state. What'll you give me for it—right here and right now?"

They agreed on a price, shook hands, and in good ol' Alaska fashion, the deal was made right there on the spot.

Dan continued to fly, finally earning his ticket and buying a nice Cessna 172 with a 180-horsepower engine. A great performer and a great plane. Phil agrees that, except for the "sissy" little wheel pants, the airplane is a dandy. Course, Alaskans aren't much on the accouterments, and wheel pants seem to fall into that category for most of us.

In retrospect, and if he had it to do again, Phil probably would have put in a few extra flying hours with the new Stinson before lighting out down the Alaska coast. Some of that country is pretty awesome. And sometimes pretty lonely . . .

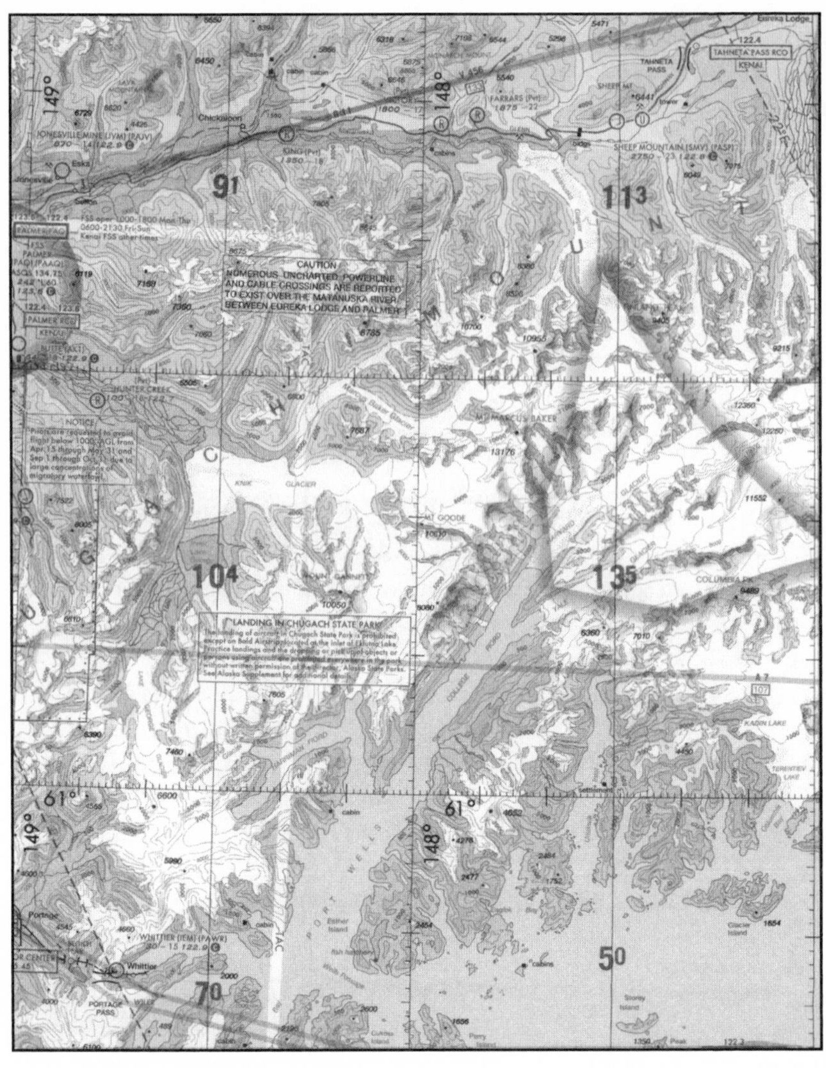

Sheep Mountain shown enlarged from an Anchorage Sectional Aeronautical Chart.

Chapter 7

More Flying

Never let your airplane take you somewhere that your brain didn't get to first.

During the last few days of July in 1980, I flew Harry Geron and a friend of his, Gwen, to Johnson Lake, a little puddle in the Chugach Mountains of the Kenai Peninsula. Both were serious fly fishermen—or perhaps it's one fly fisherman and one fly fisherwoman—who wanted to try the float fly fishing there. This fishing technique requires that the fisherman—or woman, as the case may be—float around in sort of an inner tube arrangement, dunked chest-deep in the water. A bag attached to the tube suspends the fisherman or woman and protects him or her from the cold water. I admit that it looks sort of goofy from the shore, where nothing can be seen except for the head and shoulders of the fisherman, the flashing of a busy fly rod, and the lazy curves of the line itself. Harry and Gwen would set up a tent camp on the shore of Johnson Lake and fish for several days. I would return to pick them up later on.

When I returned several days later, they both reported a marvelous short-term vacation at Johnson Lake. They had caught no end of great rainbow trout, having eaten a few and released the rest. I shared a meal with them—delicious pan-fried rainbow trout, of course, with bacon, eggs, and boiled camp coffee—and then we broke camp for the return trip to Anchorage.

Johnson Lake isn't much of a lake for a loaded, normally aspirated Cessna Stationair on big Edo floats. In fact, it's pretty tight, everything considered. I thought it best to break the flight into several segments. First I would take Gwen and the camp gear to Trail Lake, a larger lake at a somewhat lower altitude. I would then return for Harry and his personal gear, dropping off at Trail Lake to pick up Gwen and the rest of the camp. From there, it would be only a short thirty-minute hop back to Lake Hood in Anchorage. All that went well, and by late that afternoon, everything was in order and we were all comfortably back in Anchorage.

* * *

It's always something of a puzzle when the pilot has to break up a party to ferry it piecemeal from one lake to another. It would be highly unusual for a party to travel with two complete sets of camp gear, so the question always seems to be how to break up the party and gear to make the ferrying both safe and comfortable. There is always the chance—admittedly small, but nonetheless always there—that something may happen to interrupt the sequence. For example, what if the pilot punches a hole in one of the floats while the party is separated? Who has the camp gear: who has the cooking stuff and food, and who has the sleeping bags, insect repellant, firearms, and other bits and pieces that make a short stay in the bush comfortable? Or even survivable, for that matter. . . . In some cases, separating a party can conceivably become a death sentence for one or more of the party.

Let's say, for example, that a pilot had to separate a party and transport it from someplace like Black Lake, a small, grass-green puddle in the Talkeetna Mountains, to much larger Clarence Lake, where my friend and fellow guide Chris Goll had once taken president Jimmy Carter and his Secret Service wallahs for some premium arctic grayling fishing. And let's say, too, that once the party had been separated by the first flight, the pilot had crashed his airplane on the return flight from Clarence Lake to Black Lake. No one in either half of the party now knows what has happened. They do know that the pilot hasn't shown up at either lake by the end of daylight. And, while he may have the skills required to fly around up there in the mountains after a good, solid Alaska darkness has settled in, his charges wouldn't know that, anyway. They only know he is not where he should be.

In a more accurate picture, that half of the party who remained at Black Lake only know that the pilot, the airplane, and one-half of the party disappeared over the horizon some time ago. That party doesn't know whether or not the flight even made it to Clarence Lake.

The party at Clarence Lake only knows that the airplane disappeared around the mountain headed back to Black Lake a while back and still hasn't returned. Did it crash on the way out? Did it crash on landing at Black Lake? Did it crash on the return trip to Clarence Lake with the rest of the party?

Is anyone in the party left alive up there? Should we start building an emergency camp? Hey—build it with what? This country is seriously lacking in trees or brush large enough to make much of a camp. Certainly they could make some sort of shelter in the willows they would find around Clarence Lake, but it wouldn't be much of a shelter at that. And it certainly wouldn't be comfortable if the weather decided to turn sour.

And one of the scariest questions of all: does anyone out there know where we are? They haven't seen a soul in many days, perhaps, that wasn't one of their own group. They have neither seen nor heard another airplane in this quiet wilderness, and they certainly haven't seen any cities, towns, roads, railroads, or farms up here in these silent mountains.

They may have seen the odd caribou bull high on the hills, the cows probably calving somewhere back in the valley between the two lakes. Maybe they'd even seen a moose down toward the Susitna River, but they would be prepared neither to shoot it, dress it out, nor pack its meat back into camp. They would certainly have seen a grizzly or two meandering along the mountain slopes above them, looking for his next marmot sandwich along the rocky outcroppings higher up. This latter will not be accepted as much encouragement, though, since most of them will be more than a little nervous over North America's largest carnivore wandering around somewhere out there in the coming dark of Alaska's sometimes lonely wilderness night.

All this travels back to the original question of how to break up the equipment in order that neither half of the party is at serious risk. They will certainly all be nervous, but at least—if the pilot's planning was adequate—they will all have a place to sleep, food to eat, and shelter to keep them both warm and dry. If the pilot hasn't planned well—maybe he decided to throw all the sleeping bags on the last flight from Black Lake—there is a very good chance someone in the Clarence Lake party will die from hypothermia during the next twenty-four to forty-eight hours. The temperature doesn't have to plunge into minus values. Even at forty or fifty degrees above zero, wet and unprotected vacationers are at serious risk.

It might be worth mentioning here that negligence on the part of the pilot could very well lead to serious criminal charges—even manslaughter charges—in the event that one or more of those entrusted to his care, custody, and control should expire because of his poor planning or a thoughtless oversight on his part.

It is a certainty that, in this day and age, the pilot will face at least one infinitely terrible and destructive civil suit brought by the family or families of the deceased. And he truly should, though the devastating results will ultimately trickle down to his own family, who very likely had little or no influence on his inconsiderate flying at any rate.

* * *

A number of years ago, I got a telephone call from a German hunter who, along with his hunting partner, had just returned from a moose hunt down around the King Salmon River. Seems they had arranged with an unlicensed "guide" to drop them off along the river for what was a legal, though unguided, hunt. After having dropped them off on a gravel bar some distance up the river, he flew away. Neither of them ever saw the pilot again. They did learn, however, what had become of him: it appears that he had flown directly back to Anchorage—a distance of about 450 miles—and immediately caught a commercial flight that took him out of the state. Seems he was fleeing a federal warrant of some sort.

The two successful hunters had to contract with still another local pilot—who just happened to fly over and spot them waving from a gravel bar in the river—to have the moose meat and horns flown out, a requirement of Alaska's strict game management laws. Although no one was physically hurt by this errant pilot's unconscionable actions, the whole sorry thing was a black mark against Alaska's outback pilots. Still, having to flag down a passing bush pilot in the huge Alaska wilderness is a catch-as-catch-can sort of thing. What if the King Air pilot hadn't crossed that particular spot for another six or eight months? Scary thought, ain't it?

* * *

I had a situation that was in a way similar, though different in several respects. I had dropped a pair of moose and caribou hunters off in my cabin at Shadow Lake, near Devil Canyon in the Talkeetna Mountains. I was scheduled to pick up the pair on a certain date and told them to be ready to depart late in the morning of that date. I reminded them that regardless of what the weather might be like at Shadow Lake, the weather in Anchorage might be a whole lot different. That meant that some days Shadow Lake would be socked in with

The author takes off in his Cessna 206 floatplane from Shadow Lake, high in the Talkeetna Mountains, about one hundred miles north of Anchorage. *Photo by John Erskine, Anchorage, Alaska*

low-lying clouds while Anchorage was basking in bright sunlight. On the other hand, Shadow might be sunny and bright while Anchorage was flat on its face in fog, rain, or a combination of other nasty weather phenomena. That meant that if I didn't show up as scheduled, it would only be on account of bad weather on one end or the other. In any case, they were to sit comfortably in the cabin and wait until I showed up. They were at that time firmly fixed on my schedule, and I would either pick them up on schedule, or I would pick them up as soon after that scheduled time as flying conditions allowed. They said that, as Alaskans themselves, they understood all that.

When the scheduled day rolled around, the weather in Anchorage was flat on the deck, and all of the local pilots were welded to the earth.

Problem was, the weather at Shadow Lake was severe clear, as we sometimes say of CAVU (ceiling and visibility unlimited) weather. My two hunters—who had elected an economical, unguided hunt—decided I had simply forgotten about them. They packed up their personal gear, leaving their caribou meat and trophy horns behind at the cabin, and began the long trek down the mountain toward Stephan Lake and the lodge located on its northern shore. It was about a six-mile stroll for them, and the country, while not particularly difficult, did not present anything as comfortable as a hiking path or a concrete sidewalk. In fact, portions of the hike must have been downright difficult walking.

When I arrived the following day, I found a really terse note telling me that I wasn't much of a pilot and that they were going to see an attorney as soon as they got out of the wilderness. Oh—and would I fly their caribou meat, horns, and the remainder of their camp gear down to the lodge at Stephan Lake and then fly them, along with the rest of the heavy load, up to Lake Louise—about forty-five minutes away by air—where they had left a parked car?

Well, certainly I'd do that, since it was part of our original agreement. But why the hell had they departed a comfortable cabin to risk a long walk in the Alaska bush, even though they could see Stephan Lake from my camp on the mountain at Shadow Lake? Moreover, I had carefully explained that sometimes the weather interfered with even the best laid plans of mice and men, and that I would not have forgotten about them, even if I were to be a day or two late. If I failed to show up on time, it would certainly be on account of adverse weather at one end or the other. No other reason would keep me from my appointed rendezvous with them. Besides, the cabin was warm and snug and was well stocked with both firewood (which I had to fly in) and food. The beds had comfortable mattresses on them, and the view from the cabin couldn't be duplicated anywhere else in the world.

When I picked them up at Stephan Lake Lodge, they were both in a decidedly surly mood. The flight from there to Lake Louise was a grim one, and neither of them would listen to reason.

I would learn later that each had issued a stop payment against the personal checks they had given me in payment for the trip, even though it had been very successful for them. One of them would later die at his hometown in southeast Alaska when run over by a little red pickup truck. The other moved out of state and soon filed for personal bankruptcy. So—I had met a couple deadbeats and lost a couple bucks. As they say: some days chicken and some days feathers.

Still, I hope they enjoyed the caribou. We all worked hard to put that meat on their tables.

* * *

Billy Joseph and I had worked together at the offices of Jim Bridges, a local architect of some repute. Billy, too, was a pilot, though without having yet amassed the thousands of flying hours I had logged by then. Billy was one of those guys who could play a blues harp (which you and I probably still call a harmonica) as well as anyone I have ever heard. Period. He had a great sense of humor and a pleasant and quite attractive wife, Anne, and he was generally just a real pleasure to be around.

He told me that he and Anne had rented an airplane for the coming Saturday and had planned a short flight to a small fishing lodge not far from Anchorage. The place was along Alexander Creek, not quite thirty air miles from Merrill Field, and over absolutely flat country. Swampy and lake-filled, yes. Mountainous, no.

My wife Peggy and I boarded our Super Cub, N1858A, and lit out a little after Billy and Anne had lifted off. When we arrived at the little Alexander Creek Lodge strip, my radio told me that an airplane nearby was transmitting an emergency signal over his Emergency Locator Transmitter (ELT), and the airplane was damned close by! A little investigation revealed that Billy had made something less than a silky-smooth landing on the bumpy bush strip, and his ELT was happily calling to all and sundry that he and his aircraft were in serious trouble.

It wasn't long before a USAF Search and Rescue helicopter dropped out of the sky to see what all the racket was about. With a sheepish look, Billy turned his ELT off and, with sincere and abject apologies, saw the helicopter and its relieved crew depart for greener pastures. Hey, those things happen, right? Since ELTs are designed to lead rescuers to downed aircraft, they are also designed to activate upon impact. Some rough landings are rougher than others, of course, especially with less than high-time pilots and under bush conditions. In this case, that's exactly what happened.

Surely Billy's face wasn't as red as mine was on an occasion that occurred several years later. I had been doing some flying for one of the truly world-class Alaska fishing lodges, Painter Creek. This unique lodge sits about one hundred miles due south of King Salmon, on the western slopes of the Aleutian Range. I guess it's still my very favorite fishing spot. Anyway, I had flown my new Cessna Stationair amphibian from the lodge to King Salmon airport to pick up some new clients. The lodge manager, J. W. Smith, had gone along for the ride. On the route back, he had me fly back into the mountains in several spots so he could point out a few "hidden" strips in there. Most of them were only suitable for Super Cubs, though a few were usable by skilled bush fliers operating Cessna 180s or 185s. None, of course, was suitable for the tricycle-geared Cessna 206 or its heavier amphibious counterpart.

As we slipped through a small pass very near to the lodge, I began the routine of letting down in preparation for the landing. At about that time, I allowed J. W. to steal my attention away from my own business of flying the overloaded amphibian so that we could sneak a peek at another of those rough, steeply sloping, and highly questionable little dabs of real estate frequently used by the mentally challenged who fly Alaska's outback. That was a mistake because now I was involved in a conversation with J. W. and not paying attention to my own business.

As a result, I landed the seriously overloaded C-206 with its amphibious gear still tucked up warm and snug inside the big Wipline floats. I didn't realize it until I heard the aft section of the aluminum keels touch the sloping gravel runway surface. Although I was landing uphill, as was usual there, and hanging on forty degrees of the big Cessna barn-door flaps, even full throttle and maximum rpms on the low-pitch, three-bladed prop didn't help much. Except to make the landing a little more controllable, I suppose. At any rate,

the more-than-four-thousand-pound aircraft g
its embarassed pilot finally shut down the bi
was spoken.

I could see Joe Maxey and Dan Steele alr
that we would need to raise the airplane in or
main landing gears. The nose gear wheels wo
place without a problem, once we raised th
ground a little.

Did I learn something from all that? Sure, but I
anyway: always fly the airplane! Gabbing away on short final is almost as
tippling on short final. Both will one day lead to disaster.

And for all those many folks who have flown with me in the past—and who believe that I not only can walk on water but can safely land a heavy bush plane in a tall cottonwood tree—you now know the truth.

As most of Alaska's bush fliers, I've had passengers who have sworn they would fly anytime, anywhere, with me at the controls. Others have gone so far as to say they wouldn't fly with anyone else. Now, I'm sorry to have burst your bubbles.

On the positive side, the only damage I did to Bill Wiplinger's wonderful Wipline floats was to sandpaper the paint from the aft six inches of the heavy aluminum keel. Tough floats, those Wiplines! And they'll always be my absolute favorites, for many reasons.

Another flight I may as well mention, now that I'm airing my dirty laundry, was a trip I made back in August 1977. I was flying a party of two (the Ridgways from Palo Alto, California) to meet Larry Todd at Iliamna. We would then scoot across huge (about two thousand square miles!) Lake Iliamna to its drainage into the Kvichak River. Some of Alaska's finest trout, grayling, and salmon fishing can be found in this wonderfully productive river, and the strip at Igiugig, where the lake drains into the river, is a good place to start. Igiugig, by the way, isn't pronounced the way it's spelled. Most Alaska villages have that disturbing nicety about them. Igiugig is pronounced "Ig-ee-ah-gik" by most of us. It is not "Iggy-ugh-ik." Admittedly, some call it simply "Iggy-gik."

Anyhow, here I was, pooping along in a Beechcraft C24R (Sierra), a low-wing, retractable-geared, underpowered little beast that is a pleasure to fly, has a wonderful instrument platform . . . and is in no way a bush airplane. On that day, August 19, I was a bit overloaded, as usual, and flying into a wet, trip with teeny-weeny little wheels. Plus the teeny-weeny one out front there. All in all, not a smart move on my part.

an that, the little airplane's performance charts just about dupli- strip's particulars. That is to say, the strip was noted as being 2,700 ng, which was just about the performance limit of a normally loaded hcraft Sierra.

Well, we got in, did a little fishing, and got back out with no one being the wiser about this pilot operating that close to the performance limits.

It's true that I knew halfway down the strip whether or not the machine would fly away with the load aboard. If it wouldn't, I could just have aborted the flight, left one or two passengers at the local lodge, and ferried the party in two short trips back across the lake, only twenty miles wide, to Iliamna, where the 4,800-foot airport would have accommodated just about anything we could put on it.

* * *

We met Harry Geron, the fly fisherman, earlier in this chapter. Harry hand-made the most exquisite fly rods, and he was once sufficiently off his feed to make me a present of one of them. Built on an Orvis split-bamboo blank, the beautiful rod, built for five-weight gear and terminal tackle, served me for many years, taking the greatest of several species of Pacific salmon, both rainbow and steelhead trout, arctic grayling, arctic char, and Dolly Varden, plus a variety of other freshwater fishes.

Harry was also a past master with a Spanish guitar, and he often sat before our fireplace, softly playing his personal favorite, a truly mellow instrument. He was extremely intelligent and made most of his living as a consultant, specializing in the writing of technical specifications for architects and engineers.

He also had a big black Labrador retriever, name of "Red." I had several times asked Harry why in the world he would name a black Lab "Red," and his answer was always the same: "Always wanted a dog named Red, ever since I was a kid." Well, he had one, and a good one at that.

Neither time nor the tides wait for man, it is said, and the sad day came when old Red just lay down and sighed his last sigh. He had become slower of gait and shorter of patience over the past few months. Harry could see the end in sight, I guess, but, knowing Harry as I did, I wasn't really surprised to learn of Red's passing before I had learned of his gaining infirmities.

“I want him buried in one of our favorite fishing holes,” he said to me. “I guess you’ll understand that.”

“Sure, Harry. I do understand that.”

“Well, I thought maybe you could fly us down to Johnson Lake one more time. Red and I could get in a last fishing trip before I scatter him around the place.” Harry had had old Red cremated, and his ashes had no business being scattered anywhere near civilization, he figured. Rightfully, I certainly agreed, for what use did old Red have for civilization anyway, when you stopped to think on it? So the trip was scheduled in honor of old Red, best damned friend Harry’d ever had.

On the twenty-first day of June, 1979, Harry, Red, and I boarded N756VR, my normally aspirated Cessna 206. Nothing was said between us as I checked the engine and prop, took off, and, in sunny, calm weather, turned on a heading for Johnson Lake, deep in the center of the Kenai Peninsula. Harry was fondly rubbing the box with Red’s remains, and I kept myself busy minding my own damned business.

After settling smoothly onto Johnson, beaching the heavy Cessna, and tying her down, Harry and I got in a couple reflective casts. We caught a few of the native rainbows, and then I saw Harry carefully set aside his Orvis split-bamboo rod and pick up the small wooden box.

It was time for me to take down my own rod, case it, and put it with the rest of my fishing gear in the baggage compartment of the big Cessna. By the time I had finished with that chore, Harry was walking toward the airplane, all his fishing gear in hand.

After we had taken off from the mirror-like lake, hemmed very tightly all round with mountains, we circled it once in a salutary flyby.

Harry said, “It’s a good thing you did, flying us down here. I won’t forget it.”

“No, Harry,” I replied, “it’s a good thing you did. I’m sure old Red appreciated your concern. I guess he couldn’t have chosen a nicer place to rest, and I guess he finally had the rest coming.”

“Yeah,” said Harry. “Yeah, he did.”

* * *

It was only a few days later that I received a call from some FAA guy, calling to ask if I was the owner of a Beechcraft B24, a Sierra, with the registration numbers N2230L. I told him I was, and he informed me that the airplane had been reported missing on a flight from Merrill Field to Iliamna. Did I know anything about it?

No, I told him. We had purchased the ship, new, from Gil's Aircraft at Merrill Field. The airplane had been operating on a lease-back arrangement, used in Gil's flight training program as an instrument platform for hopeful instrument-rated pilots. The call had come in late in the evening, and there was no way for me to chase it until the following morning.

When I did that, I learned that the pilot, who had been working on his commercial and instrument ratings, had rented the airplane, planning to fly his own family to Iliamna for some early run salmon fishing. Oh-oh! That Beechcraft was not a bush airplane, and the student pilot wasn't an outback pilot, as far as I could determine.

Then came another call. The wreckage had been spotted on the eastern flank of Slope Mountain, just outside Chinitna Bay and across Cook Inlet from Kenai.

I lit out in N756VR and flew directly to Slope Mountain, where it only took a moment to locate the wreck site. Just a big burned spot against the sloping island mountain, black and brown against the wild green, at the one-thousand-foot level. Eventually, the story came out.

Ceilings had held at one thousand feet throughout the area for twenty-four hours or more. Below that, though, the weather was good, and visibility was probably out to more than fifteen miles. Occasional light rain cut this down a bit, but for the large part, the weather was quite good. Who needs a ceiling of more than a thousand feet?

Apparently this pilot did. He had reported to both Kenai Radio and Homer Radio that he had tried several passes through the mountain range that was keeping him prisoner on its eastern slopes. Lake Clark pass was closed, Chinitna Bay was closed, Bruin Bay was closed, Pile Bay was closed, Pedro Bay was closed. . . . He had apparently tried each of them several times. Finally, he had tried to sneak around Slope Mountain and back into Chinitna Bay again but was reluctant to come out of one thousand feet to do it. With ragged bottoms to the overcast, he was asking for trouble staying that far above the earth.

I know what that country is like. I've spent no end of hours in that neck of the woods. The cold water is terribly unfriendly, especially at night, and there are virtually no beaches fronting the eastern side of the mountains for the pilot's use. With rain and a little turbulence, poor visibility, and ragged overcast bottoms, it's not flying for the timid. Even with floats, the pilot knows that ditching in this cold and rough water is a maybe thing at best. He knows that, under the very best of conditions, he won't be able to taxi to shore at any rate. He's just bloody well doomed. I can't imagine how it must feel with your children aboard, sharing a fate over which they have absolutely no control. And after all that white-knuckle, sweaty-palms flying, the pilot finally arrived at the fate he was almost certain to find the moment the Beechcraft's wheels left the runway at Merrill Field. Unfortunately, so did his children.

Oddly, he was only three wide-open miles from a little oil exploration strip at Iniskin. But he didn't know the country around there, and even in good weather, he might have passed it up. It was really a bit short for the Beechcraft, it does not show up on any aeronautical chart, and it was by then overgrown with small willows. Still, it would have beat slamming head-first into Slope Mountain at a cruising air speed of more than 125 miles an hour.

The largest remaining piece of the wreckage was the little red T-handle designed for emergency extension of the retractable landing gear. I still have the handle, though I don't know why I've kept it. Guess I really did like that little airplane, even though it wasn't designed for Alaska flying.

* * *

During the fall of 1978, Rich Nesbitt contacted me to ask if I'd fly his wife, Sherry, along with some grub, to land on the Stony River beside their cabin. Certainly, I told him. When? Well, it wouldn't be until next spring, but he wanted to fix the date and time right now. So we did, and I agreed to fly out at mid-morning on June 30 the following year, that day almost seven months away.

On the morning of that date, I loaded two sled dogs, a whole raft of grub, some dynamite that he needed to clear stumps around his property on the Stony, and his wife, Sherry. And off we went.

His directions had been explicit, as far as Alaska pilots are concerned, but I suppose rather sketchy for stateside fliers. He had asked if I knew the Stony River country, and I told him that I did. Okay, he said, my place is on the north side of the river, about a quarter-mile upstream from that big rock in the middle of the river just upstream of the big curve. And before you get to the Lime Hills, right? Right, I had replied. Hey, you got any 100-octane low lead out there? Or do I have to cart some of that along, too? He said he had plenty of canned avgas, including 100-low lead, and I would be welcome to all I needed.

The trip, if I could hit the nail right on the head in finding their place, would be within minutes of being a two-hour flight. If I had to stagger around looking for their cabin, it would take longer. Perhaps much longer. With two hours of fuel left aboard the Cessna floatplane by then, that wouldn't leave me enough to return comfortably to Lake Hood at Anchorage. And if the weather turned sour, I might be in a real pickle, if he didn't have that fuel for me. Still, that's flying the Alaska outback, and such edge-of-common-sense flying was just about an everyday occurrence.

Sherry, of course, wasn't much help in identifying anything from the air. She wasn't a pilot and had spent very few hours in the air as a passenger. But that wasn't all that unusual, and I wasn't going to depend on her navigation at any rate.

When I got to the big rock just upstream of the big turn, I throttled back, rolled into a left 180-degree turn, and began the descent that would place me slightly upstream of the place I expected to land. Sure enough, their cabin was right where it was supposed to be, and there was Rich, standing patiently on the high-cut bank beside the river. When he saw that I was approaching for the landing, he moved upstream a ways to reach a spot where the steep bank dipped down closer to the water and waited for me to coast up close enough so that he could throw me a line. When I tied off to a rear float davit, he secured the bitter end to a riverside tree, and the deed was done.

He did have the avgas, and he did have the cash; the latter sometimes can be a bit of a problem. But he had sounded sincere seven months ago, and my faith in them paid off. I would fly for them again.

* * *

In August of 1979, I had set up sort of a main camp—though it was only an army surplus, sixteen-by-sixteen mess tent—on the north shore of a spot we named Two Lakes. It lay between Twin Lakes and Turquoise Lake and was both notoriously shallow and clear as gin. I needed the float-equipped Super Cub over there for runs to smaller and relatively inaccessible spike camps and had to hire another pilot to fly the Cub from Anchorage to Two Lakes. This pilot didn't know the area, but all he had to do was follow me with the Super Cub.

I told him I'd fly right down the middle of the lake when we got there and wait for him to land in the Cub. When he saw the lake, though, he thought it was too shallow for the floats and didn't want to land there. Well, that's where I needed the Cub to be, so I told him I'd land first in the loaded Cessna 206, and he could follow me in after I had convinced him that the lake was deeper than it looked to him. Actually, it was about waist deep, but it truly was clear water.

After we had both made our landings, we off-loaded the C-206, tied the Super Cub up on a spruce-log ramp I had built for the purpose, and boarded the Cessna for the return to Anchorage. I would have to repeat this procedure at the end of the season.

As this pilot later explained to me, he had flown many hours in a saltwater environment—meaning open water—but had flown almost no rivers or lakes. He wasn't able to "read" these waters, and I understood his trepidation over landing in a crystal clear, inland lake. Ah well, I hope he flew away with something added to his flying repertoire.

* * *

I have to write just a little bit about one of the most refreshing characters I've ever had the privilege of flying into the Alaska outback. His name is Claude Hebraud, and he arrived in Alaska as the personal chef of a successful real estate mogul, name of Paul Argence, from France. Now, Paul was nothing short of a genuine, dyed-in-the-wool, eighteen-karat horse's ass. Truly! He's the chap who, against repeated warnings, proceeded to shoot a bull moose that was standing placidly in the waist-deep water of a quiet lake. Can you imagine what a cleaning, skinning, and butchering job that action presented for us? Needless to say, he wasn't quite at the very tip-top of my most favorite clients list.

Anyhow, Claude, the great French chef, not only arranged to oversee some pretty exotic and delicious meals while in camp, he was careful always to have a two-cup pot of fresh coffee waiting for me whenever I landed where he was living at the time. He would hear the airplane coming—he had quickly learned to differentiate between the sounds of Super Cubs and the heavy Cessna 206s—and, by the time I had beached the airplane, he would be standing at the water's edge with a saucepan full of hot water. Immersed in that hot water would be his special two-cup, heavy metal pitcher of camp-made coffee, hot, strong, and truly the most delicious coffee I had ever tasted. The things he could do with fish, ducks, game birds, and big game animal parts would knock your eyes out, and I was sorry to see Claude leave Alaska. Especially in the company of his wealthy employer who, like a spoon in the soup, would lie in it for a thousand years and never know its flavor! Claude was a gentleman and a gentle man. Though I don't expect it ever to happen, I would give two nickels and a jellybean to see him again and tell him how very much he added to my life in the short time he spent in our camps.

* * *

During that same period, I had flown the Tuxen/Petersen party to the same neck of the woods, the Stony River country on the west side of Merrill Pass. Niels Tuxen and Henry Milhaus Petersen had arrived together from Denmark (they spell it Danmark, I guess). Niels had been the spokesman for the two of them, having a truly marvelous command of English, German, Danish, and who knew how many other tongues. At first we corresponded quite a bit, but over the years Niels seemed to find other interests, and I finally lost track of him. Henry Petersen and I, however, have remained friends for more than thirty years now, and I look forward to his letters. Though he hunted in Alaska with a rifle, he now favors the bow and arrow when he hunts in Europe. During his first week in Alaska, Henry presented me with a small man that he had whittled from a piece of spruce while he camped in the great Alaska outback. I was amazed by Henry's carving skills. He would probably resent my use of the word "whittled," but how else can you describe a piece of art made by hand with a sharp hunting knife? Whittling will have to do. . . . Henry, if you read this, please forgive me.

It was the Tuxen/Petersen party that finally talked me into trying Merrill Pass one more time, from west to east, in an attempt to get them back to Anchorage for their connecting flight to Europe. While I knew it wouldn't be successful, I did make a stab at it. I finally gave it up and turned south, sneaking through the mountains to find Lake Clark Pass and tiptoe around that way. Henry was so pleased at being able to find a route through the mountains in a nearly blinding snowstorm that he broke out his favorite cigars and passed them around. It wasn't long before the ventilators and my driver's-side window were opened against the stifling fog that threatened to overcome all of us.

* * *

Back in the summer of 1980, a friend of mine came to me with the notion of panning gold along the foothills south of the West Fork of the Yentna River. Farther north, such places as Nugget Bench and the area around Sona Mine behind Skwentna had produced more than a little color in the form of flakes or dust. Fact is, the crew originally working the Nugget Bench claim had constructed a thirty-inch pipeline from a water source high in the hills behind the claim. With a tremendous head pressure from the altitude drop, the huge Morgan Pit was sluiced out, resulting in a recovery of more than six million dollars in gold. And that was back in the days when gold was only sixteen dollars per fine ounce! So, my friend's idea may have been a screwy one, but who was to say?

Anyway, he and his father had somehow laid claim to a generator and a floating dredge of sorts. Trouble was, they were planning to work the streams, and water in that area is damned cold! They decided they needed some sort of protection and again came to me for help. This time, I came up with a new Poseidon dry suit for them, reminding them that this article cost an arm and a leg and to please be careful with it!

Well, they were, I guess, but the local grizzly bears—which, in retrospect, were represented by a whole contingent of the unruly characters—definitely were not. They destroyed the camp, dragged the dredge away somewhere into the brush, a place our fearsome fortune seekers were loath to investigate, chewed the dry suit into neoprene shreds, and must have swallowed the inflatable boat, since no sign of it has ever been found.

In short, it wasn't a particularly successful undertaking, and it was only a few days after I had dropped them off that I got an emergency call from the FAA station master at Skwentna. Would I please fly on up to that camp area and rescue the two petrified gold hounds?

When I arrived for the pickup, I couldn't help but burst out laughing. In an area known for the size and ferocity of its mosquitoes, these two had not thought to pack repellent of any sort. More than that, they were almost comatose with their fear of the marauding bears. I could tell at a glance that there had been a number of bears in and around the camp, for their many tracks appeared in all sizes and in a variety of shapes.

When I coasted up to the shore of the little slough where I would board the two of them, they had neither waved nor shouted. They were too busy slapping at the huge and hungry mosquitoes while at the same time looking every which way for the appearance of the next marauding grizzly. They were dancing as if both were standing before a ten-cent pay toilet with only a nickel between them. While I realized that they were scared near to exhaustion, the sight truly was remarkable, and I couldn't control myself for a few moments.

That didn't make things any more pleasant for them. They considered their plight to be at least life-threatening, while I assured them that, in the heat of this particularly hot and sunny day, any sensible bear would be cooling it until the shadows grew longer. That didn't help much, obviously. They might have elected to shoot me on the spot, but neither of them knew how to horse the big Cessna 206 floatplane out of the slough without me. I counted my blessings and quit laughing, as best I could.

* * *

Jim Repine, who authored the great Alaska photo book, *Fishing Alaska*, with the remarkable assistance of one of Alaska's most capable photographers, called me one early evening. He had two Japanese fishing clients who he wanted to take to the big rainbow and great salmon fishing areas south of Lake Iliamna. I agreed, and we set a date for the departure.

We met the two gentlemen at my Stationair floatplane—which was docked at Lake Hood—ready for our departure for a flight through Lake Clark Pass, past Iliamna and Kukaklek Lakes, and on into Nonvianuk Lake. You are free to mispronounce the name of this large lake if you want. Most Alaskans can't agree on its pronunciation, either. It's variously Non-vee-ah-nuuk, Non-vie-nik, or any one of several other pronunciations. Use whichever one you like. I prefer the first, since it sounds more native-like. Indian and Eskimo names for people and places are usually quite guttural. With half a mouthful of mashed potatoes, you should find the first pronunciation quite acceptable, especially after a warm winter brandy or two. But, to continue . . .

The flight went smoothly as we cruised south through Lake Clark Pass and then across Iliamna and Kukaklek Lakes. In only a few more minutes, we had begun the letdown that would see us skimming over the quiet surface of Nonvianuk, down near its southwest end where it empties to form the Alagnak River. At Nonvianuk's northeast end lies famous Kulik Lodge.

Kulik Lodge backs up into the Walatka Mountains, named for a friend of mine, now long gone west, John Walatka. I don't know why we all referred to him as *Johnny* Walatka, since he was the farthest thing from a diminutive

"Johnny" sort of fellow. Big enough to eat hay and pull a wagon, I'll always remember John best when he was smoking an old hawk-bill curved pipe and sitting cross-legged at the controls of one of Ray Petersen's old twin-engine Cessna Bushmasters.

In the old days, Ray Petersen was head of Northern Consolidated Airways, the Alaska airlines that served a host of bush towns, villages, and cities, including several around Iliamna and the King Salmon areas. Kulik Lake lies in the heart of excellent fishing country on the Aleutian Peninsula. It's just south of Katmai National Park, an amazing wilderness area where glaciers melt to form streams that vanish in a cloud of steam in only a few hundred yards. It is also home to a whopping collection of brown bears, protected by its national park status. It is here that the famous—or notorious, depending upon your personal evaluation—McNeil River is located. When you see large brown bears fishing for salmon on television, it is almost a one hundred percent guarantee that you are watching the bears of the McNeil River. I used to fly in there and land on the beach where the McNeil empties into Cook Inlet. The salmon, sea-run Dolly Varden, and arctic char fishing there was out of this world, if you didn't mind sharing your fishing hole with ten or twenty of the big brown bears. But, I digress. . .

Ray had taken a few of Cessna's old light twin-engine Bamboo Bombers (so called on account of their wood and plywood wings), with their small 225-horsepower engines, and made real flying machines of them. First he replaced the old 225-horesepower Jacobs mills with a pair of 450-horsepower Pratt & Whitney engines. Then he cut a huge barn door in the fuselage left side to improve the loading of freight and other large stuff. Finally, he had the planes certified by the CAA, mounted them on floats, and made what he termed the "Bushmaster," the model John Walatka flew while he was operating Northern Consolidated's Alaska Angler's Camps, then Alaska Paradise Camps. Of the camps, the most comfortable was the lodge at Kulik Lake.

I flew and fished a lot with John in those days. Many of us will miss him forever, for he was an accomplished pilot, a complete stranger to panic, a gentleman—and, by George, not a bad fisherman, either.

Anyway, to get back to business here, after landing, taxiing up to the rock beach at the north side of the mouth of the lake, and tying off to a few small scrubs back about thirty feet or so from the water's edge, we geared up the two Japanese doctors. While they began their first Alaska fishing adventure, Jim and I made a comfortable tent camp for the party.

We knew that, about two hundred yards downstream, there was a camp that consisted of a cookhouse and several comfortable cabins. We also knew that a young brown bear had been visiting the camp almost every night for about a week. First, the bear had smashed flat the door to the cook shack, had walked over it to enter the frame structure, and had then proceeded to tear the place apart. After scattering flour, various and sundry condiments, and a wealth of other unidentifiable stuff around the place, the bear had turned toward the river and walked right out through the cabin's south wall. That wall, by the way, was the food preparation wall and had been lined with a galvanized metal-topped sink and counter. Neither the wall nor the counter slowed our young bear in the slightest, and the south side of the cook shack looked worse than the west side, where the door had previously been.

It was against this background that we had erected our camp of North Face geodesic dome tents, flimsy compared to the cabins, which were now quite clearly being decimated, one each night, by our inquisitive and destructive young brownie.

Having finally seen the damage the young bear had wrought on the cabins and cook shack, our Japanese clients were really, really nervous about tent camping on the shore of a wilderness lake and directly in the path of the marauding brownie. I finally convinced them that the cabins were presenting the real challenge to the bear, and I doubted that he would show any interest in our tents, especially since we would be sound asleep inside them. My argument finally won out, and everyone decided to sleep in the tents.

I admit that, a time or two, we would see the shadow of the bear move across the face of our tents as he passed by our flimsy but comfortable camp, but we never had a problem with him. The cabins, though, continued to receive their nightly assaults with a silent acceptance. By the time our party lifted off several days later, there wasn't a whole lot left of that camp to rebuild.

Jim Repine is a wonderful camp cook. I don't mean to categorize him as such, since his claims to fame are as a fly fisherman and as an outdoor writer. He is a master at both. His camp cookery, though, leaves precious little to be desired.

Like many cold-weather camp cooks, he favors cooking with real butter as often as possible. His meals are delicious, to say the least. As usual, our Japanese guests seemed to enjoy the fare. They both ate with admirable gusto. I was pleased to see that they were enjoying both the grub and the very productive fishing. Jim, of course, being both the chef du jour and the expert fisherman, was in his glory. What we didn't know, and what the two very polite Japanese guests were much too thoughtful to mention, was that we were killing one of them.

No—*seriously!* The cooking was about to do one of them in, and both were successful and famous internists back in Tokyo. One had a condition that heavy eating, especially eating greasy—or, in this case, buttery—food, seriously exacerbated. At the time, he didn't say anything to his American hosts, nor did he give the outward appearance of being seriously—even life-threateningly—ill. It wasn't until we had dropped them off back in Ted and Mary Gerken's Iliaska Lodge that we heard anything about his condition.

Upon our return to Anchorage, Jim and I were notified that the two Japanese men had been air-lifted to Anchorage, and one of them was now in the ICU unit at Providence Hospital. We caught up with them about the time they were boarding a JAL flight back to Tokyo, one of them on a stretcher!

Nonetheless, each thanked us profusely for the wonderful vacation he had enjoyed with us. And both promised to return to fish with us again. Now, each of those gentlemen was a piece of work, I'll tell you!

* * *

Late in July of 1978, I got a call while pooping around Midway Lake, northwest of Anchorage. It seemed that a Citabria had gone down in Cook Inlet, and some help was needed at the site, which was near the village of Tyonek and just off the mouth of the Chuitt River.

I told Anchorage Approach that I'd divert immediately and would join up with a helicopter that had also been diverted. The chopper was unable to land in the silty waters of Cook Inlet, but he was hovering above the slowly sinking Citabria when I arrived with the Stationair. The rising 39-foot tides would soon cover the little Citabria, and when they went out again, the plane would doubtless be gone. The chopper pilot wondered if we had any line aboard. He figured to lift the Citabria and somehow save it.

I told him that I had a one-hundred-foot length of three-quarter-inch laid nylon rope and that it would certainly fill the bill for him. He waited for me to arrive, and when I had, we decided that I'd just drop the line on the beach, where his partner was waiting.

I dropped the line, and, after a time, the pilot and his helper lifted off to hover again above the little plane. Most of it was still above water, but that wouldn't be true for much longer. The Cook Inlet tides come in quickly, and what once may have been five miles of beach very soon becomes a strip of gravel only twenty or thirty feet wide.

The chopper pilot let his helper down on the line and held a steady hover while the poor guy hit the water, swam to the Citabria, and proceeded to tie the line onto the wings' lifting rings.

I radioed the pilot as soon as I saw what they were up to. First of all, had he secured the owner's permission to do what he was doing? And, second, if he was going to proceed with a lift of the Citabria, his partner had better slash the wing fabric so the water could quickly drain. Otherwise, I told the pilot, those wings—filled with silty water that would present a terrific negative load factor on them—would fold up like a house of cards!

The chilly swimmer pulled his trusty Buck knife from his belt and proceeded to perform the necessary surgery. After that, it was a piece of cake for the chopper to lift and drag the wet little airplane to the beach where it could be secured against its loss to the outgoing tide.

Meantime, the airplane's pilot and passenger had been plucked from the water and were even then en route to Tyonek, shivering aboard an old wood fishing boat belonging to and operated by one of the helpful Indians of that village.

I took off, followed their wake, and landed at a point that would intercept the boat and its wet passengers. No sense having them stranded in the village of Tyonek when I could have them warm and safely home in Anchorage in less than twenty minutes. We made the transfer while floating down the inlet, and I was soon in the air with the two wet, shivering fliers.

It seems that the pair of them, in a borrowed airplane, had been salmon fishing—with no success at all—in the nearby Chuitt River. By the time they had decided to leave, the incoming tide had left precious little room for their takeoff on the narrow little beach, and, during their takeoff run, the pilot had allowed the right wheel to drift into the advancing surf line. That's all it took, and the next thing you know they were inverted in the cold and silty waters of Alaska's infamous Cook Inlet. Both escaped the inverted airplane and made it ashore—no easy trick in and of itself—but the airplane had begun drifting offshore with the winds and against the incoming tide. At the moment, it seemed a hopeless situation to the both of them. Alaska, though, seems to come through every once in a while, and time and motion were clearly on their side that day.

The airplane's owner, though, was looking at some serious expenditures. Cook Inlet is mostly salt water, of course, and the little plane's instruments, radios, and, indeed, the engine, would require either lots of work or outright replacement. Some days chicken and some days feathers, I reckon.

* * *

It was about a month later that I flew a German hunter, Heimo Freitsritzer, to our lodge at High Lake. He wanted to camp out in the great Alaska outback, and this place, deep in the Talkeetna Mountains, offers a lot of that. He elected to set up a tent camp across the lake from the lodge and airstrip, and I helped him in that effort. He was using a big canvas tent, sixteen feet on a side and with plenty of headroom. Though I knew he would be comfortable in that setup, which was only about a fifteen-minute walk from the lodge, I was careful to caution him about the many bears in the area. I told him to always keep an extremely clean camp, and to faithfully hang all his food and cooking gear high in a remote spruce tree so as not to attract the bears. All my words apparently had fallen on deaf ears.

By noon the next day, his camp had been decimated, including his sleeping gear and the huge tent itself. Later, Heimo would be successful in his search for a big blackie, but in the meantime, he was a little on edge. Seems the bears came around even during the middle of the day, and while he was still in the tent! Welcome to Alaska, Heimo. I later flew him to a place I called Why Lake, where he was again successful, this time with his hunt for a fine caribou bull.

* * *

In September of 1978, I flew Leif Erickson, the popular western TV and movie star, to Talkeetna during the filming of a series of television commercials for Tesoro Oil Company, the San Antonio, Texas–based petroleum company that by then owned Alaska's first and only petroleum refinery at Kenai. Leif, and his wife, Anne, quickly became good friends with Peggy and me, and we shared many fine dinners and several good flights in Alaska's outback. It wasn't until later that I learned that while he was cooling it with us at my main camp on Kelly Lake near Lake Louise, Leif had serious—it turned out to be life-threatening—emphysema. Anne later wrote to tell us that it had finally claimed his life. She reiterated, though, how very much they had both enjoyed Alaska with us. And that Leif always remembered, with a faraway gleam in his eyes, our flights together in the remote Alaska outback. I'll always miss the tall man with the gruff voice. In spite of his penchant for those horrible little blackberry-flavored cigars!

* * *

On September 6, 1981, I flew a good friend, Reuben McNeill, and his fall hunting gear through Mystic Pass, very near to Shellabarger Pass, in the Alaska Range. Reuben and his G.I. friends from the U.S. Army base at Fairbanks, Fort Wainwright, commissioned me each fall to fly them into Scotty Lake where the four of them usually collected four moose, four caribou, and four black bears. They were excellent hunters, and all were good men. I've lost track of them over the years, but they have left with me great memories.

Anyway, on my return trip to Anchorage's Lake Hood, I spotted a large *SOS* on the beach at Highline Lake, at about the halfway point of my return flight. Well, a guy can't pass up an *SOS*, especially one lined out on the lonely beach of a really distant lake, so I reduced the throttle setting, descended a bit, moved the propeller pitch to high rpms, and dropped a few degrees of flaps.

When I skimmed the trees and put down on the long, calm lake, it was raining moderately, and the area was thick with patches of fog. This weather seemed locked in on the lake, since it hadn't been all that bad up to that point.

I raised the flaps, opened the cowl flaps, and dropped the water rudders, turning to find a family of four or five lined up on the beach. They looked particularly somber as I glided in to ground out on the gravel beach near them. After I had pulled the mixture control to the cutoff position, and the big, three-bladed prop had stopped turning, I switched off the mags and climbed out. One of the party, a woman, had approached the plane, and I could plainly see that she had been crying.

It turned out that her 81-year-old grandfather, Bill Sweetman, had gone for a stroll the evening before and was still away from camp somewhere in the bush. This was mosquito country in a big way, and the swampy area around Highline Lake bred a zillion of the big, thirsty monsters. Their concern over Bill's overnight absence was well founded.

The temperatures around Highline Lake, though not into the freezing zone, had dropped into the high forties and low fifties. These temperatures, coupled with wet clothes and hunger, frequently led to hypothermia and, ultimately, disaster. A body doesn't have to freeze solid to die from exposure. The simple lack of calories is enough to start the downhill process, and I guess we all knew it.

I had been in the air for more than two hours already that day, but I knew I had fuel for about that much more, especially with an empty airplane. I took off and began a low-level search of the area around Highline, looking for a slow hiker or—and I didn't even want to think about it—a person lying on the ground somewhere.

There wasn't really much chance of spotting the elder wanderer, what with all the rain and fog that reduced the visibility to only a little above nothing. More than that, though, was the fact that he had very likely worn himself out in the cold rain and last night's darkness. It was most probable that he had pulled himself under an uprooted spruce or some other cavelike hideout. In that case, he would be extremely hard to see. If he were standing on a naked ridge and waving his jacket, that would be another story. Still, I had to make the attempt. The old gent was in a serious pickle, if he were still alive at all.

I was beginning to run a tad low on fuel, finally, and made a general radio call on "Guard" frequency, 121.5. This is the VHF emergency frequency that all airliners and military aircraft "guard" on one of their radios. Most of Alaska's bush pilots do, too, so there was a good chance I could get somebody on the other end of the radio.

I did, in fact, and it happened to be an Alaska Fish & Wildlife Protection Officer flying nearby in a state-owned Piper Super Cub. What a stroke of luck!

I explained the problem to him, told him where the family was camped on Highline Lake, and lit out for Lake Hood where I could pick up some more fuel.

I had another flight scheduled into Scotty Lake, on the other side of Mystic Pass, to get behind me that day, and even in the scabby weather I was sure I could make it. That flight consisted of transporting two more of the hunting party and some of their gear and food.

On my way back to Highline Lake after having finished my commitment at Scotty Lake, I found that the weather had turned even worse in that area. In fact, it hadn't been all that good at Scotty Lake, either, and I had decided to come back above the overcast. Once through the pass, I was able to find a hole that allowed me to descend through the cloud layer and once again take up a search with the F&W Protection Officer. About an hour into that depressing search, I heard the F&W plane give me a call on 121.5, asking me to come up on 123.45, a frequency not assigned for the purpose but one that many of us used in the bush to communicate air-to-air. It wasn't really used for anything else at that time, so we were free to chat without taking up valuable air time on the real emergency frequency of 121.5.

The other pilot informed me that he had located the elderly wanderer, that he was a little hungry—and a little put out over Alaska's voracious mosquitoes—but generally in fine shape. After all, he told his rescuer, he had been a farmer most of his life. What was a little cold weather and hard walking, for Pete's sake? Besides, it rained one helluva lot harder where he came from, anyway!

Some fellow, he must have been. I didn't get to meet him, and I'll always be sorry that I didn't. It is easy to build a lot of respect for that kind of character, especially in Alaska, where it is often required but not all too frequently found.

* * *

One of my more memorable flights, though not a particularly remarkable one, occurred on September 17, 1981, when Jim Hubbs, my number one assistant guide, and I flew to High Lake to pick up the pair of Super Cub floats that I had dinged up earlier at Madman Lake. I had already had to threaten a pair of bush thieves who were trying to make off with them, and I didn't want the things to lie there throughout the winter, chancing another attempted theft. The next try might be a little more successful than was the last. So I was happy to be able to finally pick up the floats, since freeze-up was roaring down on this part of Alaska. Termination Dust, the first of the local snows, had begun to slip down the mountains, and it would be only a very few days more before the lakes began to ice over. One morning, it would be obvious that the lakes had begun freezing at the edges. By nightfall, they might well be frozen completely over.

With the floats tied securely atop the big Edos of the Cessna 206, the trip back to Anchorage took just an hour and six minutes, only a dab above the usual flight time between these two points. I would later sell the floats, new but damaged, and keep the Cub on wheels or wheel-skis until I would finally sell it, too. Last I knew, the little Cub, N1858A, a 1952 agricultural, flat-back model, was still flying the Alaska outback, somewhere on the west side of the Alaska Range and out near the village of Aniak, enjoying its performance with the Borer high-rpm prop.

* * *

About the middle of September of that same year, I was puttering around in the Kelly Lake area of the Upper Susitna River valley. Shuttling back and forth between Kelly and Lake Louise, a huge lake about twelve minutes east of my main camp on Kelly, I suddenly picked up a strong emergency signal on my second communications radio, which is always tuned to 121.5 in the Very High Frequency (VHF) band. This signal almost blew my earphones off, so I knew I was quite near the source.

N756VR, my normally aspirated Cessna 206 floatplane, was equipped with a DF 88 direction finder. That radio was linked to a display that showed 360 degrees of direction on a dial. The display also included a needle—super accurate!—which pointed unerringly toward even the weakest of radio signals.

Following that needle, I soon came upon a Super Cub that had obviously attempted an overloaded takeoff from a very small lake and had failed in the attempt. Most likely, I thought, a moose hunter that had tried to put too much meat aboard and just hadn't made it off the small puddle.

I continued to Evergreen Lodge at Lake Louise, where I met my friend and fellow guide-pilot, Paul Holland. Paul had a Super Cub on floats at the lodge, a plane that could handle smaller water better than my oversized Cessna. Moreover, Paul was experienced in the bush and had even gone so far as to pick up an Airline Pilot Rating, the crown jewel of pilot certifications.

Paul buckled himself into his high-performance Cub, and we both lit out to the northwest. Again following the needle in order not to waste time, I led Paul directly to the injured Cub. From there, Paul could do the honors of helping the downed pilot drag his Super Cub back into the water after unloading at least some of the moose meat. After that, it would be just another day in the bush for all of us.

* * *

On September 27 of that year, I attempted to fly Chris Batten, noted outdoor writer, through Merrill Pass to the other side of the Alaska Range. Over the east end of Chakachamna Lake, I looked ahead to see the strangest cloud formation I had ever laid eyes on. It appeared just as it might have if I had been looking down the inside of a giant pipe, just one big swirling mass of weird and tightly packed dark cloud. Frankly, it unnerved me, and I was happy to decide that Merrill Pass was closed in cloud. Later that same day, we were watching a demonstration back at Lake Hood by a Maule floatplane. The plane was wearing a new type of fiberglass floats. They lacked a keel and had instead a half-tunnel cavity along the bottom length of each float, giving them better directional stability, the pilot had said.

The floats also boasted individual water rudders, and these were actually turned ninety degrees to the path of flight. Each could be operated independently, allegedly acting as individual brakes and, thereby, helping to steer the aircraft while on the water. To this day, I don't know what went wrong, exactly. What I do know is that as soon as the Maule had touched the water on its first demonstration landing, it nosed over with a huge splash. The pilot wasn't hurt, and there were no other souls aboard, of course. The plane would suffer a lot of damage, though, through a good soaking. The elaborate collection of radios would suffer most, probably. The whole mess would no doubt cost somebody a pocketful of change. For my own part, I've never found anything that I'd care to substitute for Wipline or Edo floats. And, yeah—I know. PKs are the easiest to repair in case of float damage, which occurs often in the world of the Alaska bush pilot. Still, give me Edos or Wiplines every time. For one thing, their angle of incidence, which is very important in attaining an early takeoff speed, isn't so critical. If you fly floats, you'll know what I mean.

* * *

On December 1, 1981, I had a bad-weather flight between Tok Junction and Anchorage. I had stuck my neck out by flying in blinding snowstorms before, but this time the weather would finally beat me.

I had flown the C-206, by now mounted on its original 8.50x6.00 tires, tubes, and wheels after coming off floats at the end of the season, from Anchorage to Tanacross, where I topped the tanks. When I arrived at Tanacross, there was a measured nine inches of fresh snow on the runway. By then, I was already wishing for skis.

After topping off, I flew on down to Tok, where I would be involved in a meeting with the school board. The meeting went quite well, and, after a quick sandwich dinner, I took off again for Anchorage. A lot of you who read *Flying the Alaska Wild* have written to tell me that you follow these flights on aeronautical charts. If you want to follow this one, I'll tell you that it took me through portions of the "North" side of the Anchorage Sectional Chart.

Flying north out of Anchorage, and after passing Palmer and Sheep Mountain, I overflew Eureka, Tazlina, and Glenallan (Gulkana). Making a *slight* left turn, I headed over Chistochina, Posty, and Barnharton on my way to Mentasta Lodge and tight little Mentasta Pass just beyond it. Pouring from the east end of the pass, a left turn of about seventy degrees would fly me over Mineral Point and on into Tanacross, for my fresh fuel. Tok would be about a right ninety-degree turn from Tanacross and more or less ten miles down the valley of the Tanacross River.

Those of you who are stateside fliers have long ago realized that Alaska doesn't have such a quantity of cities and towns as you'll find in the Lower 48. Well, it doesn't have your wealth of radio navigation facilities, either. This trip, for example, lasted two hours and fifteen minutes. The pilot can expect dependable radio communications with Anchorage, Gulkana, and Tok. If flying IFR, the environment will provide radio navigation facilities. If you're down there where most of us fly most of the time, you'd better get used to enjoying the really quiet scenery, even if visibility is only out to slightly more than one-quarter mile in snow or rain and fog. I guess what I'm saying is that the majority of Alaska outback flying is anything but boring. Most of those places I noted above as landmarks for this flight are lonely spots, some perhaps even closed during the winter. A few are nothing but small roadhouses, consisting only of a lodge with dining facilities and,

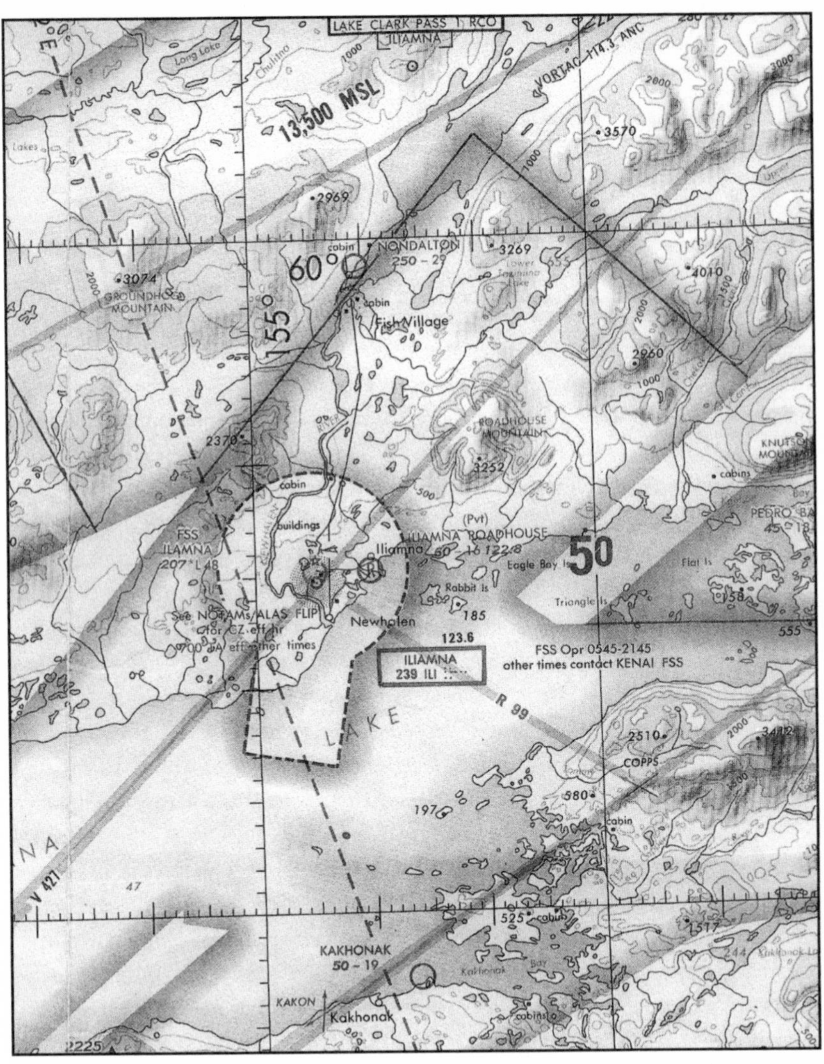

The home of the legendary Big Man is rumored to be near Roadhouse Mountain. Here is an enlarged view of Iliamna and the Newhalen River area from a Kodiak Sectional Aeronautical Chart.

perhaps, a sleeping cabin or two. And two or three buildings don't make for much of a landmark from the air. Especially when they are covered with snow.

It was on the way back to Anchorage late in the day, though, that the weather finally caught up with me. When I had checked in with Gulkana Radio while passing Glenallen, the flight service specialist there had warned me that Sheep Mountain—actually Tahneta Pass—had been reported closed in snow showers.

Since I didn't know what type of aircraft had given this pilot report—some of us use that kind of extraneous information to determine whether or not the pass is *really* closed, or just frighteningly marginal—I decided to go have a look for myself.

It was snowing at Tolsona Lake, Tazlina, and Snowshoe Lake as I followed the Alaska Highway toward Anchorage. When I passed Tazlina, I reflected that my main guiding camp at Kelly Lake lay just about fifteen minutes off my right wingtip. If things really went south on me, I could always make it into Kelly and bunk up warm, snug, and well fed. Getting back out of deep snow without a ski-equipped airplane would be a chore, but I'd have to confront that later, if need be.

By the time I reached the roadhouse and small dirt strip at Eureka, I found that the snow hadn't let up one bit, and I was beginning to think the PIREP had been accurate. Still, it hadn't quite shut me down, and so I flew on ahead to see what it looked like at Sheep Mountain and Tahneta Pass.

By the twenty-first day of December, the shortest day of the year in the Northern Hemisphere, there would only be about five hours of daylight in this area. Flying in a snowstorm late in the day didn't provide much daylight, either. Still, it was sufficient, and I plowed ahead, passing Sheep Mountain, the mouth of the Chikaloon River where it dumps into the Matanuska, and on downstream past Jonesville Mine. It was shortly after passing Jonesville that I knew I wasn't going to make it into Anchorage that day. Pinched between the Chugach and the Talkeetna Mountains, the Matanuska River is only about three miles wide at Chickaloon. The valley provided plenty of room for a comfortable 180-degree turn, though, and I knew I would have to make one now. Back to Northway, Alaska's U.S. Custom's Station. There would be good food there, plus a good bed and a nice fire. Couldn't beat that, except it represented a wasted flight of two hours or so. Ah, well, better warm, well fed, and safe than cold, hungry, and sorry on some snow-covered gravel bar in the silty Matanuska River. Besides, finding a gravel bar big enough for the C-206 in a blinding snowstorm wouldn't have been an easy chore, anyway.

The next morning, admittedly after a wonderful breakfast at Northway, I saddled up and tried Sheep Mountain and Tahneta Pass again. This time I made it on through, though the weather was minus twenty-one degrees Fahrenheit with dense fog. The pass was reported "marginal" that morning, but I had been flying through there for more than twenty-five years by that time, and "marginal" wasn't a real deal-breaker for me. Had I been carrying passengers, I would have turned back to Northway again, of course.

Chapter 8

The Abominable Snowman

GOOD JUDGMENT COMES FROM EXPERIENCE,
BUT EXPERIENCE COMES FROM BAD JUDGMENT.

It was on April 8, 1978, that my wife, Peggy, and I loaded Jim Repine, his Rhodesian Ridgeback, Jubal, and Ron Hyde, one of Alaska's premier fly fishing guides and fishing guru of the Goodnews River area, aboard our Beechcraft Sierra, N2230L, and lit out for a trip through Lake Clark pass to Iliamna. The reason for the trip was a reported sighting of Alaska's own Abominable Snowman—our Sasquatch—locally known simply as Big Man. Over the decades, perhaps centuries, Alaska natives in these parts have reported seeing—and, indeed, interacting with—this mysterious creature. Everyone around Lake Iliamna believes firmly in his existence, and many will report, with straight faces, their personal sightings of or confrontations with him. Or her, of course.

This latest report held that one of the FAA personnel at the Iliamna Flight Service Station, located adjacent to the large gravel-runway airport there, had left work after a shift change only to find the abominable snowman seated comfortably on the concrete foundation of one of the FAA radio tower's steel legs. Clearly surprised—and displaying an alarming lack of self-discipline—our shaky FAA rep fired a shot, apparently hitting the hapless creature fair and square. It should be said here that anyone who lives beyond the limits of the City of Anchorage packs heat of some sort. Fifty percent of those who live within the city do too, of course. This chap, however, may not have carried within him the restraint usually considered to be a prerequisite to responsible firearm ownership.

Anyhow, the injured beast allegedly bolted, surely an impressive sight in and of itself, I'd have to suspect. Big Man headed himself, with huge strides, directly for the nearby village of Iliamna and, possibly, to the Iliamna

Roadhouse. It was here that he could either (a) get help with his purported gunshot wound, (b) find a temporary hiding place, or (c) toss down a few in an attempt to forget as quickly as possible the recent abuse to which he had so surprisingly fallen hapless victim.

Our hero, now caught up in the heat of the chase, followed behind in his bent-up pickup, careful not to get too close lest the monster turn on him and swallow his vehicle, maybe even with the unfortunate driver still inside it.

The report also held that the fleeing brute, very likely—and quite understandably—no longer in control of his senses, had scooted through a family backyard that lay directly in his path. Unfortunately, the backyard, like so many others in the area, was rife with pole-mounted clotheslines. Iliamna was without the electrical transmission and distribution lines to which most of us have long become accustomed, and washed clothes in that neck of the woods are hung outside for the sun and breeze to dry.

It was said that, with several items of clean laundry now draped unceremoniously about his thick neck, our victim proceeded to cut across the narrow dirt road, leap down upon the snowy surface of a small frozen pond, cleverly reverse his direction of travel, and bound with ever more impressive strides back in a northerly direction. He was now headed generally back toward the scene of the original confrontation, but slightly to the east, apparently heading for the low hills and higher mountains there.

Not far ahead of him, as the crow flies, that is, there is a stream that empties into the beautiful Newhalen River, just downstream and across the river from the village of Nondalton. I won't name this stream, but a clue for you lies in the fact that there is, not far upstream from its confluence with the larger river, a truly beautiful waterfall. It is said that there, behind the falls themselves, lies hidden a very large cave. It is here that Big Man allegedly lives in relatively undisturbed tranquility. Mostly.

Our hero now presumed that his quarry was headed for the safety of that remote spot. No longer able to drive his truck in the chase, since the creature had left the hard-packed road and scooted off into the snow-covered tundra, he gave the whole thing up as a bad thought and reported the whole escapade to his cohorts back at the field. It was from there that the tale reached me. And, always excited over the prospect of doing something outlandish, I was following up on it. As was Jim Repine, of course, experienced fisherman and prolific outdoor writer that he was. And still is, by the way, though now plying his skills somewhere deep in the Andes Mountains of South America.

Ron Hyde, much more in control of his senses than either Jim or I were, was probably with us just for the great fishing along the Newhalen. But, back to the search . . .

We had indeed found blood spots on the concrete radio tower foundation pad. What's more, we examined a set of absolutely huge footprints—*bare* footprints, and alarmingly akin to human footprints—that were left in evidence as they disappeared across and beyond that small lake back by the village. The prints were clearly left by someone, or some *thing*, quite heavy, since the snow on the little frozen lake had melted around them, leaving the mounded prints as small islands spaced about eight feet apart. As I looked at these prints, I couldn't imagine anyone carrying a pack heavy enough to stomp those prints into snow packed so tightly it might as well have been clear ice. And if someone *could* have carried such a pack, how the hell could he have run barefoot—*with an eight-foot stride*—through the deep snow at any rate? Besides, there was the missing clothesline and scattered laundry to consider.

It was getting dark by the time we had finished our confused, and definitely confusing, investigation of this whole episode. Peggy and I returned to the airport, only to learn that our erstwhile fishermen, Jim and Ron, had apparently forgotten our flight schedule. The weather was a bit on the scabby side, and with darkness now descending rapidly, we could wait no longer. Our patient German shepherd, waiting inside our home back in Anchorage, would be looking to go out for a few minutes, we knew. I figured that I could fly back tomorrow to pick the guys up.

I warmed the little retractable while Peggy settled in for the ride through Lake Clark pass, and we were soon taxiing out to take the active runway for our departure.

I couldn't climb very high after liftoff, since the cooling earth had allowed the cloud cover to settle even lower than it had been for most of the day. By the time we got to the tight ninety-degree right turn at the east end of the pass, darkness was full upon us, it had begun to snow, and visibility was down to something only a bit better than a quarter-mile.

Had I been flying alone—or driving a Super Cub or one of the Cessna taildraggers—I suppose I'd have punched my way on through. As it was, and with my wife aboard, I considered the little, low-wing Sierra to be a poor piece of transportation for the attempt. I aborted the flight, much to Peggy's relief, and we returned to Ted and Mary Gerken's Iliaska Lodge for a grand dinner and a good night's sleep. After listening to Ted hold forth with some Robert W. Service, of course. Ted had a great memory and could recall at will any number of Service's rhymes. Our favorites, of course, were *The Shooting of Dan McGrew* and *The Cremation of Sam McGee*, definitely far north fare. Ted, accomplished Alaska pilot, fly fishing master, and friend, is yet another who has unfortunately gone west before his time.

Later, I returned with a TV cameraman to the mysterious waterfall. I figured that with the low water of deep winter, we might actually get a look into that legendary cave. We landed on the frozen lake above the falls and hoofed it downstream to look down at the spot where local lore claimed the giant lived. Lo and behold—no cave at all behind the waterfall, now striving valiantly for the stature of even a wintertime trickle. Solid rock, through and through.

So—am I now a firm believer in Big Man? I can only tell you what I saw with my own eyes and admit that I don't have an answer for it. If any of you can shed light on the matter, I'd be more than pleased to hear from you. I will tell you that everything you've read above is true. Or was told to me for the truth. The evidence seemed to support the event, certainly.

I later heard that folks in the village of Kakhonak, across the lake from the village of Iliamna, had once caught and kept in a cage one of the smaller representatives of the legendary Big Man. My source even allowed as how the village youngsters would occasionally go play with him. He later escaped, of course, and the story is now just that—a story. But, like other stories of the region, it is repeated with wide eyes and the ring of truth. Certainly the locals believe it.

Lake Iliamna has its own sea monster, too. With a surface area of around two thousand square miles, it's certainly a large body of fresh water. Moreover, it's as clear as gin. Like Lake Tahoe, there seems to be no end of visibility in its water.

Many have reported an encounter with the monster, at one time or another. Steve McCutcheon, popular Anchorage photographer and another Alaska pilot long ago gone west, reported having fished for the huge fish. If fish indeed it is.

McCutcheon's fishing gear consisted of a huge man-made treble hook, a generous cut of moose meat, and a steel cable attached to one of the front float davits on his old Aeronca Sedan. His story is that, if the cable hadn't parted, the mysterious underwater denizen would have pulled his four-place airplane into the lake's cold depths. Who knows? Steve wasn't known to be one to stretch the truth, I can say that for him.

Alaska is huge. There have been reports of a year-round green valley somewhere north of Fairbanks. Allegedly, those extinct prehistoric giants like the dinosaur still live and roam there. Though geographically and meteorologically impossible, the stories keep cropping up.

And who am I to throw cold water on a good warm story?

The author adds avgas from one of his hidden fuel and oil caches to his Super Cub on the gravel beach at the mouth of Chinitna Bay, along the west side of Alaska's Cook Inlet. *Photo by John Erskine, Anchorage, Alaska*

Chapter 9

The Difficult Years

You start with a full bag of luck and an empty bag of experience. Try to fill the bag of experience before the bag of luck runs out.

I wasn't going to write these tales. By the time you have finished reading them, I suppose you'll understand why. In one case, the events you will read here culminated in the most severe penalty ever handed down by any Alaska court to an Alaska registered guide. But let me give you a little background first.

A nonresident hunter who wishes to hunt Dall (or Dahl) Sheep, brown bears, or grizzly bears within the State of Alaska must first retain the services of an Alaska registered guide. That's the law, and the penalties for trying to avoid it are quite sobering. Briefly, everything involved in an illegal hunt is subject to immediate seizure by the State of Alaska, Department of Fish & Wildlife Protection (an arm of the Alaska State Troopers). This is in keeping with Alaska's sincere, and quite effective, approach to sport fish and game management in the nation's largest state. It is through these efforts that the state can now boast a larger population of brown and grizzly bears than at the time Alaska became a state way back in 1959.

In Alaska, a binding contract must be executed by the parties—that is, by both the hunting client and the registered guide under whose license the hunt will be conducted—and a copy of the executed agreement must be timely filed with the State of Alaska at the state capital in Juneau. One signed copy must be given over to the hunter who has signed it, and one copy is then retained by the guide for his own records. It is interesting to note that a guide may not guarantee the results of any big game hunt for which he contracts; nor is he allowed to take any big game animal while on a guided hunt. That means he can't shoot an animal for his client. He *can* shoot one, of course, if the animal becomes a threat to life or property.

Conversely, a nonresident hunter may hunt *without* a registered guide for such Alaska big game species as mountain goats, black bears, moose, and caribou. There are other exempt animals, of course, such as wolves and wolverines, but these are usually taken incidental to the taking of big game animals or else are trapped—along with beavers, marten, lynx, mink, ermine, and others—as fur-bearing animals. A separate trapping license is required for this activity from both resident and nonresident trappers.

Hunters will note that Alaska is broken up into game management units—if my memory serves me correctly, there are, or were, a total of twenty-seven such units, each divided further into several additional parts or subunits. As a result, the Alaska Game Regulations are a bit complex, but what can you expect from a state that is nearly one-third as large as the rest of the continental states combined?

Occasionally, one or more of the Alaska big game animals will appear within the hunting regulations as something of a special case. The musk ox, American Bison, and at least one variety of caribou are among those animals. That is, certain parts of one or more of those game management units may be closed to a certain species, or one of the subunits may be a "permit only" hunting area for a particular species.

Moreover, Alaska is, or used to be, broken further into guiding districts. A registered guide could conduct guided hunts in only those areas for which he was licensed. Finally, he could be licensed to conduct guided hunts in a maximum of only three of these areas, called exclusive guiding areas or, if shared with one or more other professional guides, nonexclusive guiding areas.

This doesn't mean that Alaska guides are restricted to areas as small as are their Canadian counterparts. In Canada, I am told, a guide's area may be limited to as little as ten square miles. In Alaska, one of my areas contained *more than seven thousand square miles*. We weren't really cramped up there, to say the least.

The larger of my guiding areas contained several subunits of Game Management Unit 13. And in one of these subunits, caribou were a "permit only" animal. This meant that the hunter must have submitted for a "drawing," and must have been successful in that drawing, for one of a limited number of permits issued for caribou for that particular licensing year. Having said all that—which by now must have bored the hell out of you—we'll move on with the story.

By August of the 1980 hunting year, my flying schedule had become really heavy. Sheep camps had to be set up and provisioned, and the early hunting season for several of Alaska's big game animals had already begun. My flight records show that I flew a total of 77 flights that month. September seems to be the guide's busiest month in Alaska, and my flight records show a total of 153 flights during the month of September that year, an average of 5 separate flights each and every day. The longest of these flights was 3.1 hours, while the shortest was only 6 minutes in duration. Even at that, an average of 5 flights each and every day is a lot of flying, not to mention servicing of the aircraft, loading and unloading, checking weather, routine maintenance, the filing of flight plans, and all the rest of those chores that are inherently attendant to the privileges and responsibilities of commercial flying.

In the midst of all this activity, there were still the chores of buying grub and supplies, and of flying and concealing aviation fuel and oil supplies at various hidden locations in the bush. These are the pilot's secret service stations, without which not much real bush flying could be accomplished during the fall hunting seasons.

Throughout the late summer and early fall of that year, my schedule was so packed with activities that my wife, Peggy, and I seldom crossed paths, it seemed. On August 2, a Sunday, Peggy elected to fly with me to Seward. It had become necessary to fly to Resurrection Bay so that Bruce (not his real name), one of my recent assistant guides, could remove some faulty parts from his small charter fishing boat, the *Avenger*. Little did I know how well that name would later describe the attitude of my new assistant guide!

Bruce was very possibly Alaska's most skilled rifle shot. He had won every turkey shoot that he had ever entered and had both a keen eye and a steady hand. He hand-loaded his own ammunition, of course. To suggest that he was a gun nut wouldn't be far from the truth, and I doubt the classification would have offended him. He also hunted Alaska's big game each season and had been as successful as most amateur hunters seemed to be when hunting on their own. Professional hunting, of course, is a whole 'nother ball game, but a guy has to start somewhere, right? Anyway, I had recommended Bruce to the Guide Licensing and Control Board for an assistant guide license and had later scheduled him to help with several of my clients during the 1980 fall hunting season. Only a licensed Alaska registered guide can contract with nonresident hunters, though he may retain up to three assistant guides to help with those guided hunts.

Elmore Maynard, a former client from California and a very good friend, had asked if I would accept a father-and-son combination for an Alaska wilderness experience for the late summer of 1980. Elmore had hunted with us before, and, even though impressively into his eighties, he still performed well in the bush. In fact, he had earlier passed up several good opportunities to bag a large Alaska bull moose because he didn't think that any he had seen up to that point were quite as large as he wanted. I admired Elmore for that, since he had put in no end of planning for his first big Alaska trip. He had even made his own Whalen .35-caliber rifle for the trip. And he could shoot the big smoke pole, too!

Anyway, at Elmore's request I had accepted Carlos M. and his son, Carlos Jr. (again, not their real names), for a short stay at Shadow Lake. My senior assistant guide, Linc, had helped set up housekeeping at the Shadow Lake cabin in preparation for my arrival with the Maynard-Carlos-Carlos Jr. party. I would leave Bruce with that party, flying Linc on up the valley another seventy miles or so to our main camp at Kelly Lake.

I should probably tell you that this party was not a "guided" big game hunt, per se, and my leaving Bruce with them served two purposes: first, it would give me an idea about how Bruce would later behave with clients in the mountains, and second, it would provide camp help to the three California visitors. They could still hunt black bears and moose in this area, of course, provided that they had the proper nonresident licenses and big game tags. Caribou, however, were off limits, since this was a "permit only" area. The party would see caribou every day, of course, since there was a captive herd that seemed to stay on that particular mountain year round.

Our camp cook at the main camp was Cindy Shaw. She was a whiz in the galley, and she could easily be mistaken for a *Playboy* "Playmate of the Month." Blond and beautiful, she broached absolutely no foolishness from anyone in camp. Period. She had confided in me that she didn't think Bruce was going to work out and that I should be very careful of him. In fact, she just didn't want him at the main camp at all. She simply considered him to be trouble, and trouble in the bush can be big trouble, what with loaded guns on hand. After that appraisal, I would be paying special attention to Bruce, naturally.

While I've come to know that I'm a very poor judge of character, I've never been quick to admit it. My wife, known to me to be an *excellent* judge of character, had also advised me to steer clear of Bruce. Why I didn't listen to any of this advice is now beyond me. My complacency and trust eventually led to my downfall. It happened like this. . . .

The Maynard-Carlos party had indicated that they might like a day of saltwater fishing before taking the flight into the Talkeetna Mountains and dropping in at Shadow Lake. So, on Wednesday, August 26, 1980, I flew the party, along with Bruce, to Bruce's boat at the marina in Seward. That trip would prove to be something of a disaster for everybody.

I had flown a total of only six and a half hours that day, but by the time I hit the bed late that night, I was nonetheless pretty well exhausted. When the telephone rang at about midnight, I wasn't in the mood for it. I presumed it was another German client, one of those who hadn't thought about the time difference between his home in Germany and ours in Alaska.

It turned out to be Bruce, calling from the Seward marina. He said the clients insisted on being brought back to Anchorage that same night and that I should fly down there immediately.

I can tell you that the boat harbor in Seward is no place to be flying—or taxiing around in a floatplane, for that matter—in the middle of a dark night. I told Bruce I'd have to drive down in the station wagon, a 128-mile trip each way through the Chugach Mountains. It would take me about two and a half hours each way, but if the clients had insisted on it, there was no acceptable way for me to get out of making the lengthy trip. After a relatively long flying day, I certainly wasn't excited about making a five-hour round-trip drive to Seward and back!

When I finally found the *Avenger*, she was tied comfortably at her berth, the onboard electrical system was plugged into marina-provided electricity, and everyone aboard was comfortably sound asleep, each in his own bunk. This didn't look like much of an emergency to me!

After rousing the sleeping assistant guide and the clients, I took Elmore aside to ask what the emergency was. He said that there wasn't any emergency; Bruce just wanted to go back to Anchorage. More than that, he had taken the group pretty far out into the open sea for the day's fishing trip. The weather had turned a bit sour, and the seas had come up in a most threatening and definitely uncomfortable manner. By the time Bruce had decided he couldn't really handle the seas and had turned tail to dash back into Resurrection Bay, the clients—and maybe even Bruce himself—were half scared out of their collective wits! Strikes one and two against Bruce in only one day.

Still, there was nothing for it now but to load the group and its gear into the station wagon and make the long drive back over Johnston Pass, down into Portage, and then back along Turnagain Arm to Anchorage. At least I was scheduled to fly only about seven hundred miles the following day!

On August 27, I flew the Elmore-Carlos party from Lake Hood to Shadow Lake, leaving them there for a few days of sightseeing and general prowling around in the great Alaska outback. I was scheduled to pick up the party for their return to Anchorage on August 31 (my wife's birthday, by the way), which I did.

After I had landed the Cessna 206 floatplane and tied it down at Shadow Lake in preparation for the pickup, Bruce approached me to ask if I would fly his caribou back to Anchorage.

"Your caribou! What caribou?! This is a permit area only, for Pete's sake! You can't take an animal on a client's hunt anyway. What caribou?"

"Well," Bruce allowed, "I thought it would be all right if I took one for my winter meat supply. It's all skinned and butchered and bagged. I cached it down there under that lone tree at the other end of the lake."

If I had had a single brain in my head, I would have clamped the 'cuffs on Bruce and flown him back to Anchorage in irons. At a minimum, I should have lifted off, radioed nearby Talkeetna, and asked for a state trooper to hustle in to see us. But I didn't. That beneficent decision would turn out to be the most expensive decision of my life.

At any rate—and in clear violation of restrictions against it—I flew Bruce's unlawfully taken caribou back to Anchorage. I guess I justified it by thinking that Bruce could use the meat over the coming winter. On the other hand, I personally knew several of Alaska's guides who would open sheep hunting camp several days ahead of their first clients' arrivals, and then proceed to shoot illegal ewes for camp meat. Over the years, one Alaska guide had utilized a federal ATF agent as an assistant guide, instructing *him* to break the law in this fashion. Which, by the way, the ATF agent did without blinking an eye.

Several of Alaska's very prominent guides were known to shoot trophy sheep with 12-gauge shotguns from their flying Super Cubs, later instructing their assistant guides to approach the dead ram carefully and then have their clients shoot the "sleeping" sheep to fill their licenses. Several of these guides would use a stretch of highway as their "airports," violating several more of Alaska's laws. None of this, however, relieves me of the errors of my ways as they relate to Bruce's caribou. It's just that I had always tried to keep my own skirts clean.

In the coming days, several of my clients complained to me that Bruce was something of a crybaby and that they would rather not share camps with him. By this time, I had finally gotten the picture and had stopped using Bruce for any wilderness activity at all.

At the close of that season, Bruce approached me with a business proposition. Would I give him 50 percent of my business? Why, hell no, I wouldn't! I did suggest that I would get my accountant to provide us with his appraisal of my company's worth and that Bruce should do the same. At that time, we could discuss his purchase of the 50 percent he seemed to want. Well, he said, he didn't intend to *buy* the 50 percent. He just thought I should *give* it to him. After all, he could throw his boat, *Avenger*, into the bargain. Bruce's $15,000 boat wasn't even in the ballpark, as far as I was concerned. Against our airplanes, boats, motors, lodge, five outlying cabins, and miscellaneous other gear? Hardly. Besides, if I thought I really needed a partner, it wouldn't have been Bruce!

It was several years later when I received a telephone call from a woman who introduced herself as Bruce's attorney. She said her client was moving to sue me for breach of contract. When I inquired as to what contract she might be referring, she said that I had refused to give Bruce 50 percent of my guiding business. I informed her that, even in my darkest hour, I wouldn't willingly give Bruce anything of that value and suggested that if Bruce really felt he was entitled to it, his clear avenue would be through the courts. I never heard another thing from the woman, who turned out to be a personal friend of his and who had apparently decided to just try their luck and have a shot at it.

It wasn't long after that, however, that I found our home surrounded by uniformed members of "Detachment C," Alaska's Fish & Wildlife Protection arm of the Alaska State Troopers. Complete with a search warrant, a locksmith (in case I refused to open the door to them, I suppose), and enough uniforms to start a small war. Their marked cars blocked the dead-end street before our home, and a glance out the back door revealed that they were also blocking the alley, just in case I tried to make a run for it.

"Uhm—make a run from what?" I inquired.

"Well, for an illegally taken grizzly bear. We understand that you traded an illegal bear hunt for a German hunting rifle. This search warrant allows us to search for (a) the rifle, (b) the bear hide, and (c) anything else that might be construed as attendant to that hunt."

"Well, hell, boys, come on in!" I said. My wife offered them fresh coffee while I called our attorney, who arrived to videotape the whole silly exercise.

In point of fact, I had *not* traded a grizzly hunt for a German hunting rifle, or for anything else, for that matter. Goodness, I had more than enough rifles in the first place. Among these were some pretty good ones, too. My favorite .450 Fuller, a custom conversion based upon a Winchester Model 71, .348-caliber lever action, custom stocked in Circassian Walnut; a custom .270 Winchester-Cook, put up on a 1911 '98 Mauser action, and with the really low serial number of 9096, stocked in a piece of curly maple that would knock your eyes out; a scoped .375 Holland & Holland caliber custom Ferlach that had been given to me by a German hunting client some years before; a custom .458 African on a Winchester action; and a mint condition, pre-sixty-four Winchester Model 70 in .375 H&H Magnum caliber (something of a treasure, these days), among others. Heck, I didn't need another rifle for my gun case. Didn't need any more shotguns or handguns, either, for that matter. Besides, a good grizzly in those days was worth about $9,000 to a guide, and I haven't seen many rifles worth that kind of money, at least to me. And I certainly wouldn't want to own one of those supervaluable firearms, anyway.

The search was embarrassing for everyone concerned, really. The rifle mentioned in the warrant was a three-barreled piece reminiscent of the old German Drilling guns so popular years ago for African big game. The named manufacturer of the rifle that these jack-booted gentlemen sought, though, had never—NEVER!—made such a three-barreled piece. Much ado was made over my wife's childhood teddy bear, but no grizzly bear skins were found, either. That's because there weren't any, of course. They did, however, confiscate my pilot flight records, and I think that's what they were looking for in the first place.

It turned out that Bruce had telephoned Detachment C, asking for immunity in exchange for reporting a game regulation violation by a registered Alaska guide. This is the thing that Alaska's Fish & Wildlife Protection Officers lived for! In their estimation, each and every one of Alaska's registered guides is a "pirate guide" and deserves to be drawn and quartered in the public square. In my own case, I probably did deserve it. After all, I had unlawfully flown the carcass of a dead caribou from the Talkeetna Mountains to Anchorage so that an unmarried friend could eat its meat through the coming winter. It clearly hadn't been shot for its trophy value, since the modest horns had been left to the foxes, bears, porcupines, and mice. And it certainly hadn't been taken as a profit item for me.

At any rate, that indiscretion eventually warranted a laundry list of thirty-two game violations, as I recall it. My attorney recommended that I plead *nolo contendere* to a reduced list of charges, which I did. And, as I remember it now, I received a fine of $10,000, some community service (which I fulfilled by flying a $70,000 airplane around in the bush, cleaning up the campsites of others), *and the loss for twenty years of my Alaska Registered Guide License!* A number of years earlier, the murderer of an Alaska Fish & Wildlife Protection Officer received only sixty days for her marksmanship. Which wouldn't have qualified her for "expert" at any rate, since he was seated and she was standing directly behind him in their own living room, holding his .44 Special service revolver. Some readers may remember the Bob Mahaffey story.

Bruce went ahead with his own plans to become an Alaska registered guide. Perhaps he has by now achieved that stature. I will tell you, though, that members of the Alaska Guide Licensing and Control Board swore to me at the time that he would never, *ever* be awarded the license.

I saw Bruce once more after that. Well, I didn't see him so much as I saw an airplane he allegedly had purchased. It was parked on a small gravel bar near the mouth of a canyon hard by Chickaloon, a little way up the Matanuska River. Seems he had earned his private pilot license and had decided that he was going to become a bush pilot. His aircraft of choice was a Citabria, and I reckon it might have been a Citabria Scout, which at least had flaps. If his skill and judgment with airplanes turned out to be as good as his skill and judgment with boats, it is quite likely that he is no longer among the living.

* * *

The calendar year of 1980 was also the year that I sent my head assistant guide, my Number One, to Las Vegas to take part in the Safari Club International annual shindig. For our booth display, the nice folks from Don Hanks' Boondock Taxidermy had allowed us to use several of their full-size animal mounts, which was a blessing, and for which I could never thank Don enough. I also sent our camp cook, Cindy Shaw, who would certainly provide window dressing as well as bush experience for our booth there.

I knew that my Number One had auctioned a Dall sheep hunt for two, the proceeds of which went to Safari Club International. What I *didn't* know, though, was that he had promised a *horseback* sheep hunt. I found that out when the two Las Vegas clients arrived later in the year.

My guiding area there was a pretty wet piece of work, what with lakes, puddles, swamps, and tundra and muskeg all over the place. A horse wouldn't last long in that wet ground, I was pretty sure. There just wasn't much of a way to keep a horse's hooves dry. But, more than that, grizzly bears just love fresh horsemeat. Ten horses wouldn't have lasted fourteen days in that grizzly country.

When the two hunters stepped down from the floats of N756VR, my Cessna 206 Stationair, they asked, "Where are the horses?"

"Horses? What horses?" I responded.

"Well, we bought a *horseback* sheep hunt," came the reply. Not only had the Las Vegas trip for two been a bit on the expensive side (my Number One had even called me from there, asking for a little more gambling money!), now I had to return the clients' money—and provide two sheep hunts, worth about nine thousand dollars each, on top of it all. I even had to hire another pilot to help with the hunt! Yeah, these were some of the expensive years, all right! And some of the most frustrating and irritating, too.

* * *

In those days—and perhaps even today—the officers of Alaska's Fish & Wildlife Protection Department were almost rabid in their zeal to strip Alaska registered guides of their livelihoods. At least at Detachment C, the F&W Protection arm stationed near Anchorage, the feeling was that all Alaska registered guides were "pirate guides." Every single one of us was cast as a poacher of the first water, patently unfair, perhaps, but that's the way it was in those days. I have no doubt that it still is.

I personally knew of many cases where F&W officers would swoop in with their little Super Cubs to haze both the guides' hunting parties and the very animals they were hunting. They would deny this, of course, and there was almost no way for the guide to prove it. Photographic evidence was seldom sufficient proof, since the aircraft were small and too far away for the camera to register the numbers.

One well-known guide—admittedly one of the genuine pirate guides to which F&W Protection referred—returned to one of his field camps to find his little landing area surrounded by F&W Protection officers. He was suspected of poaching in a game sanctuary—in this case Katmai National Park—and of taking brown bears from that closed area.

At any rate, it seems that shots were fired after the appropriate warnings had been shouted from the surrounding bush. The guide proceeded to set fire to his own little Super Cub, the story goes, later claiming that one of the officers had started the fire with a wild rifle shot. With the smoldering airplane as a focal point, the officers gleefully confiscated a brown bear hide and immediately arrested the guide. It was later proven that this particular bear hide had been skinned from a legally taken bear, which let the guide off the hook. He then proceeded to sue the state for the loss of his airplane, the result of which was that the State of Alaska had to buy him a new one, the story went. The guide later lost his Alaska Registered Guide License in another scrape with F&W Protection and was then reduced to owning and operating a sport fishing lodge on the shores of Lake Iliamna. He didn't seem to have been hurt much in the financial department by all this, however. He was later known to have bought brand-new Cessna 206 Stationair floatplanes for his fishing operation. Bought six of them at one time, it was said, and paid cash for the whole lot. In those days, that was probably more than half a million bucks for the six floatplanes, which could only be used from June through September.

* * *

This was about the time that F&W Protection really zeroed in on my activities. For example, I had agreed to fly some military friends of mine through the Alaska Range to their favorite hunting grounds for moose, caribou, and black bear. They were residents, so they did not need the services of a registered guide. I had flown the group to the same area the year before, in fact.

They were excellent hunters, and it wouldn't have been unusual for each of them to take a moose, a caribou, and a black bear, all during the same ten-day hunt. That would mean twelve animals, eight sets of horns, and at least four bear hides—plus all the edible meat—which would have to be ferried back to Anchorage, then loaded into the hunters' van for transport to their homes in Fairbanks, about three hundred miles farther north.

The flying route would take me through a squeaky little pass just southeast of Shellabarger Pass and then northeast through one of Master Guide Clark Engle's Exclusive Guiding Districts. Clark knew that I wouldn't guide my non-resident clients in his exclusive area, of course, but I would still have to make quite a few flights through his tiny little sheep hunting area. I only hoped I wouldn't get his sheep all stirred up, and I tried hard to be sure that I didn't. A few years later, Clark, one of Alaska's greatest and most respected guides, would crash and kill himself smack dab in the middle of that little patch of sheep hunting country. A very tight place some days, Mystic Pass.

At any rate, the G.I. hunters had been as successful as any hunting party could hope to be, and I had what seemed to be a million flights to make through that tight little slot in the mountains. Moreover, I would be flying a heavily loaded airplane each time on my return flights, and in an airplane not known for its tight-spot maneuverability in the best of cases.

In those days, and perhaps still, the State of Alaska required that all air taxi operators fill out and file a Transporter Report Form, a piece of paper that noted any game animals or animal parts transported—including all game animal meat, horns, and hides—and the area and time at which the animal had been taken. It is interesting that Alaska registered guides were exempt by law from completing this form, probably because of the other forms that they were required to file with the State of Alaska.

At any rate, I flew for days and days in getting the hunters and all their gear, meat, and trophies back to Lake Hood at Anchorage. Some days, bad weather—mostly from snowstorms in the mountains—would force me to turn back without making it through the narrow and twisting little mountain pass. Each such aborted flight meant at least another two hours of wasted flight time.

Several of my trips included loads so heavy that I would throw about half a load into the Cessna and fly to a nearby larger lake. There, I would off-load, and then return for the second half, repeating the process before I could finally and fully load the Cessna and have another run at that squeaky little pass.

When I settled onto Lake Hood with the last load of meat and horns, a Fish & Wildlife Protection officer was waiting for me at the dock. He immediately seized the entire load, transporting it all to the Detachment C Headquarters building, where a large freezer was available for the preservation of seized meat, trophy hides, and horns. The reason for the seizure was because I hadn't completed a Transporter Report Form for those flights. I tried to explain that the law was clear about my exemption as a registered Alaska guide *and even read to him that portion of the statute that clearly exempted all registered guides.* I might as well have been talking to a post. It appeared that I was just on their list of things to do and registered guides to harass.

With the help of the four hunters from Fairbanks, and a little assist from my attorney again, the matter was relegated to the legal trash bin. Still, it took several years for the false charges to be removed from my records, even though I had long before received the state's "official" letter advising me that the charges had, of course, been dropped. In the meantime, any prospective client who took the trouble to investigate my abilities and licensure would find in the records the charge against me, however hollow it might have been. I have always been disappointed that such abuse of power could be found within the ranks of Alaska's law enforcement community. I had always before expected Alaska's police force to be the most honorable in the world, right up there with my image of the Royal Canadian Mounted Police. You know, Sergeant Preston of the Yukon and his faithful dog, King.

* * *

This would be neither the first nor the last time this particular arm of the law enforcement community would harass me, though.

It was in September of 1980 that Chris Batin, an outdoor writer and good friend, asked if I could stuff him aboard a flight that wasn't too loaded and take him through Merrill Pass to pick up some background on unguided moose and caribou hunts. Chris knew that I advertised in a German sporting magazine, *Die Pirsch*, featuring unguided hunts for such Alaska game animals as moose, black bear, and caribou. Certainly legal under the game regulations of the state, these economical hunts catered to those who couldn't afford the high costs of guided hunts, or those who had little interest in brown bear or Dall sheep hunting.

Chris also had given us a big hand in getting our new Alaska magazine, named *Alaska Outdoors*, off the ground. Chris had handled most of the photographic needs for the first issue or two, and we had been thrilled with his superb work.

There are always supply flights that aren't fully loaded, and I called Chris when the next one of those that was scheduled for flight through Merrill Pass came up. Unfortunately, we had to make several trips during the last week of

September that year, since bad weather seemed to keep that pass closed for days on end. On September 27, though, we were able to sneak through, and I placed him at Underhill Lake, near the old Lime Village location. He would share a tent camp with two German hunters. That same day, I flew two other German hunters from that camp back to Near Lake, a larger (though much shallower) lake where we had a temporary main camp set up.

While Chris busied himself with interviewing the hunters, organizing his notes, and taking photographs of the local area, I was occupied with shuffling other hunters, gear, and supplies within the Stony River area. I also had to make sure that I got all the hunters back to Anchorage to meet their return flights to Germany, and to return gear, supplies, meat, hides, and horns to Anchorage.

Around the end of September or the first of October, Chris had bagged himself a fine young bull moose for his winter meat supply. He had asked my permission to do this, for while he was a resident and properly licensed, he would have to depend on me to fly the meat back through the pass. I told him that would be fine with me but that he would have to do all his own skinning, butchering, packing, and meat-pole hanging, since my crew were much too busy to help with that. He almost wore himself down to a nub with all that hard work, but he finally got all the meat properly bagged and hung on a meat-pole at the main camp. I would fly it all back to Anchorage as soon as possible, but in the meantime, it was well protected. I'm one of those who believe that game meat should hang for about three weeks at temperatures near or below fifty degrees Fahrenheit in order to allow the meat fibers to break down. This makes wild game much more tender and tasty. At any rate, it was during the first week of October, rather late in the year, when I was able to pick up Chris, his gear, and supplies for the return flight through Merrill to Anchorage's Lake Hood seaplane base. On October 11, Chris and I saddled up and tried Merrill Pass from the Anchorage side, only to find the pass closed in snow showers. On the fourteenth, we tried again, only to find the pass once again closed in snow showers. I still wasn't all that concerned about the meat, since it had been well cooled, bagged, and protected against flies with a generous application of black pepper. Still, winter was coming, and I wanted to get the meat back before it really set in. Some Alaska winters can get hard indeed. Temperatures on the west side of Merrill Pass can plunge to minus sixty degrees Fahrenheit and below. Too cold for flying, at any rate.

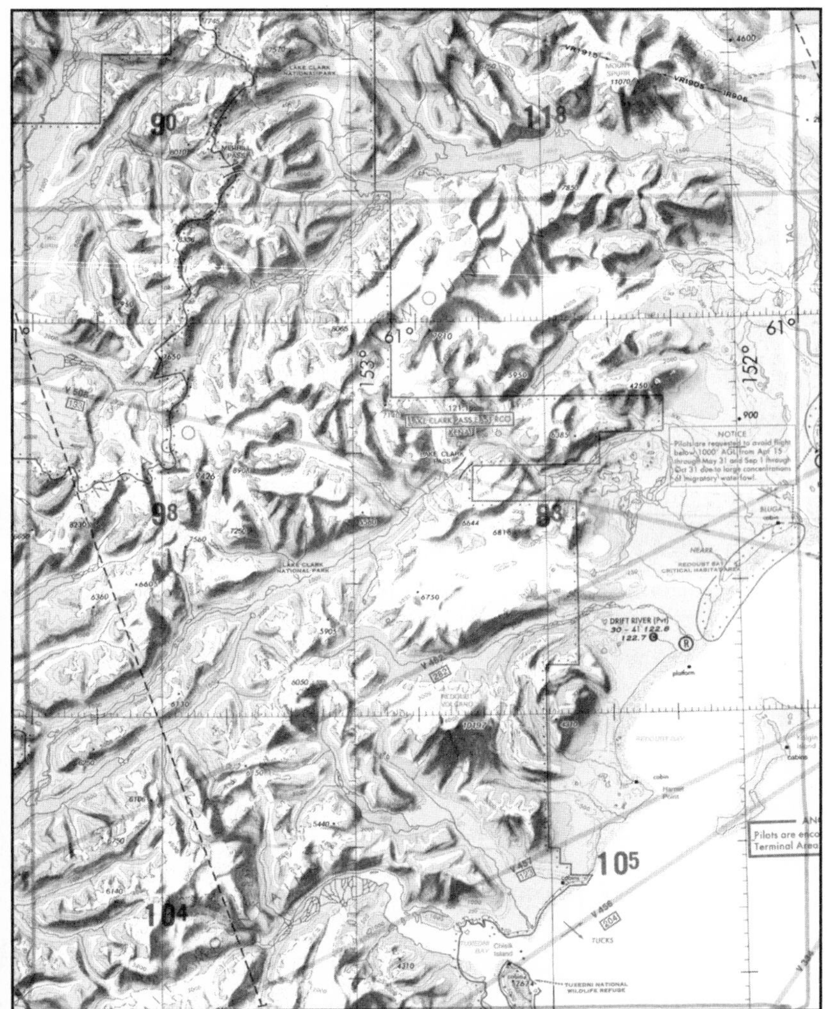

This partial chart shows both Merrill Pass and Lake Clark Pass. In bad weather, both are very difficult to find, unless the pilot is intimately familiar with the country.

On October 16, I tried several mountain passes that would allow me to get to our main camp area again, but once more all the passes were closed in snow showers. I should tell you that I wasn't a really timid pilot when it came to flying in marginal weather, but these snow showers were the real thing, and

I simply couldn't find a route through the Alaska Range that would get me to the western slopes, the place I needed to be.

Finally, on October 17, Chris and I were able to sneak through the pass, but only to find Near Lake frozen solid! I tried to set the heavy Cessna Stationair down on the ice, but, without a snow cover, the ice was too smooth and the lake much too small to allow the landing. I could never have braked the big Cessna to a stop before running out of lake. The moose meat would now have to wait until I could get back to the lake with my ski-equipped Super Cub.

In the meantime, I had advised Chris that he might be able to make a deal with one of the pilots on the western side of the range. While the moose meat would no longer spoil, and freezing wouldn't hurt it, it was still a poor idea to leave it much longer. For one thing, there are any number of wolves in that area. An Alaska wolf, standing nearly thirty-eight inches high at the front shoulders, could easily get at the meat. So, too, could any roving brown or grizzly that hadn't yet headed for the winter den, and most of them had not.

When I was finally able to get through the pass with my Super Cub, I found that the main camp had been stripped (not unusual in the bush, I'm disheartened to admit). Not only that, the moose meat had been pretty well ravaged by wolves. I dreaded telling Chris that all his hard work in packing that six or seven hundred pounds back to camp had now proved to be a waste of calories. Still, that's the name of the game, sometimes, and I would have to report to him as soon as I got back to Anchorage.

I believe it was another guide living in the area who had invaded my main camp, stripping it. I think he was also the one who then reported the ravaged moose meat to Fish & Wildlife Protection officers, claiming it appeared to be a clear case of wanton waste of a game animal. F&W jumped on it immediately and tried to move ahead with an action against me. Since a "guided hunt" had not been involved, they gave it some thought and came up with another idea. They would move against Chris Batin for the wanton waste charge, subpoena me as a witness for the prosecution, then ask the court's permission to treat me as a "hostile witness" in order to back me into a corner in some fashion. They did all those things, and the day that the matter popped up on the court's calendar, the courtroom was wall to wall with F&W Protection Officers' uniforms. I guess they were all waiting to see an Alaska registered guide finally get his just desserts. I was surprised to see that none of them was carrying a knotted rope.

After forty-five minutes of allowing the prosecuting attorney to abuse me in almost every possible fashion, the judge finally called a halt to the proceedings, stating that what the state was then trying to do had become patently clear to the bench. The judge would have no more of it, and I was excused from the stand.

Some of the proceedings are enlightening, if only for the near insanity of it all. For example, the state put one of its own F&W Protection officers on the stand. The state's attorney established that the witness was a commercially licensed pilot and historically flew a Piper Super Cub for his F&W patrols. When asked how many flying hours he had, his answer was that he had more than 2,500. When he was then asked how many times he had flown through Merrill Pass, he stated that he had only made that flight once and that the flight had been made in clear and sunny weather. Further, he stated, *he would never fly through that pass again, as he considered it much too dangerous.*

Another departure from apparent sanity was when the prosecuting attorney asked me why, if Merrill Pass had been so many times closed in snow showers, had I not flown north and through Rainy Pass toward McGrath. I told the court that it never dawned on me to fly north in order to get to a place that lay south and west of my departure point. I may not have had fuel enough for that sort of foolishness at any rate.

* * *

It might be good to point out here that the Alaska game regulations are pretty specific about wanton waste of game animals and parts. The same regulations are also clear that there are several circumstances that forgive game meat spoilage, and among these is inclement weather. It was just such weather that occasioned another of my encounters with Alaska's dedicated game law enforcement people.

On September 24, 1979, I flew a chap named Bill Blessington, now deceased, from Anchorage's Lake Hood to our main camp at Near Lake, on the western slopes of the Alaska Range. Bill was Outdoor Editor for the *Anchorage Daily Times*, at that time Alaska's largest newspaper. He had convinced me that he wanted to do a story on nonresident Alaska big game hunting. I thought that Bill seemed a nice sort and figured the newspaper exposure might not hurt us at all. I also figured it would be advertising that

I wouldn't have to pay for, so why not? It didn't work out that way, though, and I soon found out the "why not" of it.

On the twenty-ninth, I was able to fly Mr. Blessington, in the little Super Cub, from Near Lake to a little bend of the Stony River. It was a camp we had named Camp Three, and the camp from which eighty-year-old Elmore Maynard was to finally take a really huge bull moose. After Elmore had bagged his moose and then had returned to his home in California, I had placed Konrad and Erika Weinbeer in the small camp. Konrad was one of Germany's top-shelf chemists and at that time had risen in his profession to form and head his own company there. Konrad and Erika were settled in at the small spike camp when Bill Blessington finally arrived to share their camp and to record their wilderness experience. Little did I know…

Shortly after I had placed Blessington in camp, a storm blew through the area, ripping my Super Cub loose from its ramp tiedown and blowing it the entire length of Near Lake, where it hauled up against the south bank, one float completely sunk and one wingtip deep underwater. As it turned out, there was also a great gash in one of the floats, making the little ship unusable for bush work until suitable repairs could be made.

I later huddled alone inside the 16x16-foot main camp tent, listening to the wind abuse the nearby spruce trees and flinching at the bang-bang-bang of the big Stationair's floats as the ship was bounced up and down on the shallow rocky bottom where it was tied. When the wind had torn the Cub loose, it had also ripped away the spruce ramp, most of which was under water at any rate. I estimated the wind gusts to be at least eighty-five knots. Some were perhaps higher, but I didn't want to think of that. Though the Cessna itself was protected by an overhanging spruce tree, the wind-blown water was as rough as it could get in its sheltered location. And, while I thought the wind probably wouldn't blow the airplane loose from its moorings, the bouncing could absolutely destroy the expensive aluminum Edo floats! I spent a very long, noise-filled, and sleepless night in the big canvas tent, waiting for first light. And I wondered how the exposed little spike camp farther up the Stony River was making out.

By the time next morning's first weak light leaked over the mountains that pressed in tightly above our hunting area, I had checked the big Cessna, untied it, and completed the engine warmup in a slow taxi around the shallow little lake. I had already written a note that I would drop to the party at the small tent camp on the upper Stony. In it, I notified all hands that the Super

Cub had been damaged to the point that I couldn't extract the party from the winding and narrow little river where they were now located. I also gave them directions to a distant and larger lake, Two Lakes, where I could effectively pick them up. It would be a tough hike of about five or six miles through some very unfriendly country, unfortunately. If worse came to absolute worst, though, the party could hunker down at the Two Lakes cabin of a fellow guide, Jim Harrower. Jim and I weren't close friends, but I expected he would be both understanding and helpful in times of an emergency. I would certainly repay him for any kindness he would extend.

I also told the party that I would tie a flashing beacon in a tall spruce tree some distance south of their present location as something of a navigational aid. They would be able to set a path through the thick brush by that light's location, keeping it off their right side as they slogged eastward toward Two Lakes.

Returning to the main camp, I put the log ramp back in shape, then walked to the lower end of the lake to pump out the Super Cub's floats and see to repairs, if that was going to be possible. As it turned out, the hand-pumping went well, though it took nearly the entire day to accomplish this. As to repairs, those would have to wait until I could get the Cub back to Lake Hood where my mechanic could get at it.

I made several over-flights in the Cessna that day in order to keep track of the party's progress. They were struggling valiantly through the tundra and harsh willow scrub, not a pleasant hike, I knew. I noticed that Otto Obwaller, an Austrian and one of the party's helpers, was packing a huge pair of bull moose horns. Those horns alone would weigh nearly 135 pounds. The others packed their own personal gear and enough survival stuff to keep them safe and warm in the event they were hit by another storm of some kind.

Though the trek out for the party was a gruesome hike at best, they all made it safely to Two Lakes, where I could safely make the pickup. At that time, Bill Blessington was still full of good spirits and willing to humorously regale us all with the hardships of both the storm and the subsequent hike out. He also shared with us that he had been able to take a number of good photographs to go with his intended newspaper article, and to all outward appearances, he was as happy as a barnyard pig in a corn crib.

At that point, none of us knew what Bill was really up to, but we would certainly learn in only a few more days. On October 10, I flew Bill Blessington and his gear back to Lake Hood.

Looking back on that one-hour, six-minute flight back through Merrill Pass to Lake Hood, I recall that Bill Blessington and Otto Obwaller were laughing, joking, and comparing hunting tales. Bill would later skin Otto alive in his newspaper special article over Otto's alleged behavior in the bush.

It was only a few days later that Mr. Blessington's two-full-page article came out in the papers as something of a "special report" on the wanton waste of Alaska's big game animals. The spirit of his story didn't point out the storm, the damaged aircraft, or the difficult trek out for the party. It certainly didn't tell of his own involvement in the matter, which included encouragement, butchering, and packing. It only reported that one of my nonresident hunters had shot a large bull moose, had taken only its trophy horns, and had then left the entire carcass to rot in the bush. There were photographs showing Otto Obweiler struggling through the brush with the large horns on his shoulders and other shots of the dead moose on the ground before the butchering had commenced.

Needless to say, F&W Wildlife Protection once again descended upon me, this time suggesting they would try to confiscate both the Super Cub and the Cessna Stationair, since both had been used in the hunt. And since I had driven the party from Anchorage to Lake Hood in my Buick Station Wagon, they would also look to placing a claim against that vehicle as well. Of course, all firearms, binoculars, cameras, and other such trivia would be confiscated, too.

To top it all off, another windstorm had immediately punished the upper Stony River country, and these winds were followed by several days of hard rain. In spite of the care that the party had taken in butchering, packing, bagging, and hanging the moose, the elements got to it before I did, and the whole animal had to be left for the wolves. Clearly, that was another case of inclement weather and "acts of God," things over which no guide has any control. F&W Protection finally decided that bringing charges would be a waste of the state's time and resources. But they weren't pleased about it.

And, to make matters worse, someone had dropped in at Near Lake while I was ferrying hunters, helpers, and gear back to Anchorage and had stolen the client's moose horns! Though I was sure I knew who the culprit was, there was no way to prove it, and the client had to go home to Germany empty-handed. All in all, not really a good trip.

* * *

It wasn't the first time, and it wouldn't be the last time, that another guide stole trophies from us. Speaking of "pirate guides" . . .

I suspect that much of my trouble with F&W Protection began in about 1976, when I had asked the Guide Licensing and Control Board for consideration of an "exclusive guiding district" in the Port Heiden area, way down there on the Alaska Peninsula. At a guide board meeting, I had pointed out that I could verify historic use of the area, a very important point in petitioning the State of Alaska for an exclusive guiding concession in a given area.

Though this exclusive guiding district concept was clearly unconstitutional—a law that lay waste to a man's right to work—it was still the law in those days. Most of us didn't have the money required to fight the state over the matter, though someone later did, and, as a result, the law was finally set aside. In the meantime, it had seriously damaged many otherwise registered, qualified, and capable big game guides.

At any rate, Lt. Bill Pennington, the state's F&W Protection representative to the Guide Licensing and Control Board, stated that his records didn't show any such historic use. I reminded him that I had my copies of several nonresident hunting clients' contracts, as well as my own pilot flight logs, showing historic use dating back to May 1957. That was a full *nineteen years* of historic use!

Lieutenant Pennington told me that he didn't have any of my contracts on file—and if I had filed them, he would *surely* still have them—and, if I *really* had such contracts, could I provide him with copies? I certainly had my "pink" copies and told Bill that I would make copies for him. Moreover, he had only to read the May–June 1965 issues of *Gunsport* and *Guns & Ammo* magazines. These told of the world's largest moose and world's largest caribou ever taken by a handgun hunter. The stories, by Alfred J. Goerg, told of our hunts in that area during the 1964 hunting seasons. And, finally, such hunts had been pointed out in the book *Pioneering Handgun Hunting*, in which Al wrote about some of our Alaska flying and hunting adventures together.

Well, I was pretty sure that those contract copies that I had originally filed with the state hadn't just up and walked out of Lt. Pennington's files. On the other hand, it would do me no good to get in his face about it, so I agreed to again provide copies to the board through his good offices. Which I did. And those copies *again* mysteriously disappeared from the state's files.

I finally retained the services of an attorney and approached the board. Eventually, I was awarded a couple of guiding districts in which I could work.

But I had ruffled the feathers of some of the F&W officers, and I would never escape the effects as long as I continued to hunt and guide nonresident hunters and fishermen.

* * *

At one time, one of my assistant guides (again my Number One, would you believe it?) made a behind-the-back arrangement with a nonresident for a mountain grizzly bear. He did so without my knowledge but in my name. The problem with that was that he couldn't later produce a contract signed by the registered guide as required by state law.

He had hired another pilot and off they flew, into an area that they shouldn't have been hunting in, without a legal contract for the hunt, and intending to fly and shoot the same day, a definite no-no by then in the State of Alaska! And for which he had accepted $10,000 in South African *krugerands* as payment.

The next thing I knew—and the very first notice I had received about such an illegal hunt—I got a call about the purported game infractions. I agreed to meet F&W Protection representatives in my attorney's office, where the matter was *almost* cleared up. I still had to travel to Detachment C headquarters and speak by telephone with the clients themselves, who had by then returned to their homes in Chicago. They admitted that they had never met me, had never entered into any sort of agreement with me, had definitely never paid me any money, in cash, by check, with *krugerands*, or in any other fashion. Neither, they admitted, had I ever flown them into the area in which they had indeed shot an illegal grizzly bear.

It is interesting to note, perhaps, that the pilot who really did fly the party into the hunting area was later killed when his airplane crashed into Knik Arm, a silty body of glacier-fed water that empties into Cook Inlet near Anchorage. Please don't judge me unfeeling when I tell you that I didn't attend any memorial services for that pilot.

* * *

I don't want to leave you with the wrong impression of my appraisal of Alaska's Fish & Wildlife Protection officers. By and large, they are a hardworking and dedicated group of law enforcement professionals. They are undermanned, admittedly, and yet are charged with enforcing the fish and game regulations of a wilderness area almost two and one-half times the size of Texas. Certainly the area they police is absolutely huge. In point of fact, if someone should cut Alaska in two, it would make Texas the *third* largest state.

Most of these state troopers—for that's what they really are—will very likely travel more miles in a single week than "game wardens" from the other states will travel in an entire year. And they will do so in the worst weather this planet can dish up!

The next time you begin to feel that forty degrees above zero is a bit on the chilly side, imagine what it must be like to travel at thirty or forty miles an hour through a dark, snow-covered landscape at temperatures of minus fifty or even minus sixty. The wind chill factor under these conditions will be *considerably* below minus one hundred degrees Fahrenheit.

Are their efforts effective? Well, there are more brown and grizzly bears in Alaska today than there were when Alaska became our forty-ninth state back in 1957. (To be accurate, we knew on June 20, 1957, that Alaska would become our newest state. It wasn't made official, though, until January 3, 1959. Still, it was in June 1957 that Anchorage burned forty-nine tons of wood on the park strip between Ninth and Tenth Avenues to commemorate the change.) I'd have to say that they have policed, in fine fashion, the game regulation prohibiting same-day flying and shooting. That has saved a lot of brown and grizzly bears, I'll tell you! The regulations that govern the size at which certain of Alaska's big game animals may be legally hunted have also been effective. In some areas, you can no longer take a bull moose with a horn spread of less than fifty inches, for example.

The same is true for some of Alaska's serious "catch-and-release" fishing regulations. Some rainbow trout, you have to realize, will live for thirty-five years or more. These older giants are still breeding fish, and to load up on the big rascals is to shoot yourself in the foot. If everyone did that, there would soon be no more rainbow trout, a game fish that tops all others in this hemisphere, perhaps.

I've been of two minds as far as the snagging of salmon is concerned. After all, these fish will die as soon as the spawning run is over anyway. The no-snagging rule (and I don't argue with it!) may have some validity *before* a fish has spawned. Still, I'm not sure it really goes far to conserve a resource. Very few salmon spawning streams are fished at all, and even fewer enjoy heavy fishing pressure. And the number of folks who try to snag salmon for their winter larders will use every possible ounce of edible flesh from their catch. Many of the snagged salmon will be home-smoked for families' winter sustenance. I just don't see that the few active salmon snaggers are putting much of a dent in the overall numbers of spawning salmon in Alaska.

For example, the very first time I ever flew out over Bristol Bay in search of the first of the annual red salmon runs, I spotted a school that was *three miles deep and seven miles wide*. I suspect that a thousand salmon-snagging fishermen could have yanked and tugged on those monsters until their boots wore out and still wouldn't have made much of a dent in the count. Still, it's certainly not sportsmanlike, and I have always agreed with the regulation, if only for that reason alone.

So, yeah, even though F&W Protection seems to have had me square in its sights, I'm still on their side. Imagine where Alaska would be without them!

* * *

There were the routine difficulties, too. Like housekeeping chores, these little things just seem to keep cropping up at times. Like they did, for instance, between June 5 and June 9, 1979. And each of these little irritations popped up when I had my son, Mark, with me.

The first little irritation was on June 5, when Mark and I had planned a short flight from Anchorage's Lake Hood to Big Lake, only twelve or fifteen minutes away to the north, for some good pie and coffee. The fuel pump in the normally aspirated Cessna 206 failed on takeoff, and the engine wasn't getting its full share of aviation fuel for the takeoff power required. We just aborted the flight, settled back down onto Lake Hood, and taxied to Alaska Bush Carrier where my mechanic, Art Conchin, would take care of things.

Mark and I tried the flight again on the eighth, but the left magneto failed twice during takeoff attempts. And while the big Cessna could certainly fly on only one mag, that's a poor choice of options for the pilot. Especially with a passenger in the plane!

On the ninth of that month, Mark and I were finally able to make it to Big Lake, only to have the vacuum pump fail during our return trip. All this, needless to say, was something more than a pain in the neck. I had always—always—paid close attention to preventive maintenance on my airplanes. To have this one nearly fall apart at the seams was a pest, to say the least. It would be another five years before I traded this grand old airplane for a new turbocharged model, though the next one would be a model that would be mounted on Wiplinger's Wipline 3750 amphibious floats.

Chapter 10

Belize and Mexico

There are three simple rules for making good landings. No one knows what they are.

After having flown down to Florida for the second time in late 1985—the first time was in May of that year—I was contacted by two different television producers about doing some flying for them in our new turbocharged Stationair amphibian. One of them was putting together a video periodical that his group had named *Sea Fans*. According to the producer, the underwater film crew would travel the world looking for outstanding diving spots. Several such areas would be included in each quarterly videotape. The idea was that subscribers, for about one hundred bucks a year, would be the recipients of a thrilling and educational skin and scuba diving video every ninety days. Because John, the producer, knew of my turbocharged amphibious Cessna 206, he was interested in filming a dive trip that featured the plane in the Bahama Islands. The video would illustrate the possibilities for a flying and diving vacation to those islands. Since I hold several scuba diving instructor certifications, National Association of Underwater Instructors (NAUI) and Professional Association of Diving Instructors (PADI) among them, I was especially interested in flying this group of divers and underwater photographers around the Bahamas. And I was certainly interested in having the crew feature my amphibian in the segment on seaplane diving on the upcoming videotape. It might be good advertising, I thought.

So I quickly agreed to do the flying for this group. Eventually, I found the amphibian and me included on one of the later videotaped publications. It was very well done, and I was most pleased with the end result.

At about the same time, though, I received another provocative telephone call having to do with underwater videotaping. This time, the activities were to be centered on a small island just offshore from Belize City, Belize—St. George's Island—and would include an underwater wedding.

The Reverend Wayne King, of Belize City, had been commissioned to perform the underwater wedding ceremony. The bride was a really knockout blond who had formerly been a Dallas Cowboys Cheerleader and was then one of the cheerleaders' managers. Her groom was a handsome young fellow from Dallas, and we quickly came to refer to the all-American couple as Ken and Barbie. My part in all this was to provide any ancillary flying.

My passengers on the flight from Florida to Belize and back were to be the travel agent and the underwater cinematographer—in this case, videographer. I would be flying all the camera and underwater housing equipment, too, of course. Our route was to be from West Palm Beach, Florida, past Key West, and then across the Gulf of Mexico to the island of Cozumel. From there, we would fly south along the east coast of Mexico to Belize City, a one-way trip of about 875 total air miles.

We would have to worry about customs and immigration in both Mexico and Belize, so I made sure that my passengers had all the required immunizations and were carrying their passports.

Normally, a U.S. Pilot Certificate is sufficient identification for a pilot on this continent, but I have never trusted immigration and customs inspectors to be intimately familiar with all the regulations. I always make sure that my own passport is included among my flying papers, along with my license, medical certificate, aircraft papers, and all flight plans.

While planning the best route to the island of Cozumel, our first stop beyond Key West, I determined that it was possible to fly too close to Cuba if one weren't sort of careful about one's course. There would be no VORs to help, since we would be too far offshore during most of the flight, and I would have to rely upon my II Morrow Loran-C (long-range navigation) for course (magnetic compass course) and track (actual track across the Earth) purposes. We would be beyond sight of land for several hours, so contact flying was out. Using the Jeppesen Latin America High/Low Altitude Enroute Charts and a handful of sectionals, I charted a course by feeding a series of waypoints into the Loran-C. With the early evolution set that I had installed in the amphibian, this was no minor task. That original II Morrow wasn't particularly user-friendly, and it certainly wasn't automatic or preloaded. Loading and verifying all the correct waypoints took almost two hours.

Once in the air, I knew that each time I reached one of those longitude and latitude waypoints, the little display numbers would change to read a flashing "H-E-R-E" on the screen. At that point, I would select the next waypoint, turn to the proper compass heading, and proceed to that waypoint. The Loran-C would also give me speed and time-to-waypoint information. I would fly this system until I had locked on the Cozumel VOR at 112.6 and their nondirectional beacon (NDB) on the Low Frequency/Automatic Direction Finder (LF/ADF).

I had successfully used this Loran-C unit in Alaska, where it had been most helpful a time or two in finding Painter Creek Lodge, and other out-of-the-way places, in some pretty scabby weather. Up there, for instance, I had set the Painter Creek runway as a waypoint into the unit while parked on the east end of the long dirt-and-gravel strip. I could always find the approach end to the lodge's five-thousand-foot runway quickly using that waypoint setting. That particular Loran-C model might have been a pain in the neck to load, but it was extremely accurate.

The course I had set for the trip across the Gulf would keep us safely north of Cuban airspace, though I would still keep a nervous eye on the skies to the south, watching for Cuban fighter aircraft during that phase of the overwater flight.

We loaded the amphibian on the morning of November 25, 1986, at Palm Beach International, where I kept a rented hangar for the Cessna. Just after takeoff, departure control vectored us southward into clear, blue skies. Passing well west of Miami traffic, we crossed the shallow waters of that part of the Gulf of Mexico, occasionally spotting large hammerhead sharks cruising around the many small sand islands and bars. We carefully avoided the tethered balloon that the charts noted as reaching upward to fourteen thousand feet. I presumed this balloon had to do with the interdiction of air and sea drug traffickers, allegedly traveling with disturbing regularity from such places as the Turks and Caicos Islands.

One hour and fifty-five minutes after having left West Palm Beach, we let down at Key West for a quick lunch and a little more than sixty gallons of 100-octane low-lead avgas. I had calculated that when we finally arrived at Cozumel, we should have a reserve of about thirty-five gallons, slightly more than two hours of flight at cruise settings.

The weather across the Gulf was spectacular, the flight smooth and routine, and we finally settled down to land straight in on Cozumel's

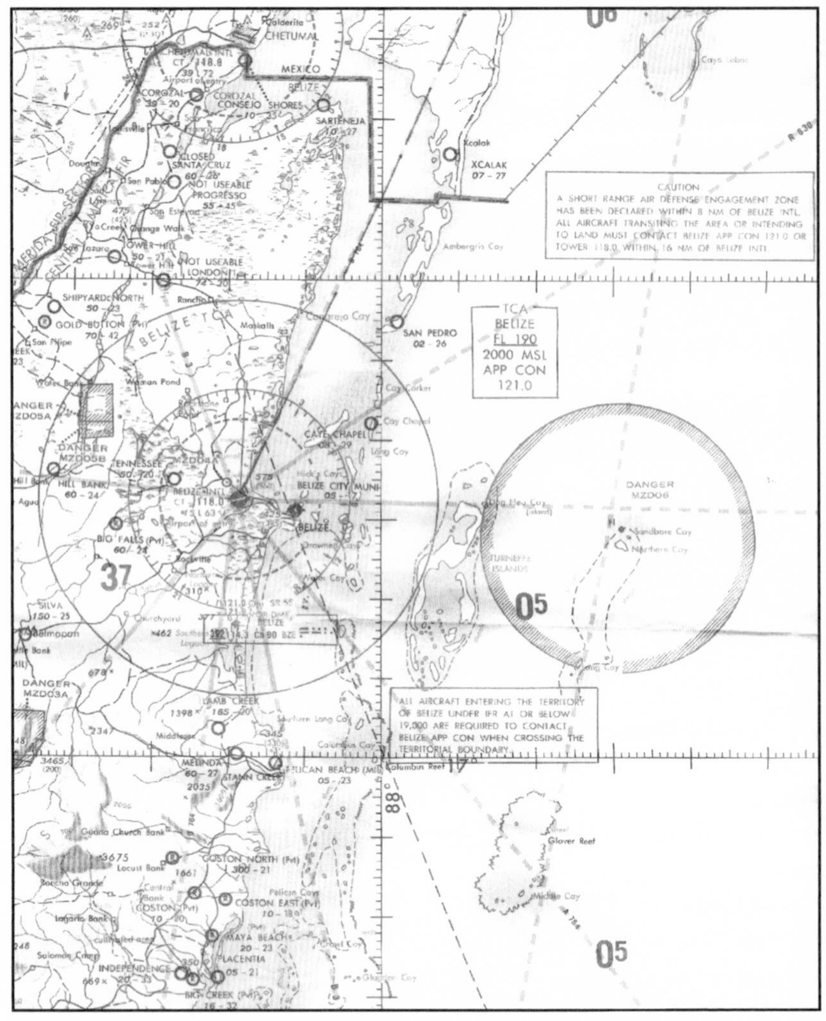

The events related in the chapter "Belize and Mexico" occurred around this area near Turneffe Islands, offshore and to the east of Belize City.

Runway 29. The fact that Cozumel traffic is controlled from Cancun, on the Mexican mainland and several miles across the water to the northwest, would prove to be something of a problem on our later return during a dark and rainy night flight.

We cleared customs and immigration at Cozumel without trouble, once again topped the tanks, and lit out along the west coast of Mexico, headed south for the country of Belize. We passed some truly magnificent, though dramatically isolated, homes, as well as some Mayan temple ruins, on that leg. We arrived on schedule over Belize City exactly two hours after liftoff from Cozumel.

It was getting to be a little late in the day when we finally cleared customs and immigration at the airport in Belize City. Our final destination was St. George's Island, a sand island about twelve miles offshore. Seems an easy flight, but it was proving to be more of a problem than I thought.

To begin with, it was dark by now, and the customs folks at the airport were not comfortable with our flying at night. I think they suspected we couldn't successfully land on the water in the darkness. More than that, though, was the fact that they didn't know exactly how much money to charge us for permission to land on their ocean. *Their* ocean? That was a new one for me. We were going to have to rent the danged thing?

We finally haggled, horse-traded, and negotiated to a mutually satisfactory price of twelve dollars and fifty cents, American, for the use of that part of Belize's ocean for the next seven days. I guess a buck-eighty a day wasn't bad, though the thought of paying to land in the ocean somehow offended my Alaska sourdough sensibilities. Still, it wasn't as bad as the $16.50 I would sometimes have to pay for landing privileges at Miami International, back in my own country. That Miami landing fee ticked me off then, and it ticks me off still.

Since Belize wouldn't back off on their night flying restriction, we had to rent a small boat and skipper for the trip to the island that night, planning to return for the plane the following morning. I have to say that I could have found the island from the air by the few lights at the lodge, or by lights at the British Army's recreational facility there, without any trouble at all. Besides, the waypoint had been loaded into the Loran-C. And I could certainly have landed in the dark on the bay at St. George's western side with no problem. The boat trip, however, was a most sobering experience for a pilot.

There wasn't a light to be seen to the east of us when we left the river mouth at Belize City. How the boat's skipper found the low-lying island in the pitch black of that dark night is still beyond me, but he certainly did. He drove that boat in a perfectly straight line for twelve miles across the absolutely dark water. The ride was smooth enough, but I wondered every moment whether we would either run smack into something hard or maybe fall right off the edge of the world in the impenetrable black. I guess our captain was using the stars. I presumed the old timer had spent a lot of years on the water and no doubt knew exactly what he was doing and where he was going. When he pulled directly up to the wooden dock at the lodge, I still couldn't see a danged thing, even from only twenty feet out!

George and Penny welcomed us to the lodge as though we were long-lost friends. Their hospitality left nothing to be desired, and they were more than perfect hosts. They knew the waters, too, since they were both NAUI instructors and operated a diving service from the lodge. George said he would boat me back to Belize City for my Cessna early the following morning. Having put that problem to rest, we stuffed away a late dinner and shared a few drinks and tall tales. I learned that George could hold his own with first-liar-doesn't-stand-a-chance stories, and I was still impressed when I walked around the elevated lodge to my thatched-roof cabaña. Right at that moment, I thought the tropics had a whole lot going for them. Pretty laid back, all right. And frostbite was virtually unheard of down here.

The next morning I was ferried back across the water to Belize City again where I made my way to the city airport. There was another small strip nearby, the "river strip," but most light aircraft traffic used the larger city field.

I arranged to top the tanks again, since I didn't know how much flying I would be doing from the island. The fixed base operator asked whether I would be using the avgas for a trip out of the country, or would I be using it within Belize? When I asked if that made a difference, he told me that the avgas price wasn't the same for both options. It would be cheaper to leave than to stay, it seemed. Incredible! What would they think of next?

After returning to the island and arranging sort of a semipermanent tiedown arrangement at the lodge's large boat dock, I conducted a few sightseeing flights to the nearby islands. There seemed to be a million manatees in the shallow and protected waters to the south of each of these small islands. The water was exceptionally clear, and we could follow the big mammals easily from the air. Landing near them was another matter, since they were quite shy and reclusive. Manatees found in Florida's inland waters are much more accustomed to people and activity, hardly even moving from the danger of outboard motors, a trait that adds to the injury and death of many of these very special mammals each year.

That morning, and for the rest of our stay on the island, we were treated to the sight of hundreds of rays as they leaped clear of the warm waters, seeming to cover great distances in flight. It was quite a sight for an Alaskan, accustomed to seeing killer whales, seals, sea lions, and walruses, all of which are hardly suited for flight and clearly anchored with purpose to whatever surface they appear on at the moment.

I was told of a "blue hole" somewhere between the islands and the huge reef that lies low in the water about forty miles to the east. Wanting very much to see that, I took off alone and set a course eastward, crossing the Turneffe Islands, about fifteen miles farther out, and headed directly toward the open sea.

Finding the blue hole was easy, since it lies in a string of coral that seems to be covered by no more than eight inches of water and also lies inside a much larger and highly visible reef. That reef, by the way, is supposed to be a part of the overall structure that is second only to the Great Barrier Reef of Australia. It seems lined with freighters lying dead across her seaward face, each rusting away with a broken back. It was easy to see that severe storms had in the past driven many, many ships up onto the sharp and unforgiving reef. I wondered how many lives had been lost there over the centuries.

The blue hole had been visited several years earlier by the Frenchman Captain Jacques Cousteau and his research vessel, the *Calypso*. Wanting to explore the blue hole themselves, and finding no immediate sea route into it, the famous captain had elected to use dynamite to blast his way through the coral to drop anchor inside the protective circle of live and dead saltwater polyps and onto the sand bottom. The Belize government, not as backward and easy-going as the sophisticated Captain Cousteau might have suspected, didn't appear all that pleased with this destruction. They promptly invited the good captain, his crew, and his research vessel to ship on the first tide—with the further invitation to avoid ever returning to Belize waters.

I had found that the channel blasted through the coral by Captain Cousteau provided a water lane deep enough for floatplane operations, with the proviso that the pilot would have to take off through a slot no more than twenty feet wide. With the amphibious floats mounted at a little more than eight feet apart, center to center, there would be approximately five feet clear on either side, so this channel width appeared to be more than sufficient.

The deep blue hole lay centered in a circle of water inside the reef itself, and this shallow, sand-bottomed bowl appeared more than deep enough, at about six feet, to accommodate the amphibian's two feet of draft requirement. This larger circle of six-feet-deep water also appeared to be wide enough that a careful pilot might come in hanging on the prop to plunk down at the near edge, reefing back on the control yoke and digging in the float heels to stop before running aground on the sharp coral at the opposite side. It appeared to be about six hundred feet across, surely wide enough for a *careful* landing.

The amphibian's performance charts indicate that about 850 feet are required for a landing. Years of Alaska floatplane operations had proved that most of us could do better than that. In any event, there was not enough room for the takeoff without using the additional length provided by Cousteau's channel. Performance charts for the amphibian indicate that a takeoff run of 1,810 feet is required for that phase, though some of Alaska's flying techniques can whittle that down a bit, too.

The real problem, though, was that once on the water, the pilot wouldn't be able to see the channel beneath surface glare. He would have to take a compass course from the south side of the blue hole—and opposite the channel on the north side—where a small pole had earlier been erected in the coral for some purpose or other, probably for the tethering of a small boat.

Knowing I was going to chance a landing there, I flew south and turned to take up a course that would lead me across the single pole and straight through the narrow escape channel that had been cut through the coral, which lay no more than eight inches below the surface. It would be a white-knuckle takeoff, but I was confident that it would work. Having made that decision, I circled around to land from the west and into the middle of Belize's blue hole.

It was a cautious approach, I'll admit that, but it all went as I had thought. The hole wasn't any larger than the amphibian absolutely required, even with every short water landing technique I knew, but the plane came off the step and sank to a near stop a few feet short of the shallow coral barrier on the east side. I dropped the water rudders and turned to avoid the coral that was only a few feet ahead of the plane after it settled down from the step. Now all I had to do was get back out! There was no way in the world that I could take off in less than six hundred feet, so I had to shoot straight through that channel when leaving.

I taxied into the center of the circle of coral and shut down the big engine. When all was secure, I stepped down onto the left float deck and peered over into the dark blue depths of the first blue hole I had ever seen up close. It was quite a thrill, and a little unnerving. I thought it possible to get vertigo by simply looking down that far with nothing but blue water to focus on. I couldn't tell how deep it really might be. For all I could tell, it went right on through the center of the Earth to become just another blue hole on the other side. It was truly eerie.

Satisfied that I couldn't see anything more than empty blue water, I climbed aboard again for the more exciting part of this flight: the departure phase.

I spent a few minutes setting the blue hole's coordinates into the Loran-C so that I could fly directly to it if I should want to come here again. Then I taxied around inside the almost perfectly round circle formed by the coral, passing the channel at the north end several times and trying to validate the compass heading I had earlier established as the correct takeoff heading. I would have no outside visual reference during the departure and would have to hold a very tight compass course. The question was whether or not my selected heading would be a good one. It's at this point that the pilot begins to sweat bullets. He is committed—and no matter how convinced he might have been just a moment ago, he now questions his own judgment just a little. He also knows it's too late to do much about it. In my case, I wouldn't be able to tell deep water from shallow, once I started the takeoff run. Besides, the nose comes up so high during the initial segment of a seaplane takeoff that the pilot can't see the water ahead at any rate. And once on the step at forty miles an hour, the plane's turning radius wasn't going to allow me to step-turn around the inside perimeter of the shallow coral surround. I would just have to hit that little channel on the first shot, that's all there was to it. And I would have only about four or five feet to spare on either side of the fragile and very expensive aluminum amphibious floats.

The engine was by now certainly warm enough to reach full horsepower, and I couldn't delay the takeoff any longer. Cinching down the harness, I made sure the flaps were set at ten degrees, the water rudders were up, the mixture control was full rich, and the prop was set in high pitch. I advanced the throttle to the firewall, leaned to thirty-one gallons for best performance, and locked on my takeoff heading from the pole. It seemed an eternity before the Cessna rolled over onto the step so that I could finally see something ahead of the hurtling airplane. Little good that did, since there was nothing to see except the glare off the water. The nearest landmark ahead was hundreds of miles north across the flat sea. I might as well have been dashing toward the edge of the world.

As soon as the plane had rolled over onto the step, I had raised the flaps to decrease parasite drag and allow the plane to more quickly build up a little air speed. By the time I had trimmed the elevators to that smooth spot known to all floatplane pilots, I had also lowered the electric flaps to twenty degrees. As the airplane slipped smoothly into the air, I could see that I had bisected the narrow little alley right down the middle. It had been a perfect takeoff, but I knew it had also been as much luck as skill. A steady diet of this blue hole business would be a fool's move! In a Super Cub, maybe it would be all right. In the much heavier Cessna 206, it was definitely not a thing to repeat too many times.

After several more days of filming and foolishness, the underwater wedding took place. The Reverend King officiated. The minister, the bride, and the groom were all communicating with underwater throat microphones. The ceremony went so smoothly that only one shoot was necessary. The bride wore a veil and a white two-piece bikini that she could easily have stuffed inside a small clutch purse. The groom was wearing a custom-made wet suit that looked for all the world like a tuxedo, black tie and all. It was quite a wedding, and the couple was very handsome. George and Penny had laid out a marvelous spread back at their lodge, and everyone had a wonderful time that afternoon.

Our underwater cameraman and a friend of his wanted to dive the blue hole to get some video footage, and I agreed to take them back there. The next morning found us following the straight-line Loran-C course to the blue hole waypoint. Twenty minutes later we were descending under twenty degrees of flaps toward the small landing area in the center of the very shallow coral bed.

The Cessna settled onto the water just inside the nearest coral. I hauled back on the yoke and jammed in a hard left rudder to land as short as possible. Once again skill and cunning overcame fear and superstition, as we often said up north, and the amphibian slid off the step to stop just short of the coral on the far side again. Just barely! Boy, I wouldn't want to make a steady diet of this place.

I anchored the amphibian on one side of the deep hole itself and watched as the two divers geared up and disappeared over the side of the right float. I could see them descend slowly into the clear blue depths, the cameraman's bright yellow camera housing a target all the way down.

The hole, I later learned from the divers, dropped to about 100 feet before it closed in on itself. The center of the hole at that depth was perhaps 30 feet across, then it belled out again in sort of an hourglass configuration, falling away to who knew what depth. At 185 feet on their gauges, the divers could see a number of really huge fish circling below them. By huge, they both later estimated, they meant that these beasts were easily more than 12 feet in length. Sounded like sharks, to me. Looked like sharks to the divers, too, and they quickly turned to follow their smallest bubbles straight back to the surface, occasionally glancing down past their moving fins to check on the traffic below them.

Still, the cameraman had taken some great footage, he said, and both of them had enjoyed the dive. For my own part, I wouldn't have dived into that wet blue empty for a hundred bucks!

After the gear had been stored, the passengers climbed aboard and buckled in. I raised the anchor and stowed it inside the right float locker, then crossed the steel cable stretched between the toes of the floats to climb back up into the pilot's chair. Harnessed in and buckled down tightly, I dropped the water rudders, checked the cowl flaps as open, then hit the boost pump and throttle, checking with the Fuel Flow Meter to verify the necessary 12 gallons per hour fuel flow required for a start.

The big engine started immediately, and we began the slow water taxi that would allow the big 300-horsepower engine to warm up a little. There are no brakes on a floatplane, so once the engine has started, the plane is in motion until it is again shut down or else bangs itself into something solid. The latter isn't usually recommended, by the way.

As we taxied around the small blue hole, I checked and set the gyroscopic compass, even though the HIS and RMI compasses had automatically set themselves when the radio master switch was closed. I'm used to watching the gyrocompass and would use that for the takeoff heading.

After one last look at the channel on the north side, I taxied around the hole to my marker pole at the south, began a left turn to take up the heading I wanted, then poured full power to the engine and raised the water rudders. It didn't matter what was rushing past the windows at that moment. The only thing of any consequence at this point was the compass heading, much as in a zero-zero instrument takeoff. I had to hold a really precise heading every second until we were off the water and climbing.

I had gone through the routine of flaps down, up on the step, and flaps back up again to get the shortest possible takeoff run, and as we roared along now, I lowered the flaps to twenty degrees for the takeoff itself. This procedure was the Alaska tried-and-tested method of the best takeoff performance in a float-equipped Stationair, though it meant exercising the flaps more times than most pilots care to mess with during the busy takeoff period.

Just as the Cessna flew itself off the water, there was a terrible BANG! from the right float, and we felt a big bump. I thought for a moment that we might be plowing through the shallow coral and would soon grind to a halt. Not so, though, and the amphibian lifted clear of the water and began its climb. I started the shallow left turn that would take us back to a western heading and began to set up for the short climb to five hundred feet. There was no need to climb to any great altitude for the short trip back, since the return flight would take only twenty minutes, even with the huge and heavy amphibious floats.

I was convinced that I had punched a big hole in the right float and could have kicked myself for having missed the little channel I had been aiming for. I didn't want to chance another water landing until I had inspected the damaged float, so I called Belize to get clearance to land at the city airport. If nothing else, perhaps they had a maintenance facility that could perform a little temporary float repair for me. I knew there wouldn't be a Wipline float specialist in Belize—or even a good float mechanic, for that matter—but any port in a storm.

I received clearance to the airport, was given the current weather advisory, and was assigned to a landing runway. There was no other traffic right then, although one of the airlines serving Belize from Miami was expected to arrive a few minutes later.

I tiptoed in for a smooth landing on the asphalt runway and took the first available left taxiway to the transient tiedown area. After shutting down, I got on my face under the right float to have a look at what I expected to be a heartbreaking sight. What I found instead was a flat tire on the outside wheel of the main gear pair on that side. The Wipline amphibious floats have dual main wheels on each side. The coral had punched a hole in the right outboard tire. There was no other damage, though it had surely been a damned close thing.

After making a few calls, I located a commercial pilot at the smaller river strip who said he'd take one wheel from his own Cessna 185 and sell it to me for 125 bucks American. That was a lifesaver, and I jumped at the deal. The tire turned out to be as bald as a billiard ball, but it would certainly get us around until I could find a new tire back in West Palm Beach.

Two days later I would tell the fixed base operator that the avgas I was then buying would be used in a flight from Belize back to America. He gave me the better price that time. What I didn't get, though, was my jacket from the customs office. In it were my license, medical certificate, passport, and everything else of any importance at all.

We filed IFR to Cozumel, got the clearance, and then took off headed north. It was late in the day, pretty dark in fact, and it was beginning to rain as we approached Cozumel. I contacted Cancun, and they asked if we were instrument equipped. What with an instrument flight plan on record, I thought that was a pretty goofy question, but I simply affirmed to Cancun that we were indeed instrument equipped. Was I instrument rated, Cancun asked? Certainly, I replied. Okay, then, cleared to the ten-mile DME (distance measuring equipment) arc for the ILS (Instrument Landing System) runway 29 approach to Cozumel Airport. Ah, that was better. Now we were back on familiar ground. Or back in familiar air, more accurately.

I set the course selector on the King KI 525A HSI (horizontal situation indicator, which, in this case, was really a PNI, pictorial navigation indicator) to 029 degrees and then flew the ten-nautical mile DME arc until the needle had begun to creep up on the lubber line. Then we just rolled into the gentle left turn that would intercept the inbound radial to the threshold of Runway 29 at Cozumel. I reported the position to Cancun, and we were immediately cleared for the landing.

We were on short final, with the gear extended and flaps going from thirty to forty degrees, when suddenly the whole world went from dark and rainy to completely black. The runway lights disappeared in a blink. I didn't remember any mountains on Cozumel, but my Alaska experience had trained me to realize that only a ridgeline or total blindness could shut all the lights off that quickly.

I added power, raised the flaps to ten degrees, and hit the gear-up switch, trimming for the climb. I knew I was going to have to execute the missed approach procedure, but I still wasn't sure why. I only knew that there was something between the airplane and those runway lights, and I had to miss it, whatever it was.

About that time, Cancun came back in the David Clarks, asking for our position. I told them that I had been almost on the ground until the environment had disappeared and was at that precise moment just a little busy with the missed approach procedure and airplane configuration. The voice in my ears came back with, "Oh—sorry." With that, the lights went on again. The controller had simply forgotten about the little amphibian descending from the rain somewhere out there in the Mexican dark. He had casually turned off the lights, presumably saving electricity. *Aw, Jeez . . .*

I decided to hell with the missed approach procedure, having already secured the landing clearance, so I quickly reconfigured the aircraft, went to full flaps and gear down, and descended steeply to the landing.

It wasn't until we began to check through customs that I discovered the missing jacket. Now I was really in a pickle. Flying into a foreign country, at night, with no identification at all. Oh, man, what could happen next, I wondered? I'm sure we looked exactly like three dopers with a half ton of white powder buried somewhere inside the plane or hidden deep within its big floats.

The major with whom I was now making weak excuses asked if I was at all familiar with the famous white rum of Belize? "Well now, Major, I certainly am," I answered. Seems as though he would just love to have a bottle of that superb elixir. I allowed as how a bottle certainly wasn't sufficient for such a sterling and responsible authority as himself, and if I could but get a few hours sleep on some nearby pallet, however Spartan and uncomfortable, it would be my genuine pleasure to fly two hours south again, just to find a full case of that tasty stuff for his future enjoyment.

It was necessary to conduct another conversation by way of teletype with the Belize customs office in order to convince the major that I wasn't really a dangerous drug smuggler but had simply just left my damned jacket in the customs office at the Belize airport. After a seemingly endless series of those little yellow sheets had been blazed back and forth, Belize reported that my black flight jacket had indeed been left there and that, yes, all my papers were in good order and safely tucked inside the pockets of the said flight jacket. With that out of the way, I was allowed to find a good meal and a night's sleep.

First thing the following morning, I flew alone the two hours back to Belize, got my jacket, and then returned to Cozumel. By the time we had eaten again, topped the tanks, and filed our IFR flight plan back to Key West, it was once more dark and raining. We couldn't have cared less, just then, and away we went.

We climbed to ten thousand feet and began following the Loran-C as it pointed our return path across a wet, dark Gulf of Mexico. There wasn't much point in being on the alert for Cuban fighters this time, since we couldn't see a thing through the rain anyway.

The Loran-C flagged "H-E-R-E" several times for me, and I finally contacted Key West, requesting that U.S. Customs meet the airplane for clearance back into the country. I also requested fuel, only to learn that it was Sunday night around here, for Pete's sake, and didn't I know that everyone with any sense at all was at home out of the rain? The nearest fuel stop would be the fuel truck at Marathon Key, a few minutes north of Key West and hard beside that damned balloon cabled to the Earth on its fourteen-thousand-foot string. Nuts!

Two really gorgeous female customs personnel met the aircraft, but they weren't anxious to step outside in the rain and ruin their hairdos simply to inspect one little-bitty ol' airplane. I reminded them that the "lil ol' thang" was an amphibian and that the float lockers might well be crammed tight with hundreds of pounds of some controlled substance or other. One of the women condescended finally to walk outside to peek in through the big, four-foot loading doors, but she certainly didn't want to stand around in the rain long enough to inspect the float lockers while losing her attractive hairdo. So be it, and we were soon off again to Marathon, this time for fuel.

We were all getting a little tired and cranky, but at least we were on American soil once more. The approach and landing at Marathon went smoothly, and the avgas truck met us right on schedule.

From there to West Palm Beach was more of the same— more rain—but an IFR flight plan, filed in the air after departure, took care of that. There apparently wasn't much traffic that night, and clearance delivery wasn't long in reading back our clearance. The next landing would be at Palm Beach International, where we wouldn't have to bother with customs again.

I later asked a friend of mine, a brick agent with the Drug Enforcement Administration (DEA), why no one at the Key West customs office seemed much concerned about an amphibian landing there after crossing the Gulf of Mexico in the rainy dark? He told me that the FAA routinely kept the DEA pretty much up to speed on air traffic in that neck of the woods. My friend knew the aircraft numbers, knew who I was, and knew where I was almost every moment of the flight. Customs had been notified who we were and were pretty much told to leave us alone. Customs had done just that.

Oh, one final word. After more than a week of wallowing around Central America with that amphibian, my clients stiffed me for the eight-thousand-dollar cost.

Added to my never-again-accept-as-clients blacklist, and among unscrupulous lawyers and a few Texans, you will now find video outfits and travel agents. Alphabetical order aside, travel agents are found just after lawyers and just ahead of Texans. I've placed Chicago doctors dead last, since there may be a few among those who won't try to fleece the pilot, or his big game guide, out of his fee.

Chapter 11

Water Doesn't Burn

Keep looking around: there's always something you've missed.

Jules Tupper, a longtime outback pilot flying the wilderness areas of New Zealand, shared this tale with me. It's so very much a part of all bush flying that I just have to share it with you. In bush areas where there are no avgas facilities for miles around, pilots know that their flying machines must live on canned avgas more often than not. And, even at those macadam and concrete airports, where several varieties of avgas can be found, contamination in the form of moisture, rust, or old fuel sediments continues to plague the pilot of internal combustion engines. Heavy rains can see water slipping directly into an aircraft's wing tanks. Driving winds can pack sand or dust around the filler necks and tank caps, eventually finding ways to get inside where the lifeblood of aviation is held in rubber or metal tanks. Even leaving the fuel tanks less than full when parked for extended periods—sometimes only overnight, in fact—can encourage moisture contamination from condensation. Checking for fuel contamination is an integral part of every preflight airplane check. It may well be the very most important preflight check, come to think of it. Even with this caution, there is always a chance that Murphy's Law will catch up with a fellow. As it finally did with Jules.

It had been a long wet period in New Zealand's Hollyford, and Jules Tupper had been unable to fly out of the valley back to his home in Invercargill. Instead, he had hitched a ride back with his partner, Viv, in Viv's car.

Viv had originally driven through to the Hollyford airstrip, located near road's end. He had brought a load of building materials that Jules had then flown on to Martins Bay. It was here that they were busy making improvements to their small lodge, one that they planned to use for their proposed walking tour parties during the coming summer's tourist season.

Jules had tied down his trusty Piper Super Cub just off to the side of the small airstrip and close beside some tall trees that were growing there. He knew that this would provide some shelter when the strong westerly winds began to blow, which happened frequently at this time of year.

It was nearly two more weeks before Jules was able to return with Viv and Bruce—one of their lodge staff—this time with the car and a trailer jammed full and with another series of freight flights planned.

Breathtakingly beautiful weather greeted them as they left Lake Te Anau and drove quietly up the magnificent Eglington Valley toward the main divide. The sun was shining, and not a cloud could be seen as they carefully crossed the ridge and descended past Marian Lookout, headed down the side route to the little airstrip. The heavily loaded trailer itself had no brakes, and both Jules and Viv were keenly aware of their soberingly poor braking and stopping ability on the downhill leg of this rough gravel road. Eventually—but not without a few tense moments—they pulled safely onto the little strip alongside the small plane. There were three really stiff, weary, and uncomfortable men who tumbled from the cramped vehicle to stretch their legs after the slow, almost two-hundred-mile drive through from Invercargill.

As the other men began unloading and sorting the gear, Jules started the thorough preflight of his faithful little Super Cub. After removing the windshield cover and tiedown lines, the first thing was to perform a fuel contamination check on each of the two fuel tanks. Along with the little bit of dihedral rigged into the Super Cub's wings, the manufacturer of the Piper Aircraft plant had installed exterior Curtis-style fuel drains beneath the wings, one along each side of the fuselage. The Cub's tanks were only about half full, and with the moist conditions they had experienced over the past few weeks, Jules fully expected to find a bit of condensation in the water traps of the aluminum-alloy wing tanks. As it turned out, he wasn't to be disappointed. About a teaspoonful from the left tank, and two or three tablespoons from the right.

"Nothing unusual about that," Jules thought as he continued with his preflight check of the rest of the little aircraft.

Among other items in the large pile of freight, there was a considerable amount of framing timber already roughly precut and semidried. The precutting and partial drying had been done in order to make the framing lumber easier to handle and to save weight by removing some of the natural moisture from the wood. There was no way they could fit some of the framing lumber inside the plane, of course, but supply-dropping racks had been added to each wing. It was quite normal for them to carry awkward loads in expandable clamp carriers that were then clipped onto the supply racks. Like Alaska bush pilots, carrying exterior loads is something of an everyday occurrence for the New Zealand outback pilot.

Apart from the convenience of this arrangement, it had an added advantage for Jules. In case of an emergency, the pilot had the option of dropping the load so as to lower his plane's gross weight and—hopefully—increase his chances of a successful outcome if it came to a precautionary, or even an emergency, landing somewhere out there in the weeds. Besides, dropping an external load almost always had the added benefit of reducing parasite drag by an appreciable amount. Seldom is an external load efficiently aerodynamic.

After loading up and stuffing the cabin with a whole lot of smaller bits and pieces, it was time for Jules to get his show on the road.

He cranked up the little Super Cub, warmed the engine until the cylinder head temperature came off the peg, and then taxied out onto the little airstrip. One of the last things Jules always did before takeoff was to perform a cockpit "drill of vital actions" (DVAs, as he calls them). He had already done the engine run-up and had checked both magnetos for proper operation, rpm drop, and the drop differential between the two mags. Everything was normal.

While still holding his position on the little strip, he checked the elevator trim, verified full movement of the controls—ailerons and rudder, along with full travel of the elevators—and then glanced up at the glass tube fuel gauges located at the wing roots on either side of the cabin. The left tank showed slightly more 80-octane avgas than the right, the tank on which he had started the engine and done the warmup, so he switched to the more full left tank—always the best practice for both takeoffs and landings—and then checked all instruments to verify that they were reading normally. He tightened his seat belt and shoulder harness and finally checked to make sure that the split door was securely closed and latched. And then he applied full throttle to the little 150-horsepower Lycoming engine and began rolling slowly down the strip.

The Cub was packing a pretty good load, and there was very little wind just then. Jules noted that acceleration was notoriously slow, and it wasn't being helped by all the parasitic drag created by the external wing loads. Jules must have coaxed the heavy little Cub through about sixty miles per hour before he finally eased it off the gravel strip and set a course down the valley.

"Not much of a climb gradient," he thought as they inched their way upward, reaching for a little more altitude.

They had only reached about three hundred feet above the bush—and were level with the end of Hollyford road on the opposite side of the Hollyford River—when all of a sudden the engine quit, dead as a stone, and right in midstride.

Instinct born of long experience took over for Jules. He immediately pushed forward on the control stick to maintain necessary air speed. He had been climbing at just above stall speed, which was now increased on account of the bothersome exterior load hanging out there on the wing racks. Still, Jules didn't want to dump that external load just yet. Maybe there was something he could do to get the little powerplant back online.

Just in front of him was a small gravel bar along the bend of the river. Jules knew that he had to put the little Cub down there, since the alternative was simply to perch like a bird in the high trees!

Why he didn't jettison the load, he really didn't know, but it was this omission that probably saved his skin. Normally, such a violent pitch change would have immediately produced a rapid increase in air speed, and Jules' chances of successfully putting down on the little bar this close in would have been minimal. He was already too close and too high for a normal approach and landing. If he *had* dropped that external load just then, he would have probably overshot the landing, and when the landing gear ultimately hit the water, the loaded Super Cub would have tipped up in the river at the far end of the beach. It's entirely possible that he might have ended upside down, hanging from his seat belt and trying to hold his breath long enough to figure out exactly what had happened and where he was. And how he was going to get out of the wet little cabin.

But the gods were with him that day. The drag from the external load gave him a high rate of descent without a noticeable increase in air speed.

It was one truly relieved Jules Tupper who thumped down at the very near end of the rough little gravel beach and bounced his way to a shuddering stop.

Shakily, he crawled from the cockpit expecting the very worst. The undercarriage looked okay to him, and the tires were still inflated, so that was a good start. The plane rested on the slope of the gravel bar, with a slightly wing-down attitude on the right side. But what had caused the engine just to stop right in the middle of things? If that sort of calamity happens at all, it usually happens during a power change of some sort, not when power is being steadily and evenly applied.

Jules went directly to the fuel drains. The right tank appeared okay, but he was horrified to find that the left tank delivered a full sampling tube full of water instead of the avgas that should have been draining from the tank and into the tube. It was not until he had taken out nearly eight full tubes of water that the red color of 80-octane aviation fuel began showing through. He must have drained close to three-quarters of a liter of water from that wing tank in all!

But how had this happened, he wondered?

He jiggled the plane around and got the right wing down a little farther. He tried the drain again, and fortunately only a few more drops of water appeared, even after he had shaken the wings severely in order to force any more water—considerably heavier than the avgas that surrounded it—that may have been present to flow inward toward the fuel sump drains.

Satisfied that he had found the cause, it was time for Jules to check the engine. As do most of us who fly the outback, he always carried a few tools with him in the airplane. Because this was a very remote area and there was absolutely no communication with the outside world, it was a matter of "helping yourself" for Jules. Not really an unusual situation, but a pain in the neck nonetheless. It may not have been exactly by the rule book, but he had a strong mechanical knowledge (from his family's motor engineering background, I understand). It was almost no time at all before he had the cowling off and the fuel filter removed. The sediment bowl was absolutely *full* of water—confirmation enough of what had caused the engine shutdown. But how far had the water contamination gone?

It was a lovely hot day, but Jules was going nowhere fast. So, with nothing much to lose, he disconnected the fuel line between the sediment bowl and the carburetor and found still more water.

"If it had got this far, I bet it got to the main jet," he thought as he continued his partial engine strip-down. He spread his jacket down on the gravel. Then, as he slowly removed one part after another, he laid them all out atop his jacket in the warm sun. The parts would soon enough be dry.

After some time, Jules was sure in his own mind that the carburetor was now clear, so he carefully reassembled everything. Then he flushed a considerable amount of fuel through the lines and into the sediment bowl. Satisfied now, he started the engine. Everything seemed normal, and full power was once again restored. He once more shut down the little Lycoming engine and then turned his attention to the takeoff area.

After he had landed, Jules had been quite amazed at the size of some of the rocks he had obviously ridden over. The Super Cub's tires had very low inflation pressures—perhaps as low as four or five pounds per square inch—and he reckoned that these soft tires and a soft undercarriage were all that saved his little aircraft from some serious structural damage.

It took Jules over an hour to move some of the larger rocks out of his planned takeoff path, but he was eventually satisfied with around 250 yards of a reasonably clear takeoff length. After rotation, he was going to have to fly down the river a bit, since the high trees across the river prohibited a straight-ahead climb after takeoff. Fortunately, a reasonable sea breeze had sprung up, and this would shorten the length of his takeoff roll.

Everything went according to plan, and the Cub bounced off the uneven little strip surprisingly quickly. Jules decided to return directly to Hollyford, since his friends were probably wondering where the hell he had disappeared to, and what the heck they should do about it. It was the right decision, as it turned out, since they really had become very concerned.

After Jules' explanations, and a further check for water in both wing tanks—with each wing individually placed high in the air to promote positive drainage to the sump drains—he was satisfied that there was no more water in his fuel. But how had the whole thing occurred, he wondered?

When they stood again at the original tiedown point before departure, it was his passenger, Viv, who pointed out the obvious. When secured, the left wing was slightly low due to the slope of the ground. The wing's dihedral was thus minimized to the extent that, if any water at all were present, it would remain in the outer section of the tank. From there, Jules would have been unable to drain it through the fuel drain at the wing root when the aircraft was sitting tied down.

Jules had done his engine startup and powerplant checks while on the right wing tank, which of course was free of water. He had only changed tanks just prior to takeoff when he went through his DVAs. Just his luck, he guessed, but he now shudders to think that if he had changed tanks in flight somewhere else, there may be a different ending to this story. There had been precious few suitable landing places along his flight path, and he would have needed all his skill and experience to have survived an emergency, power-off landing along that route.

As a sequel to this tale, it was almost fifteen years later that one of Jules' pilots had a similar problem with a leased Cessna 206 Stationair. This time, the results were a complete engine failure when approaching to land at Big Bay beach—fortunately, with no damage to either aircraft or the pilot's pride.

And once again, there was water in the fuel filter.

When they raised each wing up in the air individually, they took more than two liters of water out of the two tanks. Cessnas at that time were notorious for letting in water through the recess above faulty O-rings on the fuel cap actuating cam. And due to the flexible fuel bladders of that era, water would occasionally be trapped behind a crease—a real "wrinkle"—in the bladder. At the most inopportune time, this trapped water would cause the pilot a lot of heartache when the noise department out front went suddenly and disturbingly silent.

Fortunately, Cessna later produced a modification to their tanks. They also changed the fuel caps so that in recent times none of us has heard of similar experiences. All for the good, Jules reckons, but he will never forget his good fortune on that day back in 1969.

We live and learn, Jules supposes, hopefully from the experiences of others. He has certainly had his own share of experiences over the years. And like most of us who fly the empty outback, there are some flights that we'd much rather not share with others. We really *don't* want to stick our clients' necks out.

Chapter 12

My Personal Heroes

GRAVITY ISN'T JUST A GOOD IDEA—IT'S THE LAW.

We know where Harold Gillam came from, and we know much of what he did. We know where he died, and I guess we know why. But we don't really know how, exactly. Probably the greatest foul-weather pilot ever to fly the North Country, Harold Gillam was at once a known entity and a complete mystery.

Harold has been one of my real-life heroes since I first came to know about him. The more I read, the more I found we had in common. Oh, don't get me wrong. I wouldn't want to put myself in Mr. Gillam's class, for he stood quite alone in his abilities and accomplishments. It's just that everyone seemed to agree that he must have had exceptional eyesight, an accident of genetics that favored me with the same blessing—or curse, as the case may be.

Almost no amount of inclement weather would dissuade Gillam from a planned flight. In 1935, pilot Frank Pollack had contracted with the U.S. Weather Bureau to make three flights per week out of Fairbanks. The task was to climb to a high altitude, then circle back down, recording temperatures and humidity of those air masses through which he climbed and descended. Bad visibility had disrupted many of these scheduled flights.

Gillam contracted for the same flights with the Weather Bureau the following year, but this time they were to be made *daily*. He would climb to seventeen thousand feet and then spiral back down in precise circles, again recording temperatures and humidity in the various air masses. In Gillam's case, though, almost every flight was made as scheduled. To assist in an almost perfect record, Gillam installed a radio in the cockpit so that his mechanic back on the ground could listen to the sounds of his airplane's engine and tell him whether he was east or west of the field, and whether or not he was flying toward, or away from, his landing spot.

For those among you who are pilots, just imagine, if you will, flying in absolutely zero-zero conditions with only the two primary instruments of turn-and-bank indicator and air speed indicator—needle, ball, and air speed, as they say. Then imagine doing this day after day after day, sometimes in temperatures that plunged well below minus sixty degrees Fahrenheit. On one such flight, Harold descended through the fog, only to come out at the bottom so close to the power company's high chimney that onlookers could see the reflection of his wingtip running lights on the stack.

In 1938, Harold Gillam was awarded a mail contract for the villages along the Kuskokwim River drainage. He prosecuted this responsibility with such regularity that villagers began to line his landing strips a few minutes before his scheduled arrival time, holding every confidence that he would show up on the dot. It seems that they were never to be disappointed: the twenty villages along that 525-mile route received such dependable service that the government determined his regularity beat even the land and sea route mail delivery systems. He never missed his schedule a single time in that entire year! Along the Kuskokwim, villagers would comment, "Best finish that danged letter. Harold is due here in a few minutes." And, sure enough, here he would come, good weather or bad.

Harold Gillam had one bad habit with which I have a big argument: he would fly passengers in the same scabby weather through which he would fly alone. I have never done that by design, and I never will. Period. I admit that I've been caught a time or two carrying passengers in weather that kept the ducks and geese walking along in single file, but it never happened if I could avoid it. Not so with Gillam.

Several times I've flown into a lodge or strip somewhere only to find other pilots sitting around drinking coffee and playing cards. I've been scolded for it on occasion. Nick Sias, a much better pilot than I'll ever be, was once weathered in at Ted and Mary Gerken's Iliaska Lodge on Lake Iliamna with a bunch of his fishing clients. Nick was flying a float-equipped De Havilland Beaver, perhaps Alaska's and Canada's favorite single-engine, load-carrying bush airplane. When I arrived in my Beechcraft Sierra, a low-wing, retractable-gear single—and probably the farthest thing from a bush plane—Nick took me aside to tell me that I had embarrassed him in front of his clients. He had told them that the weather was much too bad for flying just then, and yet here I came, flapping around up there in an airplane not at all suitable for flying the bush in the first place.

I explained that I had simply been caught in the bad weather and had had no choice but to drop in for coffee where he was weathered in with his clients. I offered to explain it to his charges, but Nick didn't think that was a good idea, either. So, I just finished my coffee and then quietly lit out again, headed south for King Salmon, another hour out.

Gillam's luck finally ran out on January 5, 1943. It was on that day that he took off from Seattle, Washington, in a Lockheed Electra. He was headed for Alaska with five passengers. At the time, he was flying for Morrison-Knudson, a huge construction contracting firm.

Harold had been told of a bad storm that was approaching the Alaska Gulf Coast along his route, but he had elected to fly anyway. On board with Gillam were Robert Gebo and Percy Cutting, both M-K employees; Joseph Tippets, a CAA engineer; Dewey Metzdorf, an Anchorage resident; and Susan Baxter, a twenty-five-year-old stenographer on her first trip to Alaska, where she was going to work with the CAA.

Things went well for the first four hours of the flight. It was then that Harold encountered thick clouds. They went clear to the deck, and he was now on solid instruments. Harold was never much for radio communications, and it surprised no one that he didn't radio his position along this route of flight either.

He finally decided to make a landing at Annette Island, a place where the U.S. Army had a newly constructed field. But the low frequency radio range legs had recently undergone some changes, and Gillam didn't have the current navigational charts. Though he was plowing along at six thousand feet and trying to bracket what he thought was the southeast leg of the Annette Island low frequency radio range, he was now actually flying along the *northeast* leg. It was about here that one of the two engines went south on him. And then, a heavy downdraft suddenly pulled the plane from six thousand to only four thousand feet above the sea. At four thousand feet, it was impossible for him to clear all the peaks on the island. The Electra was still trimmed for cruise speed when it hit the mountain.

The plane had impacted only sixteen miles from Ketchikan, Alaska, and less than seven miles from Prince William Sound along the Inside Passage. The Inside Passage, remember, is the route taken by today's cruise liners that carry so many tourists to Alaska each year. It's also the route that found the *Exxon Valdez* piling up on a rock. In spite of Gillam's stature as a living legend, the search for the plane's wreckage was called off after only two weeks.

It was two more weeks before a Coast Guard vessel spotted two men and a large bonfire on the shores of Boca de Quadra Inlet. The two, Tippets and Cutting, weren't in very good shape.

Both of Tippets' ankles were sprained, and Cutting was moving with a broken back. And they had been among the *least* injured of the passengers. It had taken them nine days of slipping and sliding and falling down the mountainside to cover the ten miles that had finally brought them to this little piece of cold and rocky beach.

They had found an old dory on the beach and had tried to row it out of the bay. It capsized on them, though, and the men had to swim through the icy waters back to the beach. They had subsisted on some raw mussels, two Alaska ravens, and a half cup of wormy rice. Their feet were frostbitten, and each had lost more than fifty pounds of body weight. In spite of all this, and with only a few hours' rest, Tippets and Cutting tirelessly led a rescue party back up that damned mountain to help with the rescue effort. Gebo and Metzdorf, though close to the end, were rescued alive, thanks to these two. The young woman, Miss Baxter, had lived less than two days after the crash before dying of her injuries at the crash site.

As for Gillam himself, it was on the sixth day after the crash that he determined he should climb to a nearby ridge to see if he could find a landmark that he recognized. Taking a few provisions—and a parachute for protection against the piercing cold—he disappeared into the fog. None of the passengers would ever see him again.

It was some time later that a Coast Guard search party found his frozen body, wrapped in the parachute, on the beach of Boca de Quadra Inlet. Harold had tied his red underwear to a nearby spruce tree, and his flying boots had been placed, bottoms up, on two tall poles nearby. By the time he was found, he had been dead for several weeks.

It has always been supposed that Harold had found some sort of derelict boat along the beach, had tried to escape the island in it, but had capsized it—or perhaps it just plain sank from under him—forcing him to swim ashore. He most likely had hung his boots on the poles to dry and had then wrapped himself in the parachute for protection. Hypothermia very likely caught up with him as he slept, and this one-of-a-kind Alaska bush pilot slipped silently west while asleep. An ignominious end to a remarkably fearless and capable pilot.

***

I guess Jack Jefford is pretty much every Alaska pilot's hero. Raised in Broken Bow, Nebraska (strange that so many of Alaska's outback pilots came from the middle of the country!), he soloed an airplane when he was only nineteen years old. With his brother, he ran an air service throughout Nebraska in the early 1930s.

In 1935, he was making high-altitude weather flights, similar to those Harold Gillam made in Alaska. Like Gillam, too, many of his flights were made under low- or no-visibility conditions. This drove him to earn his CAA instrument rating that same year, one of the first pilots in the United States to do so.

He managed an airport in Hastings, Nebraska, for a while. He also did some stunt flying (acrobatic flying, which is really more accurately described as "precision" flying) and did a little barnstorming along the way. It wasn't until 1937 that he received a telegram offering him a job with Mirow Flying Service at Nome, Alaska. He immediately lit out for the far north and, like so many both before and after him, arrived with less than a dollar to his name.

Typical of many Alaska backcountry pilots, he once spent five days and nights huddled in a damaged airplane while fifty- and sixty-mile winds buffeted him. Perched precariously on the edge of a mountain, he expected at any moment to be blown over the edge only to plummet thousands of feet to his doom. It didn't happen, and he was eventually rescued by another outback Alaska flier.

Jefford's skills in bad-weather flying caught the attention of the master of that ability—none other than Harold Gillam—who offered him a job. Later, Jefford was contracted by the federal government to perform aerial surveys of the Territory of Alaska's reindeer herds.

In 1943, Jefford was flying with the CAA when they bought him a new DC-3 twin-engine airliner. Jefford named this airplane *King Chris* in honor of Chris Lample, who was at that time Assistant Superintendent of Airways in Washington, D.C. This ship wouldn't be utilized for civilian air travel, however, and Jefford made some modifications to it that he felt would be necessary. A four-foot-wide loading door, for one thing, nearly twice as wide as the standard DC-3 passenger door. He also had a winch and pulleys installed for handling heavy loads, and he even had an A-frame with a hoist made that could be carried in the plane so that he and his co-pilot could handle the heavy loads by themselves.

I guess every one of us who flew out of Anchorage in the "old days" will remember seeing the silver DC-3 at the CAA hanger at Anchorage International Airport. We'd seen it come and go with such regularity that we never gave it a second thought. Yet Jefford racked up more than ninety-three thousand passenger miles—and almost fifty *million* freight-pound miles—in only a single month of flying the silver bird.

What places Jack Jefford so high on my own list of heroes is his history of instrument facilities check flights. With an instrument airways system (in the "old days," that is) of more than eight thousand air miles, Jefford was responsible for maintaining both the accuracy of its many low frequency radio range legs and the operating personnel at all the range locations. Not only that, but he virtually established both the fields and the navigational facilities single-handedly. Because of his constant facilities checking and verification flights, Jack Jefford probably had more pure instrument time than any other living pilot of his day. He was one of those truly rare characters, a real live bush pilot and the smoothest and most precise of instrument pilots. Without doubt, Jack Jefford advanced instrument flying in Alaska by leaps and bounds. Flying *King Chris*, he virtually single-handedly checked and rechecked every instrument facility along the Alaska airway routes. Given the incredible size of Alaska, that was a lot of air miles, and no end of precision flying. He was the master of the airways. Those of us who knew Jack have a very special place in our hearts for him.

***

There are many heroes in the fraternity of Alaska outback fliers. They are not limited to the pioneers of Alaska flight, either. There are heroes flying the Alaska bush even as this is being written. Oh, sure—the equipment available to today's bush pilot is revolutions ahead of the stuff the pioneer bush pilots had to contend with. But the environment hasn't changed a bit. It is still huge, it is still forbidding to the inexperienced, and it is still edge-of-the-envelope flying.

The powerful engines hanging out front of today's single-engine bush planes are incredibly dependable. Yes, some of them will, on occasion, cough and sputter with carburetor ice, if the pilot isn't careful. And they still quit every now and then. It's rare, but it does happen. When it does, life gets much, much closer to the edge. It is then that the pilot knows his advance planning wasn't all for nothing. He does have his survival gear aboard, and someone really does know just about where he is flying. Unfortunately, it's usually the pilot's wife or girlfriend, though, and the FAA is very reluctant to begin any search activities based upon a request from these sources. I've chased emergency locator transmitter squeals for more than an hour over trackless wastes on occasion, only to come upon the source to discover the pilot didn't want to be rescued. In most cases, he was up to something he shouldn't have been up to—most often with a girlfriend who clearly was not his wife.

At other times, though, a pilot that goes missing in the Alaska bush had best be pretty innovative, in regard to temporary aircraft or engine repairs and his temporary living arrangements. A huge part of Alaska is virtually without trees, and making a suitable shelter against the elements can become something of a challenge. And it is almost always a life-threatening situation. Summer or winter, it doesn't really make a whole lot of difference. Between the awesome mosquitoes, the ever-wet ground, and dropping temperatures with the usual precipitation, the Alaska environment isn't just another walk on the beach. Flying the Alaska bush sort of demands heroes, though precious few of us ever thought of ourselves in that fashion. Hell, we just flew until something bad happened and then went about fixing it so we could fly some more. And none of us wanted to do something as risky as becoming an Alaska crab or pollock fisherman. We always thought of those two Bering Sea occupations as two that really do stare death in the face for so many hours and for so many days on end that even the cold, wet end of it all seems to lose its impact. And like pilots, neither Alaska crab nor pollock fishermen would give up their professions for anything else on earth. Those guys are nuts, though, and Alaska's bush pilots, of course, are not.

There were, and there still are, plenty of "heroes" in my own neck of the woods, too. Ketch Ketchum and his son, Craig. Not to mention Marguerite, Ketch's wife. Hank Rust, certainly. His son is following in his dad's footsteps, I believe.

At the top of my personal list is probably Dave Klosterman, who has perhaps by now seen the error of his ways and retired from actively sticking his neck out on a daily basis. Bill Cunningham, whose brother was the astronaut we all knew. Bill took his Grumman Super Widgeon to Hawaii and retired several years ago. Still, we always knew he would show up at Big Lake when the Widgeon Owner's Club would meet for its annual summertime fly-in.

Oren Hudson, of course, who still flies the bush in his Super Widgeon. Oren is now over eighty years old. But quit flying? What for? Don Sheldon, the Hudsons—father Cliff (not long ago gone west, I'm sorry to say) and son Jay—Lowell Thomas, Jr., who began flying the world with his famous father and who now flies the special challenges of Mt. McKinley (or Mt. Denali, if you're a newcomer), highest mountain in North America. Redheaded, fully aerobatic, and absolutely fearless Doug Geeting, who knows as much about Mt. McKinley flying as any other living man. He's been known to make zero-zero letdowns to a glacier more than eight thousand feet up on the slopes of the great mountain using only his compass and his watch for the blind approach and landing. All these from the small town of Talkeetna, jumping-off place for all Mt. McKinley climbers. I guess that just about every one of those pilots who flies out of Talkeetna is a hero, come to think of it.

Alaska's former governor, Jay Hammond, master guide and bush pilot of no small accomplishment, was surely another. Jay has gone west, too, but there are still a handful of real outback fliers around the Big Empty. And they all hang it out there on the very ragged edge of the flight envelope all day long, every single day, and day after day after day.

There are too many really good Alaska outback pilots for me to mention here. It may be enough to say that any of them who toughs it out attains the status of hero without really trying. And, typically, they don't see themselves as heroes. They don't concern themselves with the fact that they may be saving a life on this flight. They only focus on the flight. Saving that life is only a by-product of their profession. As most would simply tell you, "Hey, it ain't no big thing!"

Chapter 13

Aviation Christmas

One of the really neat things about having my first book, *Flying the Alaska Wild*, published was the incredible number of great people I've gotten to meet since it first hit the bookstores. I've lost count of the many e-mails I've received in the past three or four years, and I hasten to add that I've met some really great folks at book signings, too.

One of those grand folks—actually *two* of them—were Maeva and her husband. He had been a pilot for many years, and he certainly enjoyed the many memories my little book brought back for him. Unhappily, he was suffering a very debilitating illness and was not to live long after we met. Maeva, who had been at his side for no end of decades, would read to him from the book in the quiet of their gentle, golden evenings. It broke my heart when Maeva told us that her husband had finally gone west.

Another of those readers has shared with me the following Christmas story. A rhyme, actually, and I know you'll recognize its predecessor.

The Night Before Christmas, Aviation Style

'Twas the night before Christmas, and out on the ramp,
Not an airplane was stirring, not even a Champ.
The aircraft were fastened to tiedowns with care,
In hopes that—come morning—they'd all still be there.

The fuel trucks were nestled all snug in their spots.
Gusts were two-forty at thirty-nine knots.
I slumped at the fuel desk—at long last caught up—
And then settled down with my cold coffee cup,

When the scanner lit up with noise and with chatter,
I turned up the volume to see what was the matter.
A voice clearly heard over static and snow
Called for clearance to land at the airport below.

He barked his transmission so lively and quick,
I near missed the call sign he used: "Ol' St. Nick."
I ran to the panel and turned up the lights,
To better welcome this magical flight.

He called his position, no room for denial,
"Ol' St. Nick One, turnin' left onto final."
And what to my wondering eyes should appear,
But a Rutan-built sleigh, with eight Rotax Reindeer!

With vectors to final, down the glideslope he came.
As he passed all the fixes, he called them by name:
"Now Ringo! Now Tolga! Now Trini and Bacun!
On Comet! On Cupid!" What pills was he takin'?

While controllers were sittin' and scratchin' their heads,
They phoned to my office—I heard it with dread.
The message they left was both urgent and dour:
"When St. Nick pulls in, have him please call the tower."

He landed like silk, with the sled runners sparking.
Ground said, "Left at Charlie and taxi to parking."
He slowed to a taxi, then turned off three-oh,
And stopped on the ramp with a "Ho-ho-ho-ho."

He stepped from the sleigh, but before he could talk,
I ran to meet him with my best set of chocks.
Red helmet and goggles all covered with frost,
His white beard now blackened from Reindeer exhaust.

His breath smelled like peppermint gone slightly stale,
And he puffed his clay pipe—but he didn't inhale.

His cheeks were all rosy and jiggled like jelly.
His boots were as black as a crop-duster's belly.

He was chubby and plump, in his suit of bright red,
And he asked me to "Fill it with hunnert low-lead."
When he came dashing in from the snow-covered pump,
I knew he was anxious for drainin' the sump.

I spoke not a word but went straight to my work,
And I filled up the sleigh, then just stared like a jerk.
He strolled from the restroom, he sighed in relief,
Then he picked up a phone for a Flight Service brief.

And I thought, as he silently scribed in his log,
These reindeer could land with one-eighth mile in fog.
He completed his preflight, from front to the rear,
Then he put on his headset, and I heard him yell, "Clear!"

Then laying a finger on his mike's push-to-talk,
He called up the tower for clearance and squawk.
"Take taxiway Charlie, the southbound direction,
Turn right three-two-zero at pilot's discretion."

He dashed down the runway, the best of the best,
"Your traffic's a Grumman, inbound from the west."
Then I heard him proclaim, as he climbed through the night,
"Merry Christmas to all!—Nick has traffic in sight!"

The author on a photographic safari at one of the beaches on the north side of Chinitna Bay. He preferred to use his Hasselblad camera for wilderness photographs, when he had time to use the complicated camera and its many attachments. *Photo by John Erskine, Anchorage, Alaska*

Chapter 14

Julius and the Bear

THE THREE MOST USELESS THINGS TO A PILOT ARE THE ALTITUDE ABOVE, THE RUNWAY BEHIND, AND THE FUEL LEFT AT THE AIRPORT.

Julius Harris. I think of him every now and again, though I reckon I haven't seen him now for going on fifty years. He was a gentleman, Julius. And a gentle man. He was also the funniest danged person I think I've ever met, bar none.

Now, Julius didn't tell many jokes around a wilderness camp, as some do. He didn't set out to do funny things, either. And he wasn't a prankster. He wasn't even overweight, a condition that we too often tend to associate with humorous personalities, good dancers, and opera singers. Come to think of it, Julius was downright thin, mostly, and pretty tall in the bargain. Without being really gangly, of course. He was also as black as a March night.

Julius owned a string of barbershops—which he proudly referred to as *tonsorial parlors*—back in New Jersey. In the early spring of 1965, he had traveled north and west to test his mettle against the legendary Alaska brown bear.

I don't recall exactly how it was that my party had found itself in the Chinitna Bay area of Alaska's Cook Inlet. I do remember that I had returned from Lake Tahoe with a Cessna 180 strapped to my backside. When I unloaded it in Anchorage, there emerged a Californian by the name of Jay and a longtime friend—whose name is probably known to just about every serious big game hunter in the world. That was Brad—Basil C. Bradbury, ASC, now deceased—a Hollywood cinematographer at that time and later to become my first assistant guide in Alaska.

We were, among other things, supposed to be field-testing a new line of gear for a prominent fishing equipment manufacturer. Going to get a slew of photographs of Alaska's bigger sport fish. Maybe with a brownie or two in the background. That's a little hard to do, early in the spring, though it's not completely impossible.

But the lakes and streams everywhere around us were still locked in winter wear, so we were shuffling from foot to foot and waiting for the first sign of a weather break. In the meantime, we were stormed in at Chinitna Bay, where we were warmly, if not too safely, packed into a small fishing shack near the head of the bay.

The weather couldn't have been much worse. It was still spitting snow, off and on, and howling like a banshee down the full length of the bay. Our plane, pulled as high on the beach as we could get it and securely tied to a huge spruce close beside the cabin, was my first concern. If that went, everything else would stay. For a long time. From the relative safety of the cabin, we could hear the occasional breaker crashing down on the beach, only a few feet away, showering both the cabin and the plane with water, snow, sand, and silt. None of us was all too comfortable with the whole thing, right then.

It was during the third or fourth night of this howling mess that, after having put away an embarrassingly large quantity of clam-foot burgers and boiled camp coffee, we had begun the old Alaska hunting camp game of "First Liar Don't Stand a Chance." Each tale got bigger, of course, until one or another of us began to regale the others with some of the many things that he had never seen. Well, it's easy to fall into the spirit of that sort of conversation, and we were getting really warmed up to it there for a little while.

Along with horse flies, house flies, and cowslips on a hill, we allowed that there just wasn't all that much that one or another of us hadn't laid eyes on somewhere along the trail. Among those things, however—and we all had to agree about this—two rarities had escaped us all. None of us had ever laid eyes on a black pilot, first off. And never had any of us seen a black bear hunter. That is, a black man who hunted Alaska bears, no matter the color of the bears.

No sooner had this curiosity been aired than—above the roar of the wind, the shrieking of tortured spruce, and the horrendous pounding of angry surf against the exposed beach, the threatened Cessna, and our suffering little cabin—there came a loud banging at our flimsy door! A banging that was a fright in and of itself, since we were now camped almost two flying hours from the nearest city or town of any size and locked in the chilling grip of a storm that was keeping even the moose and caribou huddled in stands of shivering birch, spruce, and aspen.

When I opened the door against the storm, no mean feat, I thought I must surely be looking at an avenging and determined representative of a Higher Authority. There, before my unbelieving eyes, stood a really tall, and truly black, man. He was only inches from my frozen face and, at first glance, was as motionless as a boulder. I was a little unnerved to think that he might have overheard the latter portions of our foolish camp chatter, even over the awesome racket of the serious storm that continued to abuse us with both frightening malice and grim determination.

Given his surprise appearance at our flimsy portal—for the storm was getting much worse rather than much better—and his Pennsylvania deer-hunting costume, it was a moment before I had gathered enough wits about me to shout against the wind, "Come in the house!"

As this strange apparition entered, I noticed another shadowy figure standing behind him. I was relieved to realize that I knew this second figure. Frank Griffin, another Alaska registered guide and, among his other accomplishments, an expert on Musk Oxen. It turned out that Julius was his client. They were planning to thin out by a total of one the brown bear population around West Glacier Creek. West Glacier is one of the creeks that feed into Chinitna Bay at its head, by the way.

After finding enough hard, flat surfaces to provide seats, of a sort, for everyone—and after having done away with several more makin's of camp coffee, spiced with a couple more hours of camp tales and lies—we three bid our visitors a good night. We had learned that the two of them were staying in an abandoned log cabin on the back side of the slough that lay just behind our shack. In fact, that's where they had come from just prior to Julius' having scared the wits out of me with his loud door banging.

We had agreed to meet them early the following morning to accompany them on their hike into West Glacier country. We did that, just at early light, and while Julius fiddled with one last-minute preparation after another, Frank confided to us that Julius had planned to spend the previous night sleeping in a two-man tent along the beach that fronted the old cabin. Said he wanted to be near to the bears that he had come to Alaska to pester.

Now, sleeping alone in a tent in the middle of brown bear country is not considered, by most city folk, to be an especially restful undertaking. As it happened, this wasn't really Julius' cup of tea, either, and he was soon back in the log cabin, his sleeping bag under one arm and his tiny tent under the other.

Julius had learned, by this time—and in spite of less than ideal weather conditions—that Alaska's mosquitoes are not made of myth, legend, and fertilizer. They are real, they are large, they are vicious, and, according to the sworn testimony of my friend Julius, they appear to have an abiding preference for dark meat.

Two and two added up to four, as far as Julius was concerned. Clearly, the old log cabin would discourage both the unknown quantity of the Alaska brown bear and the now known hazards of associating with the Alaska mosquito. Thus convinced, and with admirable if confusing determination, he proceeded to pitch his tent on the top bunk, after which he fluffed up his down bag inside the tent and was then prepared for a more comfortable night's rest.

With a number of remarkable gyrations—for Frank was fully dressed during this telling, right down to his hip boots—we were being given a graphic description of the rather lanky Julius surmounting the second floor of his chosen home to disappear inside the one-room sleeping accommodation of his small tent. This was finally accomplished, allowing Frank once again to shut down the Coleman lantern.

Julius had been provided, as is usual, with a spray can of insect repellent. Now, this stuff doesn't kill the little beasts, of course. But choosing the proper blend will usually provide at least some minor, though temporary, relief through insect discouragement. Providing, of course, that an intelligent application of the stuff has been made in the first place. Many of us believe that this means spraying it onto one's clothing and the exposed areas of one's hide.

In all fairness to Julius, it should be noted here that there existed very few Alaska mosquitoes in or around his New Jersey tonsorial parlors. The fact that he was confused as to the accepted method of application and dissemination of his insect repellent is certainly acceptable on that account alone.

At first, Frank thought that Julius was just being naturally conservative. Frank was hearing, somewhere in the darkened cabin, the occasional short "psssssssst" of a spray can. This, you understand, was an impediment to Frank's sleep, a state which he knew he must soon acquire out of deference to tomorrow's demanding schedule.

For the non-Alaskan hunter, perhaps it is best to confirm here that the arctic mosquito and subarctic mosquito, like the common house fly, seem to winter quite well—some would say even comfortably—at temperatures of fifty and sixty below zero. But, at the very first sign of a rise in temperature, these cannibals awaken, stretch, yawn a couple of times, and begin a very serious and concerted forage for man's lifeblood. Once our hunters' cabin had been heated a bit, the moss chinking between the logs had released the hoards to peruse and pursue their new menus. Obviously, Julius was to be the entrée of the evening.

It seems that Julius, in his flawed method of application, was jump-shooting in the darkened tent at the sound of each flying marauder, no doubt confusing the little carnivores, but certainly not dispelling them.

Frank jumped up—barefoot, of course—to light the Coleman lantern again. He first carefully explained to Julius the niceties of the proper and widely accepted—not to mention demonstrably more effective—application of his insect repellent and then settled in once more against the shortening night.

After a brief but disarmingly eye-watering laugh, we were joined by Julius who, by now, gave every appearance of a successful sporting goods wholesaler.

Besides the Pennsylvania red-and-black checkered pants, shirt, jacket, and hat, he had pulled on a pair of hip boots and warm gloves. This was topped off with at least one of every portable device known to outdoorsmen, and some perhaps known only to outdoorswomen. Around his neck, each item suspended from its own tether, were camera, movie camera, binoculars, light meter, whistle (whistle?), something that (under other circumstances) might have passed for a bird call, and additional other items too numerous to inventory then or to recall now with any accuracy at all. How this slim man staggered along under this impressive, if superfluous, load is to this day difficult to imagine.

That morning, we had slogged perhaps two miles up the delta of West Glacier Creek, through an expanse of calf-deep water and lush grasses, tough going under the best of conditions, when I heard Julius say, "Uh-oh!"

"Whatsamatter, Julius?" I knew it wasn't the mosquitoes.

"Uh-oh, uh-oh!"

"Julius, what's the matter?" I knew he hadn't been snake-bit, either. At least Alaska doesn't have any of those critters.

"I lost 'em."

"Uh—lost *what*, Julius?" He'd answer directly, I reckoned.

"Muh danged binoculars!"

"Well, where were they, Julius?"

"Right here, dang it. Right around muh neck!"

"You sure they're gone, Julius?"

"They wuz good ones, too. Muh *new* ones."

Frank could see that Julius was about to shed real tears over the loss, so he volunteered to trudge back along our backtrail through the swamp and locate the glasses, leaving the rest of us to take a rest break. It figured to be possible to find the glasses. Our backtrail now stood out like a sunflower in a Kansas wind, and the water we had muddied should have by now settled out and cleared up.

So, away went Frank, slogging back down along our telltale trail. After all, what's a guide for, anyway, if it's not to track down missing bits and pieces and little lost articles?

We four—Brad, Jay, Julius, and I—took the opportunity to find a few dabs of dry hummock where each of us figured to plant his backside in relative security, dry if not really too comfortable.

Suddenly, there it was again. "Uh-oh!"

"Something else missing, Julius?" I inquired.

"Huh-uh. I found muh glasses."

"You did? Great! Where were they?"

"Uh—I guess they wuz hanging down my back and I couldn't see 'em around there behind me," he said sheepishly.

By the time a weary and empty-handed Frank had returned to report his failure in the swamp, I had moved several yards farther up West Glacier. I didn't want to be around to hear how Frank might accept the news that his walk had been pure exercise. Frank didn't really need a whole lot of exercise, you see, and I didn't know how he would take this energy expenditure, especially in light of his recent lack of sleep.

Several hours later, and much farther up the creek, so to speak, we were again taking a little break, this time for a snack. We were on a gravel bar, counting the many small chunks of ice that were floating down cold and silty, glacier-fed West Glacier Creek.

I was just sort of cooling it, Frank was carefully scanning the brittle and leafless willow scrub along the far bank for any sign of a bear, and Julius was fascinated by a pair of magpies that were fussing and complaining about something a little farther upstream.

Suddenly, and in a hoarse whisper, Frank said, "Take him, Julius. Take him!"

"Take whut? Take whut?" Julius had obviously been watching those two birds to the exclusion of all else.

A nine-foot brown bear had emerged from the dry willows lining the opposite shore, stepping down from the three-foot-high cut bank onto the gravel beach there, about forty yards away. He was big enough that his head was swinging as he walked, and he was sufficiently pigeon-toed to be classed as a keeper. Soon his back would be swayed as he became truly huge.

By this time, Julius was fumbling and fiddling with his Winchester .348 lever action and looking absolutely stricken. He hadn't seen the bear yet and wasn't just exactly sure what it was that he was supposed to "take."

He seemed to spot the bear, after a few more frantic moments, at just about the same time as his center of gravity, for some reason, shifted slightly aft on his log seat. Without fanfare, he shouldered the Model '71, torched off a quick round, and slipped ignominiously backward off the damp log that had been his resting place, all in a single, smooth motion.

Julius' shot had obviously smacked the bear a good lick, causing him to immediately whirl, make two quick jumps, and then disappear completely into the low willow scrub.

By the time Julius had sufficiently recovered to discern up from the other direction, his bear was hairy history, the willows were unmoving, and the stream seemed to have picked up a lot more ice.

Frank, of course, knew the drill as well as I did. I didn't envy him, but Julius was his client, not mine. If he wanted my help, he would ask for it. And I would give it, of course.

Frank knew that he had to cross that unfriendly creek somehow and go into the brush after the bear, most likely now deceased but most certainly hard hit. He knew, too, that the creek would be much deeper than his hip boots would accommodate. That meant either a cold and naked trip or a cold and *wet* one with clothes that wouldn't be dry again for many hours.

"You stay here, Julius. I think that was a good hit. I'll go rustle him out over there." This from Frank.

Julius, now fully recovered and anxious to get a look at the bear that he couldn't even remember having seen earlier, stood up and allowed as how maybe Frank could use a little help over there?

"Julius, you just stay put." No question, this was a command. We all noted Julius' courage, but guides prefer to go at it alone in these cases. Most of us know bears in the brush, but none of us really knows his clients in the same batch of weeds or willows.

By this time, Frank was stripped as naked as a jaybird and as white as a beached Beluga. He was holding his rifle and clothing bundled over his head now, pausing momentarily before taking his first shocking step into that refreshing, if not inviting, little glacial river.

Anxious to get this first phase of the unhappy event behind him, Frank was quickly immersed in the icy water nearly up to his armpits. I watched without envy as, one by one, chunk after icy chunk of icy glacier cast-off clouted his exposed ribs with a scraping I could almost feel.

When Frank had finally gained the opposite gravel bar, he apparently decided to settle the bear question before he bothered to settle his blue and shivering nudity. He immediately scrambled to the top of the cut bank where the willow line began.

While it was relatively sunny just at that time, there was an impressive wind coming down the valley from the glacier that mothered the ice-filled stream. Riding on that wind was a temperature of about thirty-eight degrees, cool if not really cold. But Frank, wringing wet and already chilled, was shivering like a fox hound passing corncobs. Eyes watering, goose pimples building upon goose pimples, and both hands locked around his Model 70, three-and-six-bits, poor frigid Frank tiptoed, barefoot and brave, into the stiff and leafless willow.

Visualize that for a moment, if you will. Barefootin' through a stand of scrub willow as tough as spring steel. This is certainly a little hard on the soles of Alaska feet, which do not, in the usual course of events, see daylight from one month to the next. And almost never are they allowed to touch the bare earth.

Anyhow, there was Frank, sneaking around looking for Julius' bear rug, which, hopefully, was growing cold and stiff faster than was his jaybird pursuer.

About fifteen yards into that willow patch, Frank paused, squeezed his eyes again to clear them a little, and pressed down, with the big toe of his right foot, a particularly springy and tough little willow stem. As he shifted his weight a little for the next step, the laws of chance at long last caught up with the brave and honorable Frank Griffin. That willow stem slipped from under his big toe.

I suppose you can guess that it smacked poor Frank, with no little vigor, precisely upon that most tender of all male anatomical protuberances. If one can imagine how his eyes must have watered prior to this untimely happenstance, ponder for a moment, if you will, the effect of this most recent and decidedly embarrassing injury.

It was at precisely that moment that Frank thought he saw the flash of brown that would signal his quarry.

Well, Frank is still among us, as far as I know. You are correct to suppose that the bear had already expired. Needless to say, we were all kind of pleased about that. Well, all except the bear, of course.

Back in camp, some time later, we were all speculating on the various tales we might have had to lay on the investigating officers in the event that the bear had won that one. Why was a prominent and respected professional guide sneaking around the Alaska outback in his altogethers, anyway? The explanation, while in some ways quite logical, was like one of those jokes that always seem to fall flat. You just had to have been there, I guess.

Properly skinned and fleshed, but before the lips and ears had been split and turned, the bearskin was suspended in old Kodiak fashion, more like a beaver plew than anything else. This made a good background for the requisite photographs.

As soon as the picture-taking session was completed, I had planned to fly to Anchorage for a grub run. We still had some powerful fishing to do. Julius asked if I would stop at the local Alaska Communications System (ACS) office in Anchorage and send a couple telegrams for him. Alaska didn't have Western Union, of course, which most of us still thought was cowboy underwear at any rate. Sure, that would be no problem, I told Julius. He handed me a couple folded sheets of tablet paper, which I jammed into a jacket pocket, and off I went, flying east to round the corner at Cook Inlet and settle down northbound toward Anchorage.

The weather was excellent by now, although I knew this would be just a few hours' respite. My time in Anchorage would be limited, so I had to hustle around with my chores, planning the telegram stop at the ACS offices in the old Federal Building on Fourth Avenue as my last in-town undertaking.

Julius had indeed given me two telegrams to send, both written out in pencil on folded, yellow tablet paper. The first was to his wife, to whom he was quite devoted, proclaiming his sterling performance and notable success at brown bear hunting. The second was to the boys back in his headquarters barbershop. Excuse me—*Tonsorial Parlor.*

The first, I saw as I copied it onto the appropriate ACS form read, GOT A GREAT BIG BEAR. SEE YOU SOON. LOVE, JULIUS.

The second, the one to the boys back at the shop, read simply, HAPPY MOTHER'S DAY. HOW YOU MOTHERS DOING?

I have lost track of Julius over the years, I'm sorry to say. He sent photos to me once, long ago. Shots of the bear, of course, and some of his family back east. I'd like to see him again. He was truly quite a fellow.

I'll forever remember his rich and ringing baritone voice, lifted in song and pressed against the wind, as we trudged tiredly along a shortcut back to camp that successful, funny day.

"One more river to cross, Lord—just one more river to cross."

Chapter 15

A Very Lucky Day

Keep the pointy end headed forward as much as possible.

"You don't know how lucky you are." So went the popular song back in the days when Fred Dagg was all the rage down under in New Zealand. Whenever Jules Tapper heard it played, he thought back to a flight he had made into Big Bay. That was in the late 1970s, and it was a flight that he wouldn't be likely to forget.

His passenger, Peter, had done very little flying in light aircraft. This bush flying business—flying in and out of tiny little airstrips instead of the usual big commercial airports—was all new and adventurous stuff for him.

The flight had begun on a beautiful summer morning when they had lifted off a small field north of Glenorchy and banked gently away to the northwest. Heading directly into the mountains via the Dart Valley, they were soon winging their way past the majestic Rockburn faces and impressive Park Glacier. To the left of their flight path, and on the opposite side of Hollyford Valley, the magnificent Darren Range seemed almost to pierce the cloudless blue sky. This is truly awe-inspiring country, and Jules' passenger was suitably impressed.

Jules was flying an airplane almost empty of freight. Their ultimate destination was Martins Bay on the West Coast. Jules had two loads of passengers from one of his guided tours to fly over to Milford Sound that day, but, just before takeoff, he was asked if he would be good enough to drop some mail into Dale Hunter's airstrip at the south end of Big Bay. The strip was a very short one, and quite demanding, but as they were light, and the diversion quite small, Jules had agreed to make the mail stop.

Dale Hunter was a successful crayfisherman. He was also planning to begin capturing live red deer in the special pens that he had constructed in the bush near his camp.

After sliding smoothly through Cow Saddle, they flew over a red ochre–colored vista reminiscent of a lunar landscape. From there, it was down the Olivine and on out into the wide Pyke Valley. They were now heading straight for Big Bay. In the past fifteen minutes, they had flown over a dramatically wide variety of beautiful and exciting landscapes.

Glenorchy lies in the rain shadow of the Southern Alps and is rife with typical Central Otago vegetation. Mountain beech thrived on the more inland alpine flanks, but here on the coast, high rainfall and mild temperatures ensured a dense rainforest vegetation, which predominated from valley floor to the brush line at around 3,500 feet.

Descending quickly now, Jules and Peter were soon skimming past Lake Wilmot, sparkling in the summer sun, and then, after a left turn around the corner, caught their first view of Big Bay.

Dales Hunter's little strip had been constructed at a right angle to the beach and on the south side of the bay. It lay tight alongside McKenzie Creek, just where it flowed out to the sea. The creek lay perpendicular to the little strip and was jammed in tightly between the end of the strip and the narrow beach itself.

The strip was very short, and definitely a bit narrow. It did have a good approach from the land side, though, and it had a good braking surface. Scrubby bush lay close on one side, while large, mature flax crowded the other.

The strip's major disadvantages were that, apart from being quite short, it ended abruptly at a cut bank that was a couple feet high. To overrun this strip meant a surprising drop into the creek. And, on the far side of the creek, the beach rose up to form a ridge three to four feet high before it finally sloped off into the sea. Once the pilot had his wheels planted, he had to stop right now—or he would have to execute an immediate go-around to avoid dumping it over the bank and into McKenzie Creek. To overrun the short strip and drop down into the small, shallow creek would surely mean nosing over and ending upside down. Thus, split-second judgment was needed during any landing that didn't feel just exactly right.

A light sea breeze prevailed that day, with waves about three feet high breaking gently on the beach as Jules made his final approach from the land toward the sea. He was pleased that they had a bit of headwind, since this would slow their ground speed slightly, and at this short strip, every little bit helped.

Their main wheels nailed the strip right on the threshold. Jules dropped the flaps off and applied all the brake pressure he dared in order to stop within the little bit of strip remaining.

Almost instantly, the left brake pedal went soft. Jules knew immediately that he had lost hydraulic pressure on that side. The aircraft began drifting to the right, directly toward the tall flax that crowded the narrow little strip.

It was one of those times when the pilot's instinct would take over, an instinct born of years of outback flying experience. There was definitely not enough room for Jules to stop the airplane, and a plunge into the creek with its resulting aircraft—and perhaps personal—damage and injury was obviously in the cards. Theoretically, there was very little chance of successfully aborting the landing at this point. The books would by now have painted a picture that included lots of dust, a huge spray of water, and very loud noises.

Looking back on that day, Jules thinks he must have instinctively thought it was worth trying to abort the landing, even though standard operating procedures would have argued against it. He knew the aircraft's handling characteristics extremely well, as do most outback pilots, and he had often used a few little techniques not found in the pilot operating handbook. This was especially true when operating in tight areas.

The throttle was hammered into the instrument panel, and, with an answering roar, all 310 takeoff horsepower snarled back into action. At the last minute, just a split second before they were about to drop off into the creek—and long before they had gained enough air speed to really fly—Jules yanked the manual flap handle up to its full flap limit. Immediately, forty degrees of Fowler's huge barn door flaps extended aft of the wings, and for an instant the airplane enjoyed a huge increase in lift.

They staggered across the creek in a nose-high attitude, looking more like a helicopter than a Cessna 185, while Jules struggled to keep the wobbling little airplane in the air. They were in ground effect, that volume of air just above the earth's surface where a cushion of air sustains flight at well below published flying air speeds. But they had a lot of drag sticking out there to overcome, too! The landing gear only added to the tremendous drag of the huge flaps, now hanging down all over the place.

Things were happening quickly now. The ridgeline on the beach loomed much too close. It was just ahead of them, and it was growing higher by the second. Luck stayed with them, though, when the main landing gear hit a half-buried log partway up the slope and the aircraft was bounced into the air just enough to let them scoot over the top of the ridge and then down toward the sea.

Jules was milking the flap lever now—judiciously raising the flaps in small increments—in an attempt to get the nose down so that he might regain a little air speed and continue flight. The waves, however, were just about to grab the wheels, and that would surely be the tragic end to this very short flight.

At the time all this was happening, Dale Hunter was driving around on his small tractor, en route from his house to the strip. Right at that moment, he was observing how very lucky his friends really were. The first wave broke just as Jules' aircraft was about to hit its foaming top. As the wave crested out and broke, the plane's main wheels slipped over the surface with the tail wheel running in the water, sending a rooster tail high into the air. The plane was still riding ground effect, barely skimming the sea and virtually hanging in the air on its prop. In another couple of very tense seconds, they had accelerated through to a more suitable air speed, and Jules slowly retracted the big flaps as they reached for a safer altitude. I suspect that he had no idea what his heart rate was just then—surely somewhere off the clock. Strangely, his passenger, Peter, seemed remarkably composed. In shock, Jules no doubt thought.

The next problem was to land safely with brakes only on one side. The answer to that was to land at Martins Bay. There was a good long airstrip at Martins Bay, and, with a lockable tail wheel to keep the airplane tracking straight ahead on rollout, Jules was confident he could make a successful landing there. Luck stayed with them, and there was no crosswind when they arrived. As they gently taxied into the lodge, Jules began to relax a bit.

Investigation found that on the landing at Big Bay, a rock must have zipped sideways off the wheel and torn the brake caliper bleed valve completely out at the bottom. It usually was only about six inches above ground level and, on reflection, appeared quite vulnerable. Fortunately for Jules, they had quite a good tool and spare parts selection—and plenty of hydraulic fluid—on hand at the lodge, and he was able to fit a blanking plug to the caliper after refilling the reservoir and bleeding the brake line. All seemed to be back to normal again, and after a thorough check of the rest of the aircraft, the two loads of passengers were flown to Milford in time for their boat cruise on the fjord.

Then it was back to Hollyford for a couple more quick freight haul trips with supplies that were needed at the lodge. Jules and Peter were then ready to depart for the flight home to Glenorchy.

It was late afternoon with a setting sun as they flew down Lake McKerrow, over Park Pass, and on down to their strip at Doug Scott's Rees Valley Station.

The tick, tick of cylinders cooling quietly in the still conditions permeated the atmosphere as they tied down the aircraft. Jules just had to ask Peter how he had enjoyed the day.

Peter wondered, "Does that sort of thing happen often?" Jules reassured him it didn't, just as Fred Dagg's theme line came to mind.

"You don't know how lucky you are, boy!" But Jules remained quiet—Peter may have wanted to fly with Jules again some time.

Later on, back at their maintenance base, they removed the standard bleed adjusters and fitted blanking plugs that wouldn't stick out there just to be broken off. Jules says that he doesn't want another episode like that, ever again!

The statement that "Good judgment comes from experience, but experience comes from bad judgment" summed up the day quite nicely, Jules thought.

I certainly do have to agree with Jules about that.

Chapter 16

Bad Day at Painter Creek

The propeller is just a large fan out front.
It is used to keep the pilot cool.

I had contracted to do some flying for one of Alaska's world-class fishing lodges during the summer of 1984. At that time, the owners included two local attorneys, one Alaska registered guide, and a really top-notch and longtime Alaska pilot, Joe Maxey. Along with the lodge's two Cessna 180s—wheel-mounted, since we seldom required a floatplane for our daily fly-out fishing trips—Joe kept his own Cessna 170-B model floatplane tied up downstream a little way from the lodge, about where Painter Creek and Mother Goose joined waters. I kept my own new turbocharged Cessna TU206G amphibian at the lodge's five-thousand-foot gravel airstrip. Primarily, the amphibian was used for incoming client transportation from King Salmon—the nearest airport to which clients could fly commercially and about one hundred miles to the north of the lodge—and their return flight to King Salmon at the end of their seven-day stays.

I also used the amphibian, N9975Z, for grub hauls and occasional client transportation from Anchorage to the lodge, a one-way trip of around 550 miles or so.

If any of you is looking for really world-class fishing for Alaska's five varieties of Pacific salmon, by the way—or the very best of trophy-size sea-run arctic char or breathtaking rainbow trout—let me put in a plug here for Painter Creek Lodge. The lodging accommodations, the cuisine—it wasn't just grub at this lodge—the wine list even, were not to be matched at any other of the Alaska outback fishing lodges operating during those days. All in all, the place was simply five-star incredible! Course, that was twenty years ago or so, but I can't imagine it's gone to rack and ruin in the meantime.

The author with a Marguerita Creek rainbow trout, near Painter Creek.

All the guides were expert at handling the large and powerful custom-made jet-drive riverboats, and a whole lot of the fishing was done right there in Painter Creek itself. For variety, though, side trips were made to such fishing spots as the Ugashik Narrows—a very, *very* short stretch of beautifully clear water between the Upper and Lower Ugashik Lakes—where the world's record arctic grayling was caught a number of years back. Other trips were made to nearby lava cinder patches adjacent to large, clear, and incredibly productive fishing streams. "Nearby" is something of a relative term here, and these trips could range as far as twenty or thirty or forty miles from the lodge. Except for maybe Marguerita Creek, my favorite rainbow trout stream, which was a bit farther away still. I prefer that little stream over even the Upper and Lower Tulariks. Those are the two giant rainbow trout producers that feed into Iliamna Lake's north side. The Tulariks are known to almost every serious fly fisherman in the world, by the way. But only you and I know about Marguerita Creek, right?

Still other trips were made—especially during the first two weeks or so of August—to the "Pacific side" of the Alaska Range, into which Painter Creek Lodge had been set. These trips over the hump toward the east were made primarily in search of the awesome silver salmon, easily the greatest fighter, pound for pound, of all Alaska's salmon. While not as large as the king salmon, which averages around forty pounds in the Alaska Peninsula neck of the woods, silvers are certainly the most aerial of all Alaska fishes. It's been said that, when hooked, they spend so much time in the air that they are almost dry by the time the fisherman leads them into his net. They are without doubt the greatest fighter of them all, in my book, and I include here the trophy Alaska rainbow trout, the large sea-run arctic char, and the wonderful, if delicate, arctic grayling, with its great, beautifully colored and spotted dorsal fin. The silvers even outfight the mighty steelhead, in my book, though I would hesitate to say that right in front of a dyed-in-the-wool steelhead fisherman. They can get pretty much out of hand, those boys.

The silver salmon hit the streams on their spawning run in this neck of the woods sometime during the first two weeks of August, usually. The guides at Painter Creek knew this, of course, and they began keeping one eye peeled for signs of the early silver salmon runs around the first of August. As soon as the silvers had begun their first spawning run, the lodge's pilot-guides would each load three lucky fishing clients aboard each of the Cessna 180s and then slip through the mountains from the lodge to the "Pacific side" along the eastern slope of the range, dropping in at any one of several favorite fishing spots there. Never, to my certain knowledge, had a client been disappointed with the experience of fishing silvers on the Pacific side.

One of those favorite spots is hard beside a five-thousand-foot-long gravel airstrip. Couldn't ask for a better landing spot than that, though I've never seen another fishing party there. The strip isn't marked on any aeronautical chart, and very few seem to know of its existence. So, let's just keep it a secret, if you don't mind. And if you fish there, don't even bother with light tackle. Between the heavy water and the silver salmon's terrific fighting abilities, you won't catch a single fish! I've tried and tried and *tried* that spot with light tackle. It's fun, but it's disgustingly futile. I've never caught a single silver salmon there with light tackle, and I've fished those dudes for more than thirty-five years.

The Painter Creek pilots had several routes through the mountain range there. The nearest, right at the head of Painter Creek, is the easiest to use if

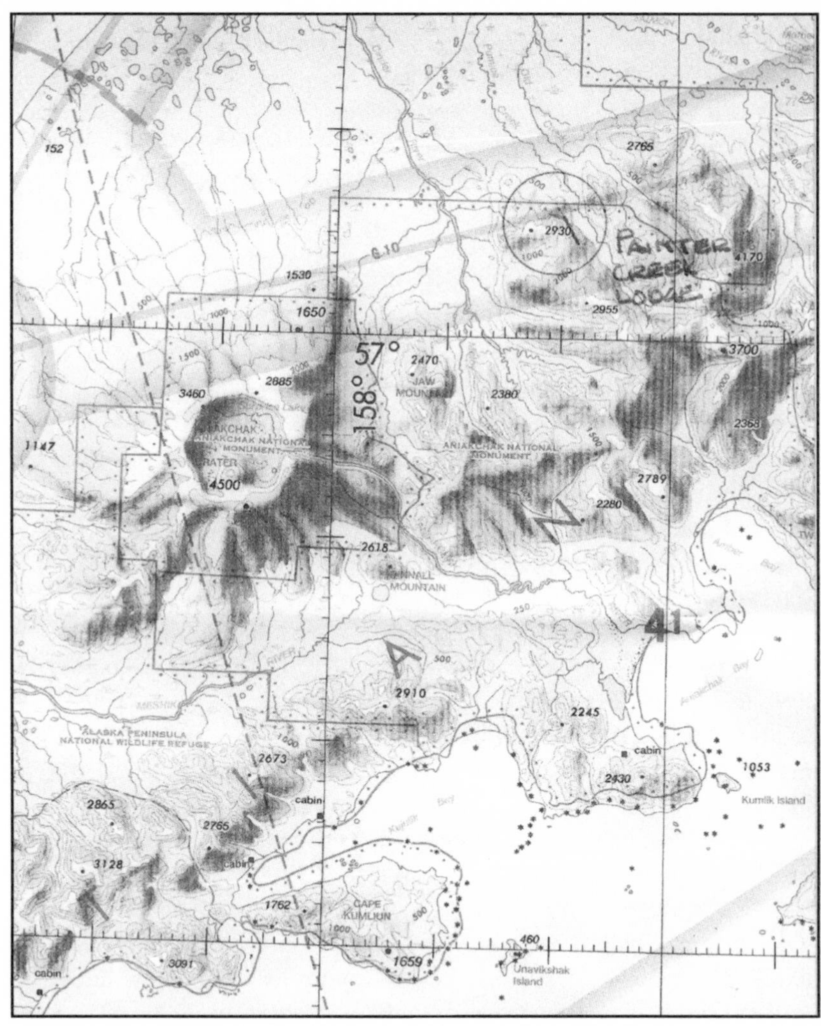

This aeronautical chart partial view shows the locations of Painter Creek Lodge, Aniakchak Crater, and Amber Bay. It was from the beach at Amber Bay that Joe Maxey took off on his ill-fated flight with three fishing guests from the lodge, only to perish in the mountain pass leading to Painter Creek.

the weather isn't too shabby. If ceilings drop to somewhere around the pilot's feet, he'll take a southern route that skirts around the north side of Aniakchak Crater, a long-extinct volcano located south of the lodge and not far from Port Heiden. He can make that route, either way—and with an altitude of less than two hundred feet—until he either gets back to the lodge strip or wends his way from the lodge, past the crater, and up the coastline to the great salmon fishing. When returning, and once he nears the lodge, he'll have to pop up a little bit, but only a few feet. It's a much longer route, though, and is only used when the weather is really bad.

It threatened to be just such a day back in August of 2001. But the silvers were running well, and Joe Maxey had decided to take some of the lodge clients over that way and have a look. He and a trailing plane from the lodge were able to get through from west to east that morning, and both the pilots and all their clients were soon enjoying the incomparable fishing. When the time arrived for them to return to the lodge, both pilots departed and scooted back into the mountains, picking up their usual route through the nearest pass.

The weather continued to deteriorate, though, and the ragged ceiling was dropping faster than either of the pilots had expected. Joe was leading the flight of two, of course, and suddenly he transmitted to the trailing pilot. The weather had worsened quickly, and he could then neither make it through the pass nor turn around to try the more southern, and much safer, route back to the lodge.

Though Joe was instrument rated, he was unable to climb through the overcast from his location deep inside the now unfriendly mountain range. He told the trailing pilot to turn around and try the Aniakchak route, since he was sure that the following pilot wouldn't be able to get through in the direction that Joe was then making a stab at.

Joe and his passengers had gone a little too far into the pass, though, and without resorting to aerobatics, Joe was now too far behind the power curve. Though he might have elected to climb through the overcast to clear skies, I'm sure he knew he was too close to the slopes to make that climb successfully. Or to turn around, either, for that matter. Joe had finally committed the cardinal sin of fliers: he had flown himself dry of options.

He perished on that flight, as did his clients. One passenger, later flown by rescuers to King Salmon, lingered for a day or two, I understand, but she later died in the hospital. Alaska weather and the wrong guess had taken still another good friend and great Alaska flier.

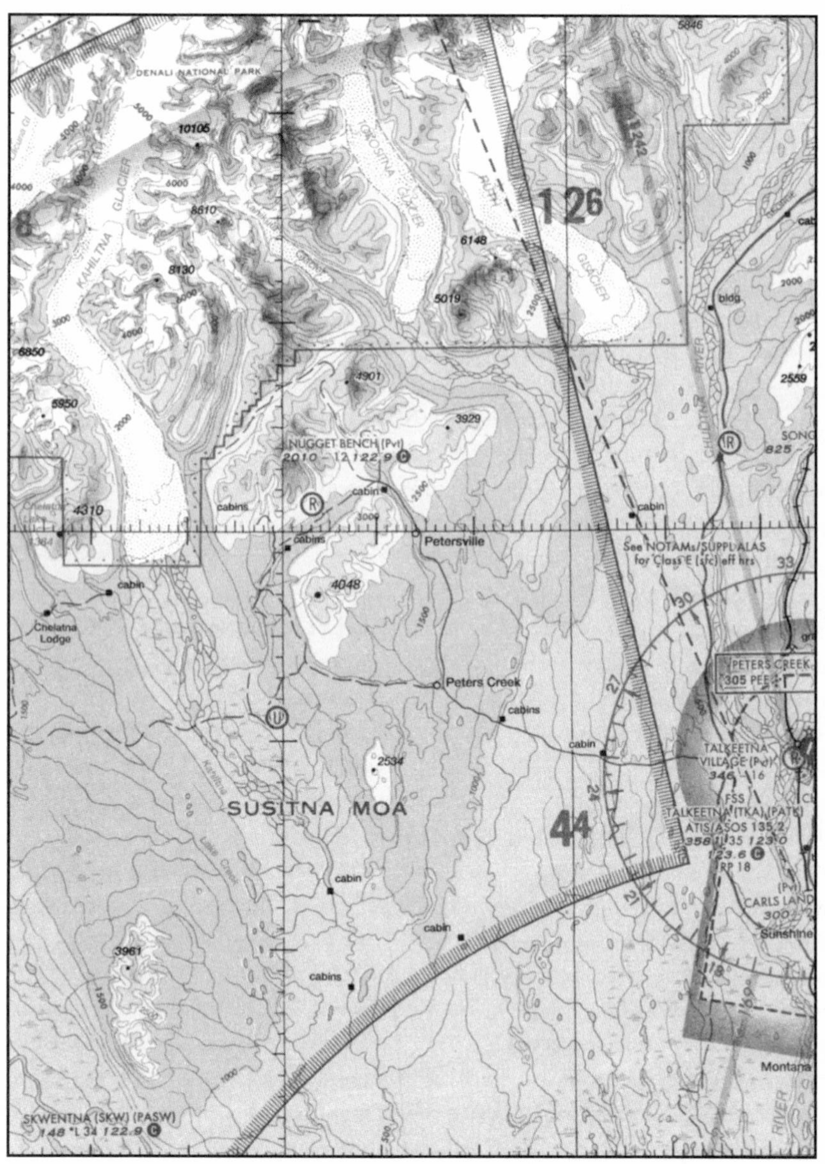

A partial view of this chart shows Chelatna Lake Lodge (at the center of the left edge) and Lake Creek. It is here that the De Havilland Beaver was forced to put down due to mechanical failure. Only one of the eight souls aboard survived this doomed flight.

Chapter 17

The Lake Creek Incident

You've landed with the wheels up if it takes full power to taxi to the ramp.

Only a few hours after the Fourth of July, 1997, fireworks display had died away at Anchorage, a De Havilland DHC-2 Beaver lifted smoothly off the water at Lake Hood Seaplane Base, crossing the cold waters of Knik Arm below five hundred feet and headed generally northwest. That altitude would keep the aircraft safely below the approach routes of incoming jet fighters stationed at nearby Elmendorf Air Force Base. Altitudes above two thousand feet would do the same.

The Beaver, registered as N5164G, was being operated by one of the pilots who flew for Dave Klosterman's Alaska Bush Carrier (ABC). The Beaver, which was manufactured in 1953, had been a part of Alaska Bush Carrier, Inc., since 1987. Today, it had been scheduled for a nominal one-plus-ten (one hour and ten minutes) flight to Chelatna Lake, a gorgeous, mountain-shrouded lake very near to Mt. McKinley The lake dumped into—or *formed*, depending upon your interpretation of its outflow—the crystal-clear and fish-laden waters of Lake Creek. This beautiful stream, which pretty much flowed southward through almost completely empty country, dumped into the busy Yentna River and then into the long, silty, and famous Big Susitna River, where it lost all its clear-water beauty and, after a few more almost sluggish miles, quietly slipped into the dark and frigid waters of Cook Inlet.

The flight that morning was a routine one for the Beaver—just one of a seemingly endless string of such flights during Alaska's busy summer tourist season. Besides sightseers, people flock to the state at this time each year to fish. They thrash and beat the cold, clear Alaska waters for all five varieties of Pacific salmon, as well as for Alaska's famous rainbow trout, arctic char, and

Dolly Varden, the delicate arctic grayling, sheefish, northern pike, lake trout, burbot, and a wide variety of other fresh- and saltwater specimens. The discriminating and dedicated angler might even find cutthroat and golden trout here. And, for the more particular fisherman, huge and delicious halibut could be pulled from the chilly Pacific waters near Homer or Seward.

This flight, unhappily, was doomed to disaster from the moment the pilot began cranking up the big 450-horsepower Pratt & Whitney R-985-AN14-B radial engine preparatory to his takeoff earlier in the day. Something of an oil leaker at times, this reliable engine has for decades powered the Beaver—and a million other aircraft—through both the Canadian and the Alaska backcountry. In fact, the Beaver is really pretty much like the old Douglas C-47s and DC-3s in that regard: flown in every remote part the world and known as remarkably tough and encouragingly dependable.

The four stateside passengers slated to be aboard this flight had arrived at the ABC dock sometime between seven and eight o'clock that morning of July 5, 1997. Upon arrival, they were each asked his or her approximate weights, along with the weight of all the gear and baggage. At the end of this short but meaningful inquiry, the pilot began fueling the large floatplane.

Satisfied that the Beaver could accommodate the roughly calculated load, he then began loading the airplane. As usual, the light stuff went in first. This was almost always shoved to the rear of the baggage area during Alaska bush operations. Heavier stuff was loaded aboard in a more forward location, presumably to keep the baggage and miscellaneous gear within the gravity envelope for that particular plane.

However roomy the Beaver seems to be, it is still sometimes not quite roomy enough. This day, a part of the passengers' gear had to be left behind. Another pilot would ferry that gear to Chelatna Lake Lodge. That second flight would occur a few hours later that same day, so the passengers wouldn't be left without their remaining gear for more than a very short time.

It has to be noted here that the pilot neglected to tie down the freight and gear that was then aboard. I'm well aware of how easily familiarity can breed contempt among Alaska's outback pilots. After days and weeks and months of routine banging around up there in our little airplanes, we tend to take everything pretty much for granted. This flight, for example, was about to lift off for a pass across virtually flat and level country, and on a bright, calm, and sunny morning. What the hell could possibly go wrong that an experienced Alaska pilot couldn't handle in the normal course of today's events? Well, they were all about to learn.

It wasn't really necessary, from a practical standpoint, for the pilot to check on the weather—heck, they could all see Mt. McKinley from the dock where they were standing. And that mountain, standing majestically tall about 138-nautical miles north of the dock, was *well* beyond their intended landing at Chelatna Lake. Every good pilot checks the weather, of course. More than that, the FAA directs him to do just that, as well as to check every other source of information for matters that might even remotely affect the coming flight.

At any rate, the weather must have been somewhere around 2,500 to 3,500 feet scattered, just then. The pilot would fly VFR (visual flight rules) at an altitude of 2,000 feet, well below any clouds they might encounter en route. He would file his flight plan with his flight operations and again with the Federal Aviation Administration.

The pilot cast off the forward and aft lines—very likely in that order—grasped the horizontal stabilizer, turned the compliant airplane just a bit to point it away from the dock, then jumped aboard the float deck, walking forward to climb aboard and enter his complex front office.

Using standard operating procedures for starting the big radial engine—procedures frequently taken directly from the *Pilot Operating Handbook*—he soon had the sturdy floatplane gliding smoothly away from the dock. Taxiing at first north, the pilot would soon have turned eastward to head through the channel that linked Lake Hood with its eastern neighbor, Lake Spenard. Once at the eastern end of that barbell-shaped, two-lake body of water, the pilot would have verified the engine temperature, run through the required magneto checks, verified the throttle's full travel and effect, checked full travel of the flight controls, and then notified the tower on 119.4 that he was ready for the west departure. By now he also would have set and checked his flaps for the takeoff setting, set the mixture control at full rich, placed the propeller at high rpms, and adjusted the airplane's trim and directional gyrocompass settings for the takeoff.

It's likely the tower had immediately cleared Beaver 5164G for the western waterway, and, with a smooth advance of the pedestal-mounted throttle and raising of the water rudders, the pilot would have pulled the nose up and waited for the accelerating ship to rise up on the floats' steps for the takeoff.

Once the loaded Beaver had lifted smoothly off the water, and as it passed through the west end of the channel, the pilot would have gently rolled into a turn toward the north, pushed the nose down in order to level off, and reset throttle, propeller pitch, flaps, and transponder code for the short Knik Arm water crossing toward Point McKinley. From there on, the flight could be expected to be smooth, sunny, and most pleasant.

It was here that the passengers began looking out the side windows, searching for moose or maybe a black bear or two. Very likely, they saw some.

Once past Twin Island Lake, the pilot would have adjusted the pitch again and advanced the throttle just a bit for the smooth climb to altitude, in this case two thousand feet.

As they passed over the Little Susitna River ten or fifteen minutes out, and probably not far upstream from Little Susitna Station, depending upon the pilot's exact route of flight, one of the passengers was comparing his personal GPS (global positioning system) to that of the airplane-mounted unit. He may have smiled to himself as he saw they were precisely synchronized.

The pilot had no doubt calculated from experience that the flight would take about one hour and ten minutes, more or less. It wasn't really going to last that long at all.

It was somewhere along about here, forty-five minutes or so into the flight, that the engine hiccupped. It cut out for about one second, then began running smoothly again. One of those mysteries that all pilots encounter from time to time, the pilot was probably thinking.

He wasn't about to let this surprise pass without his close attention, of course, and he no doubt immediately began a scan of his engine instruments for any indication of what might have just happened. Oil pressure—okay; fuel selector switch on the fuller tank—okay; magneto switch to both—okay, manifold pressure—okay. . . . "Ah," he must have thought, "A drop of water or something in the fuel, probably."

Rather than take a chance with his passengers, though, safe was better than sorry, and the pilot immediately rolled into a left turn and began looking for a suitable lake for a precautionary landing where he might sort things out. Or, if things really went sour, an emergency landing spot for the loaded Beaver.

Weather at the airplane's location around this time was recorded as a broken cloud level at 1,500 feet above the ground. Visibility was reported at fifteen nautical miles, the usual *maximum* visibility reported. You should know that this often means more than 200 miles of clear visibility in the normally dry atmosphere of interior Alaska. Remember that the group had already seen tall Mt. McKinley from Alaska Bush Carrier's floating dock.

Since the engine seemed to perform well once again, the passengers were comfortable in letting the pilot worry about the little glitch in its performance. In retrospect, it seems that he might have been more than a tad uncomfortable about this "little glitch."

For the next few minutes—probably less than five, though—the pilot continued a slow descent, still intent upon finding a suitable parking place for

The author operates one of the remote lodge's boats on Chelatna Lake, near Mt. Denali (formerly Mt. McKinley), the highest point in North America. The big mountain is just outside the photo on the right. *Photo by John Erskine, Anchorage, Alaska*

his reluctant flying machine. It had continued to cough and sputter intermittently, and now he wasn't at all comfortable with the heavy load behind him. It is likely that the disturbing coughs and hiccups occurred every ten or fifteen seconds, but there were no loud noises at all from the engine compartment. The pilot was certain that the engine wasn't even then trying to swallow something that it shouldn't.

No loud banging noises, no loud, sharp slapping sounds, nothing screamed as though being stressed or cracked, and no vibrations outside those of a slowly descending De Havilland Beaver floatplane.

The pilot was using his radio, too, transmitting and receiving to and from we can only guess whom. Perhaps his own company on a discreet frequency, perhaps to someone listening on "Guard" frequency, the international emergency frequency at 121.5. At any rate, one supposes he felt a bit rushed at this point. For my own part, I don't believe he was trying to raise his company on its discrete frequency, since no one there seemed aware that anything had gone wrong with this flight.

The earth was now approaching his airplane a little faster than he liked, one can presume. He hadn't spotted any lakes that really thrilled him, and Lake Creek was not in any way suitable for his float-equipped Beaver. Nor for a little two-place Super Cub, either, for that matter. With vertical walls and shallow, rushing waters, nearby Lake Creek was the least inviting of his choices at that moment.

Finally, the pilot realized that good fortune wasn't what was going to leap up and smack him on the forehead this morning, and he turned to advise the passengers that they were going to land. One of the passengers asked, "Where are we going to land?" and the pilot pointed to a small lake directly beneath the airplane.

It is understandable that the pilot found it encouraging to hold his faltering airplane near to that small body of water. Sort of like a moth to the flames. I was in much the same situation once, and I know the attraction of perceived warmth and safety. On the other hand, he was in a bad place if he was directly above the small lake with a faltering engine. Both he and the passengers had by this time realized that they were much too high to land on this particular body of water, if the airplane finally did decide to give it up for the day. Descending straight down becomes something of a high-speed descent, as it were. A lay person, in fact, might even apply the term "dive" to such a descent.

From this point forward, the pilot's actions—or perhaps his lack of action—can only be presumed. He certainly knew he was in the cow pies up to his ears. Whether or not he lost his cool at this point can only be conjecture. What is clear is that the float-equipped Beaver finally impacted the boggy terrain in an almost vertical attitude.

The Beaver met the earth at the edge of a small lake that later measured about 1,200 feet long by 700 feet wide. It seems possible to me, seated now at my computer and buried in the comfort of my Knoll office chair, that the pilot, with proper approach techniques, might well have made a successful emergency landing on this lake. After all, it was as long as three football fields placed end to end. Moreover, the airplane manual states that the landing distance for this floatplane—over a 50-foot obstacle!—is 1,500 feet. Unless the little lake was surrounded tightly by tall trees, which I think was not the case, an *emergency* landing surely was possible. Clearly that didn't happen.

Perhaps the pilot was holding the Beaver in a steep turn, bleeding off air speed and trying to keep the right wing from coming over the top by using heavy pressure on the right rudder pedal, a control input that would hold that wing down for a short time. It sometimes *feels* as though this might work, but every experienced pilot knows better. If that's what was going on, it is very likely that the lower wing just stalled out at its lower air speed, giving the right wing an open invitation to come quickly over the top in the beginnings of a violent spin to the left.

The airplane's manual notes that the stall speed of this airplane when in a sixty-degree bank, and without flaps, is 115 miles per hour, faster than the Beaver's normal cruising speed. It also cautions that flight loads, in tight turns, may reach their load limits and, at the same time, increase the danger of an unintentional stall. A stall out of a steep turn has all the ingredients necessary for a full, big-time spin! At low altitudes, a disastrous result can safely be predicted.

It is noted here, too, that both lakes and other open areas larger than the lake that the pilot was fixated upon were quite near, and certainly within the Beaver's gliding distance. One has to wonder why a larger area had not earlier on been selected for the intended landing?

The Beaver came to rest at an angle of almost ninety degrees to the horizon. Virtually straight up and down! The aircraft, including its huge floats, was found buried in the boggy earth. The Beaver was so close to the lake that its right wingtip extended out over the water. The left wing was lying on the swampy ground. The left wingtip was curled upward at about sixty degrees and crushed aft.

The fuselage, tail section, and other features aft of the wings seemed undamaged. The forward portion, beginning at the wing attach points, was buried in the swampy ground.

Later investigation revealed that the hydraulic flap actuator was in its fully extended position. The flap position indicator showed the flaps to have been in the "Full Flaps" position. The vertical speed indicator (the gauge we used to call the rate of climb), indicated a one-thousand-foot-per-minute rate of descent at the time of impact.

The throttle was still set at its full forward (full power) position. Strangely, the propeller pitch control showed that the pitch had not been adjusted to its high-rpm setting, as it should have been for *any* approach to a landing, emergency or otherwise. The carburetor heat control was still in its "Off" position, which seems odd, while the electrical master switch had been moved to its "Off" position in preparation for the emergency landing. On the other hand, the tachometer was left to read 3,000 REVOLUTIONS PER MINUTE, certainly above a gliding or power-off setting one would expect to see at such a time. The emergency fuel and oil shut-off switch was still in its stowed position, its safety wire still intact.

It would appear to me—regardless of an official government appraisal—that the pilot was still fighting to fly the airplane at the time of impact. And, in fact, may have been trying even then to recover from a classic stall-spin situation.

The sole survivor of this tragedy later reported that the pilot and his front seat passenger were being held underwater by the load of baggage and other gear. Which had not been tied down, you will remember, and which had, upon impact, rushed forward to seal the fate of anything or anyone ahead. On the other hand, autopsies confirmed that deaths were caused by blunt impact injury due to an airplane crash.

Still, though, the survivor, who had been on the right-rear bench seat, said that he observed the pilot try several times to get his head above the water. He also saw the gear bags thrust upward from below a couple of times, but this action soon stopped.

The first rescuer to reach the site noted that both the pilot and the front seat passenger were completely submerged. Two other passengers were being held face down in the water by the load of gear and baggage resting atop their bodies.

Finally, the ELT was located in the tail cone. Its power and antenna cables were still firmly attached, but the transmitter was set to its "Off" position. No ELT signal had been heard from the crash site. It had been located by another company pilot who had departed Lake Hood with the party's remaining gear and baggage.

When that pilot had arrived at Chelatna Lake, only to discover that the first flight had not yet arrived, he immediately took off and back-tracked toward Anchorage. He found the Beaver at the accident site, three hours after the crash. It was noted that the site was about seventy nautical miles north of Lake Hood and forty miles from its destination at Chelatna Lake. The pilot had flown almost a perfectly straight flight route from Lake Hood to the crash site.

To make this all the more intriguing, it was found that only two days before the crash, the pilot had passed a fifty-minute FAA competency and proficiency check-ride in the Beaver. Among those procedures tested were: powerplant (engine) failure, approaches to stalls, and emergency procedures.

An interesting footnote to this accident pops up here. About ten months before this accident, on September 3, 1996, this same pilot had been involved in another floatplane accident. This one happened during a takeoff from the water near the eastern shore of Lake Clark and at the village of Port Alsworth. This time the pilot was flying a Cessna 206 Stationair floatplane. The FAA's determination was, although unfavorable winds were a factor, the accident was caused by the pilot's inadequate compensation for the winds.

Chapter 18

New to Aerobatics

TRY TO KEEP THE NUMBER OF LANDINGS EQUAL TO THE NUMBER OF TAKEOFFS.

I had decided to take some aerobatic training. The real "stunt pilots"—and it's not fair to call them stunt pilots, since what they do is really precision flying—know exactly what both they and their airplanes can do, and they have developed the skills required in order to operate right up against the abilities and capabilities of both. I had determined that, if I was to do very much edge-of-the-envelope flying, I had better get a firm grasp on the limits that I dare not cross.

It was my good fortune to tie up with a former Czechoslovakian Air Force fighter pilot by the name of Egan Knets (pronounced *Ay*-gon Ka-*netts*). Egan wasn't much for size, standing just short of my five feet nine inches. He must have weighed around 140 pounds. Between his height and his light weight, he would have made one helluva bush pilot, I thought.

As a civilian pilot, Egan was still having a hard time getting used to inside loops—which most of us called simply "country loops"—since our little Cessna 152 Aerobats and the Citabria line of two-place aerobatic airplanes performed these simple loops with an inside diameter of around three hundred feet or so. His former military fighting machines, of course, used up a whole lot more of the vertical sky for the same maneuver, and while he could certainly perform perfect loops, he still couldn't get used to the small loop the lesser planes made.

Anyway, the country loops and aileron rolls and barrel rolls came easily enough in the Citabria and Decathlon models, once I got used to the first feelings of disorientation. I was soon making those loops with enough skill to feel the small "bump" in the seat of my pants when we came out at the bottom at precisely the same place where we had started the maneuver.

I had to be a little more careful with the country loops when flying the Cessna Aerobat, though. My left elbow rested on the armrest of the pilot's door, and when I would move the wheel aft in order to begin the climb, my left elbow wanted to drop with the motion. Since the armrest stopped that downward motion, I had a tendency to turn the wheel slightly to the right. This, of course, made the airplane want to start a slight bank or roll, and I would have to look out the side windows as I went over the top to make sure that the wings were still level, even though inverted. A little attention on my part got rid of that habit.

It was the snap roll at the top of a loop that boggled me for a time. Neither of us had studied the aerobatics handbook that comes with the Cessna Aerobat, so we just approached that maneuver in the same manner that we attacked the simple inside loop. Lower the nose about forty-five degrees to pick up some air speed—in this case about 145 indicated—then begin the two and a half to three g pull-up. That air speed didn't leave us with enough left over at the top for the required snap roll, and at each attempt I found myself falling out of the sky at the top and in a dive with full power.

Well, we tried until we were both blue in the face and totally confused, but nothing would get us through that snap roll at the top. We decided to poop around with some other maneuvers, and then we returned to the home field, this time to sneak a peek into the manual.

Sure enough, the handbook told us that we needed to enter the maneuver with about 165 knots indicated airspeed. Next time out, the maneuver went much better. Neither of us had suspected that the required air speed for this maneuver would be the same as the redline speed (do not exceed air speed) for the little ship, so we had avoided that. Earlier, we finally did get up to about 160 knots for one or two tries, but it turned out that this was still a few knots short.

Inverted flight was easy enough, though anything less than a really clean cockpit left sand, grit, and dust falling "upward" toward the top of the cockpit. And loose objects in a shirt pocket found their way to the "ceiling," too. It pays to keep a clean house if you're going to go inverted.

Later, when I became bored with calm, sunny days and was flying an empty Super Cub over some of Alaska's more remote outback areas,

I would occasionally break the monotony by flying through another good ol' country loop or two. Once in a while, though only rarely, I would overfly my bush landing spot, pull up into half a country loop, and then roll right-side up at the top, headed in the opposite direction. Aerobatic pilots know this as an "Immelman Turn." At other times, I might pull the Cub skyward, go over the top of a country loop, and at forty-five degrees on the back side, half-roll it on the way down. Half of a "Cuban Eight," actually. I certainly don't condone this sort of flying, and I never, *never* did that sort of thing with a passenger in the plane. But I do admit to having done some of this foolishness from time to time, and I believe it helped to make me a safer pilot in the long run. I have to admit that it was sorta fun to execute half a floatplane Cuban Eight for an approach to some wilderness lake or other, but I surely don't recommend this maneuver, either!

For those of you who just can't stand it, I should tell you that the Super Cub has notoriously small ailerons. Takes about a week to labor one through an aileron roll, and I really don't recommend this to you. And remember—the FAA wants you to wear a parachute and fly only an airplane built to the higher stress ratings of an aerobatic airplane. Planes like the Decathlon, the Citabria, or the Cessna 152 Aerobat. There are others, of course, and much better ones. The Pitts, for instance. Both the one- and the two-holer. But the run-of-the-mill light aircraft just wasn't constructed for the g loads attendant to aerobatic flying. Especially for the heavy handed or inexperienced. So, just stay away from such maneuvers unless you wear a 'chute and are flying an appropriately rated aircraft.

The toughest maneuver I ever staggered through was a 360-degree turn with four aileron rolls at the quarter points. Definitely not a maneuver for the low-powered Citabria or Cessna lines, it's something set aside for something like a Pitts—I was flying a one-holer Pitts Special at the time.

Maybe my most favorite maneuver as a fledgling aerobatic pilot was a four-point roll. This is just an aileron roll with a pause at each 90-degree point. My first attempt at this maneuver was a shocker. I was alone in a Citabria (a 7KCAB Model, for those who care) and was doing fine until the 270-degree point. Looking back on it, I know that my air speed was a bit on the low side. At any rate, the airplane began to shudder on the edge of a knife-edge stall, and just as I was about to complete the roll, the left window blew out. I can tell you, *that* got my attention!

I realized almost immediately what had happened, but not before my heart rate had gone up just a tad. With the racket from the air blasting through and around the missing window, I limped the stricken little ship back to the fixed base operator (FOB) where I had rented it.

When I explained what had happened, the mechanic there didn't seem too concerned about it. The next day, and with a new window installed, I did the same damned thing! I'm a slow learner, but it was just about there that I determined a little more air speed was needed for the last knife-edge pause at the three-quarter point in that maneuver. I can truthfully say that I haven't lost another window since.

While banner-tow flying isn't in the aerobatic line, much the same mysterious happenstance jolted me just after I was wheels-down with the Cessna Amphibian at Palm Beach in Florida. I had decided to keep my flying hand in by towing banners along the golden beaches of southeast Florida. To do so meant passing an oral examination and then a practical flight test. And, to give you an idea how some believe banner towing to be just a little on the dangerous side, I can tell you that my FAA examiner refused to ride in the airplane during the flight portion of the exam.

I guess this shouldn't be considered all that unusual, since banner towing is an exercise in extreme "slow flying," a condition that puts the pilot on the sharp edge of aircraft performance. If the pilot somehow screws up, or if anything should somehow go wrong, especially near the ground, things can go south for him in a hurry. Knowing this, many flight inspectors are a bit hesitant to climb aboard with a pilot whose skills are virtually unknown to the inspector. It really isn't hard, for example, for the pilot to toss the big treble hook out his window only to have it hang up on the left main gear, the left horizontal stabilizer, or some other exterior appendage. When that happens, certainly no inspector wants to be aboard. Neither does the pilot, for that matter.

After answering all the examiner's questions and walking him through the banner-tow line attachment procedures, he told me to blast off and pick up a banner that had been placed on the field.

For those of you who are not familiar with banner towing, and without going into it in any great depth, here's pretty much the simplified version. The pilot attaches one end of a line to a contraption near the tail wheel (of a tandem-geared airplane, in this case) and passes the other end through the left-side cockpit window, where a large and wicked-looking treble hook is hung on the windshield cross-braces (or some other convenient place). After takeoff, the pilot tosses this hook unceremoniously out his left-side window, then sticks his head out into the slipstream and looks back to make sure the hook is still attached to the airplane. If it is, he then flies around the field, making a low and slow approach to what appears to be a miniature football goalpost alongside the active runway. A line is stretched between these two uprights. It sags in the middle, of course, but not to worry. . . .

To this sagging line, another line is attached, this one perpendicular to the one stretched between the uprights and secured to the advertising banner to be flown on that hop. The banner itself, a series of letters attached to a complex nylon webbing system, carries a long steel pipe at its leading end. This stabilizes the banner and tends to hold it upright. It's a heavy piece of plumbing, and our worst fear ever was the thought of having to drop that banner in case of an emergency. We tried sincerely to avoid flying over schools and large parking lots with that potentially death-dealing weapon following along behind us. At any rate . . .

As the examiner stood safely along the runway, I powered up the Citabria Scout that I was to fly, took to the active runway, and lit out toward the Atlantic Ocean on an east departure. As I left the ground and gained a few feet, I pitched the big treble hook out the window and looked back to make sure it was still there. It was.

After making my turns and lining up for the banner snatch, for that's what it is, I made sure I had achieved an airspeed of seventy miles per hour with two notches of flaps and approached the pickup point.

Immediately after the firewall passed the pickup standards, and at an altitude of five or six feet, I pulled up into a staggeringly steep climb, a necessary pull-up that is required to get the banner off the ground in the shortest amount of time. Dragging a banner through the grass is a good way to lose an alarming amount of air speed! At the top of this short, sharp climb, the air speed needle was usually somewhere between fifty and sixty miles an hour.

On this particular occasion, I didn't feel any drag from the banner and was rather surprised. I thought I had nailed the thing right on the button! As I rolled into my first left turn for a go-around, I looked back to discover that the banner wasn't following me and that the hook itself was gone! Impossible!

To make this long story short, I will tell you that no one has found that hook even today, and this happened more than twenty years ago. I still wonder . . . where the hell did that hook go?

Oh, yeah, I did pass the test that morning, and I did get the required low altitude waiver for banner towing operations. Turns out that it was kind of neat to fly at two hundred feet along the beaches and ogle all the bathing beauties down there. Hey—don't you guys tell my wife I said that. . . .

Chapter 19

It Does Happen

THE PROBABILITY OF SURVIVAL IS INVERSELY PROPORTIONAL TO THE ANGLE OF ARRIVAL.

It takes constant attention to overcome the tendency that allows familiarity to breed contempt. Most of Alaska's backcountry pilots have done this goofy sort of flying stuff for so many long and boring hours that it's pretty easy for us to become casual about what we do. Imagine yourself, if you will, strapped to a tiny seat in a very small—really small—office for eight hours each and every day. Then imagine that this lasted for more than nine and a half continuous years, summer and winter, spring and fall. You can't stand, you can't stretch, and you can't really change your position. You're simply strapped into your small seat for the equivalent of twenty thousand hours over those long nine and a half years.

Given that scenario, would you ever let your own mind wander, even for a moment or two? Very likely! Would boredom sometimes take over and leave you hanging on the ropes of complacency? Most certainly. Well, that's about the story of every longtime Alaska bush pilot, too. I'm here to tell you that sometimes we develop just a bit of contempt for the little things. Unfortunately, it doesn't take very many of those little things to become something really big, when you're banging around above some pretty unfriendly real estate in a bush-modified flying machine. One prime example of "one of those little things" might be the very important task of fuel awareness and management.

Many bush-capable airplanes—and this includes the workhorse Piper Super Cub and the comfortable Cessna 185 and 206 lines—have a fuel management system that won't allow the pilot to select fuel from both wing tanks at the same time. He must choose to use fuel from either the left or the right wing tank.

It was my habit to fly for either thirty minutes or one hour on one tank—depending upon the airplane model and the gross load—and then move the fuel selector valve to allow an equal amount to flow from the opposite wing tank. This kept the aircraft pretty well in balance, laterally, and neither wing was allowed to become too "heavy" with fuel when compared with the opposite wing, which would in turn demand either a change in a trim setting or constant control pressure to keep the heavy wing up and level with the lighter one.

Unless the pilot keeps track of the time when he started using fuel from the first tank, then when he selected the second, then when he went back to the first, and so on, he has allowed familiarity and complacency to become contempt for the potential penalties of any error.

For example, let's say the weather isn't as good as it might be, you've flown several hours to reach your destination—which, by the way, doesn't usually present much in the way of an improved airstrip—and you're ready for a good stretch and maybe a hot cup of camp coffee. As you approach your intended landing place, the weather turns even worse, and you have just about run out of alternates for your landing spot. The upcoming landing is going to tax your skills. Just visualize a narrow, gravel bar along a small stream in a very tiny valley with dramatically steep sides. You get the picture. There's almost no room for turnaround—which means precious little room for error—and the weather is now even worse over the rising ground up ahead.

You're most likely less than eight or ten seconds from touchdown. Are you now flying on the fuller of the fuel tanks? You sure as hell aren't going to stop to figure that out right now, so you'd better have it firmly planted in the back of your mind. Maybe it won't matter. But—maybe it will.

What if you have to execute something of a missed approach and go around for a second try. I promise that your turns will have to be steeper than "standard" turns. If your fuel system relies upon gravity—it almost certainly does—and you suddenly enter a steep turn with an empty tank in the high wing, trouble is just about to smack you on the back of the head.

And all this fuel management business was pretty small potatoes, just a few moments ago, wasn't it? Well, it ain't now, partner.

It's this sort of familiarity coupled with the potential for trouble that has caused a whole lot of really serious problems. Sometimes it's only a matter of a bent airplane lying almost helpless in some very remote and hard to reach location. Sometimes it's a matter of an injured pilot or passengers. And sometimes it's even more tragic, with bodies that must be removed and returned for their last rides and last rites. Consider some of the following accidents.

The matter of repeated preflight inspections sometimes seems so mundane as to be almost a waste of time. Still, a small bolt in the flap/aileron interconnect system in a Cessna 180 floatplane caused a problem that ended in near disaster when the left aileron went into the trail position and the right aileron drooped during an approach to landing. This occurred near Big Lake, Alaska, only ten flying minutes from Anchorage. An uncontrolled descent followed, and the airplane was substantially damaged. Fortunately, the commercial pilot, flying alone, wasn't seriously injured. His airplane, though, was a complete loss when it plunged into the water. Mechanical failures, while extremely rare, do happen. Closer attention during preflight inspections *might* have made this failure a non-event. The Cessna's last annual inspection surely should have. After all, that's what they're for!

Sometimes, the reason for equipment failure is never determined. Take, for instance, the Piper Super Cub whose pilot noticed a drop in both engine revolutions and oil pressure while about fifteen minutes out of McGrath, on the far side of Alaska's Rainy Pass. He elected to put the little plane down in an area of brush and small trees bordering a swampy area. The airplane was substantially damaged, but the pilot escaped without injury. Let's hear it for cool Alaska pilots and Mr. Piper's great little Super Cub!

Another Super Cub pilot and his passenger escaped injury—even though the little airplane was completely destroyed—when the pilot allowed it to stall while they were scouting for moose in the mountains near Soldotna, Alaska. Slow flight and steep turns are a very poor mix, and it was always my policy that I would do the flying while my passenger did the looking. There may be nothing more final than a low-wing stall close to the ground. This is true even with the fabulous Super Cub, which, as I've said before, has notoriously small ailerons.

When the low wing stalls, it tends to plunge toward the earth, with the high wing—flying farther and faster than the lower wing—coming very quickly over the top. It happens so quickly, in fact, that the pilot, if not trained in aerobatics, can be completely disoriented for just a moment. It's here that a violent spin begins. While spins aren't in and of themselves dangerous, each revolution may require the loss of between five hundred and seven hundred feet of altitude. If the pilot had his aircraft down at two or three hundred feet at the time, you can see how that flight was going to end. Very badly indeed.

Then there are the truly mysterious accidents. Like the Cessna 182 that plunged into cold and unfriendly Cook Inlet near English Bay on September 4, 1985. Neither the aircraft nor its pilot was ever recovered, and the National Transportation Safety Board (NTSB) holds the causative factors of this accident as: "Reason for Occurrence Undetermined."

Sometimes pressure from outside sources leads to something less than a happy landing. This was the case of the Cessna 207 pilot who was told by his employer to make a pickup flight to Chuathbaluk, Alaska. Fuel quantity aboard was apparently unknown. The reason given was a broken fuel tank cap on the right wing. I frankly don't understand the reasoning here, but that's the stated excuse for not knowing the usable fuel load aboard.

The operator nonetheless ordered the pilot to take off with no idea how long he might be able to fly before the engine starved out and quit. Fortunately, the pilot was flying alone when the engine finally did give up, forcing him to make an emergency landing in a nearby river. I think the owner/operator of this small charter service should be thankful for a pilot with the flying skills to safely dead-stick such a big floatplane out there in the bush. On the other hand, I can't imagine why the pilot agreed to take off in the first place. Needed the job, I guess.

There are times, too, when pilot error is so flagrant as to be almost obscene. Take the commercial pilot who was headed through Merrill Pass with two passengers during the last few days of May in 1985. This was an air taxi operation based out of Anchorage, and the airplane involved was one of the greatest of all bush planes, a De Havilland DHC-2 Beaver, Registration Number N5317G.

The pilot had obtained a weather briefing before takeoff and learned that the pass was forecast closed *in deteriorating weather*. That means the weather wasn't getting any better. The pilot had made radio contact with the McGrath Flight Service Station and, in a PIREP, he advised that the weather was at that time marginal, with visibility out to only two miles in snow showers and moderate turbulence.

Now, two miles visibility is not really all that bad to most Alaska bush pilots if they are flying through a really familiar part of the outback. Many can get along just fine with only one mile, a half-mile, or even a quarter-mile. This last is true only when flying over flat, unobstructed, wide-open country or along a beach, of course.

At any rate, that transmission was the last that was heard from the Beaver pilot. The wreckage was found at an elevation of 3,600 feet. The pass itself, as

I remember it, is down around 2,400 feet, while the ridge saddle immediately beside it on the southern side of the pass soars up to slightly above 4,000 feet. What the pilot was doing at 3,600 feet confuses me, and I wonder whether or not he was really familiar with this sometimes-tricky pass.

In any event, the pilot had no business dragging passengers along on such a scabby flying day. And through such a tight little mountain pass to boot. That pass is virtually lined with the remains of aircraft whose pilots had tried the same thing in years past. Do we never learn? Or does familiarity truly lead to such contempt for our flying machines and their environments that we lose sight of common sense?

Not all light aircraft accidents are limited to Alaska, of course. Pilots do goofy things in other parts of the country, too. Take, for instance, the two pilots in a Cessna 177A, N30491, near South Hackensack, New Jersey.

The accident, which occurred just before 11 PM on the night of September 2, 2005, took the life of the private pilot, while her student pilot passenger was seriously injured. This tragedy would have been easy to predict, since the student pilot later stated that she had absolutely no idea how much fuel was aboard, while the private pilot, and pilot-in-command, only "*thought* there was enough." The private pilot had also "thought" the fuel gauges were wrong.

Let me say again that any pilot who relies on the fuel gauges rather than on clock time and known fuel consumption is looking for trouble. Period. Every pilot knows, or should know, how much fuel his airplane uses at various cruise settings. If your airplane isn't equipped with a fuel flow meter, your wristwatch or the airplane clock can be the best tool you have with which to calculate fuel availability. Use it. But, back to this unfortunate accident . . .

The pilot had contacted New York TRACON just before ten thirty that evening. Though no flight plan had been filed for their flight from Block Island State Airport in Rhode Island to Essex County Airport at Caldwell, New Jersey, the pilot was requesting flight following services. She reported the airplane level at three thousand feet and about five miles west of Fisher's Island, New York. Performance charts for that airplane show that she could have glided to that airport from there, even with a dead engine and a windmilling propeller. That, of course, presumes that the pilot sets up the proper glide speed and trim configuration. A headwind would reduce the glide distance over the ground, of course, and these two pilots were fighting about a five-mile-per-hour headwind. From here on out, it was going to be a losing battle for them. While neither could be certain of that, one can only imagine the apprehension each must have endured during the last moments of that night flight through the dark skies of New Jersey.

The pilot received a transponder code and continued the flight until about a quarter past eleven, at which time she declared an emergency, stating that "the plane is stalling." I presume she meant that the engine was beginning to miss. Whatever the pilot meant at the time, she was then requesting clearance and assistance in landing as soon as possible.

With the generous glide ratios of the Cessna line of light aircraft, the pilot should have been able to make a safe landing anywhere within a five-mile radius. That would depend, as I've said, on the pilot's having set up the proper glide speed in the first place. In this case, they would fall short of the airport's Runway 24 approach end by less than one city block! *One lousy block!*

Issued a heading then of 240 degrees for vectors to Teterboro, only eight miles distant, the pilot was told she had a choice of either Runway 19 or Runway 24. She chose Runway 24. The choice would turn out to be academic, since the two ladies were destined to land short of the airport anyway.

At 11:17 that evening, the pilot reported the field directly ahead and reported that, "I'm high enough to make it." One minute later, she changed her mind and reported that she now only "hoped" to make it to the runway.

Once cleared to land, she now stated that, "I don't think I can make it to the runway." Nothing more was heard from either the pilot or the student pilot passenger after that transmission.

The aircraft first hit a twenty-five-foot-tall utility pole about one-quarter mile from the approach end of Runway 24. The tip of the left horizontal stabilizer had been torn free at that point, and white paint was discovered on the pole, down about two feet from the top. The tip of the stabilizer was found at the base of the pole.

The path of the remaining wreckage was only about fifty feet long and headed generally in alignment with the runway. The airplane came to rest in an approximate forty-five-degree nose-down attitude. The left outboard wing section was crushed inboard, and a garbage dumpster was embedded into the left side of the cockpit area, right where the pilot was sitting strapped into her small seat.

I have to think that the pilot saw that dumpster coming at her just before she died, growing larger and more indestructible just outside her window with every millisecond. I suppose she didn't have time to think how easy it would have been simply to top off the tanks back at Block Island before they took off that night.

As an aside to this tragedy, it is noted that a review of the pilot's FAA medical file shows that she had answered "No" when responding to the question: "Do you currently use any medication?" She had also answered "No" to all entries under "Medical History," including specifically "Mental disorders of any sort, depression, anxiety, etc."

Toxicological testing by both the Bergen County Medical Examiner's Office and the FAA Toxicology and Accident Research Laboratory in Oklahoma found her blood to contain: 0.047 (ug/ml, ug/g) of diazepam and 0.056 (ug/ml, ug/g) of nordiazepam. Further, 0.134 (ug/ml, ug/g) of nordiazepam was found in her liver.

Maybe I should also tell you that the pilot reported her occupation as "psychologist" and that she was self-employed.

It doesn't make me feel any better to tell you that the student pilot passenger insisted, before departure from Block Island, that the private pilot "get night current" and that she waited inside the FBO there while the private pilot performed several full-stop and touch-and-go landings.

It's interesting to speculate on the fact that the Cessna 177 probably was flown that night at 75 percent power at an altitude of three thousand feet. The fuel rate burn was very likely about ten gallons per hour. I have to wonder whether or not the pilot bothered to use the EGT (exhaust temperature gauge) to properly lean the engine to best performance power settings. If she hadn't, then having done so would have left her with enough fuel to make a safe landing and to later taxi to both the tiedown area and the gas pumps before her next departure. Ah, well . . . these things do happen. And, unhappily, will probably continue to happen.

***

One of the world's most comfortable, and certainly one of the safest, general aviation airplanes is the faithful Cessna 172. Mild-mannered, gentle in all configurations, and as dependable as the sun and the moon, this incredible little airplane still has its limits. Witness the flight that occurred on September 2, 2005.

The owner/pilot of Cessna N5070A wanted some photographs of a little piece of property he was selling. His passenger and photographer for this short trip was seated in the pilot's left seat, while the pilot occupied the right front. Records show that the pilot had more than 800 flying hours, 640 of which were logged in the accident airplane. It is unlikely, though, that any of those hours had been logged from the right seat.

Having performed the aerial photography to the owner's approval, the pair turned back toward the airport at Yuma, Arizona. The weather was fine, and a gentle breeze at about seven knots was aligned with Runway 8 at Yuma International. It was about eight thirty in the morning, and there shouldn't have been any appreciable turbulence at that hour.

The pilot made his approach and had set things up for a full-flap landing. He later stated that everything was just fine, until the Cessna began descending too fast. Any of you who have flown the Cessna family of barn-door-flap-equipped airplanes knows that full flaps (forty-degree displacement) can put the pilot on the edge of his seat if the air speed is allowed to get too low. The gentle bird can sink like a rock under those conditions.

Exactly that was happening to this Cessna, and the pilot edged in a little power to get back ahead of the power curve. A "little power," though, isn't enough with those huge flaps hanging down out there, and at about fifty feet above the ground, the pilot held in a little too much back pressure. The nose pitched up and then fell through. A perfectly executed power-on stall.

But about three hundred vertical feet are normally required for the pullout from a full stall, though this determined pilot was able to bring the aircraft back to an almost level attitude before it impacted the earth.

The Cessna had hit the ground well short of Runway 8 and, after impact, skidded about eighty yards along its direction of travel. Immediately upon coming to rest, the Cessna burst into flames. The fuselage was burned entirely. The passenger was killed, but the pilot survived with a handful of serious injuries. And a conscience that no doubt haunts him still. Familiarity breeds contempt. Indeed it does.

The really experienced pilots seem to get into at least as much trouble as their less experienced fraternity brothers. For instance, the airline transport-rated pilot who flopped his loaded Cessna 206 into a swamp near Yakutat, Alaska, in September 2006.

With four passengers, one dog, and a batch of fishing gear, the pilot was attempting a takeoff from a gravel road that provided 1,100 feet of very bumpy "runway." That this "airport"—really just a short stretch of a local gravel road —was only ten feet wide didn't seem to bother the experienced pilot. You might want to remember that the Cessna 206 measures about eight feet eight inches from outside to outside at the main landing gear wheels. And that would leave only eight inches to spare on either side of the airplane on that little bitty gravel road. Of course, that could be enough, but it would take a really good eye and a remarkably steady hand.

Stop for a moment and imagine driving a tricycle at fifty miles an hour along a really rough gravel road and with only eight inches to play with on either side! This was one confident airplane driver! On the other hand, it can certainly be done, and I don't find fault with the pilot for having landed there in the first place. That, too, must have been pretty skillfully done!

At any rate, the rough ground bumped the marginally loaded Cessna into the air about two-thirds of the way along his little chosen strip. The pilot had enough experience to know that he would have to stay in ground effect until he could build up a bit more air speed. Didn't work, though . . .

The loaded Cessna just gave it up and settled back down into the high grass and water ahead. At least that part was handled well enough, since he was able to effect some bush repairs and fly the airplane out the next day.

***

And here's one for you! The float-equipped De Havilland Beaver with six aboard had struck the shore on its takeoff from a small lake about fifty miles south of Anaktuvuk Pass in Alaska. The pilot managed to keep the airplane in the air and flew back to his home base in Bettles.

Since the pilot thought that the floats might have been damaged at the earlier argument with the lakeshore, he elected to land on the hard-surfaced runway at Bettles, something that floats aren't really designed to do.

I believe the pilot made the right choice, since such a landing is not only possible but not really all that difficult. Many of us have done this sort of thing, and the usual result is only the loss of paint along the floats' keels. In this instance, though, I think the pilot might have been just a wee bit more nervous than the situation really called for.

During the landing, the float supports failed and the airplane sat back on its tail. Probably looked funny, but I doubt that it was heavily damaged. Still, the landing could have been a lot smoother than it was! Must have really slammed it down pretty hard onto that runway.

***

Some pilots do things that are so incredibly stupid that it simply boggles the mind. This is the case of the private pilot who lost his life in a crash on September 9, 2005.

This 682-hour pilot hadn't been behind the controls of an aircraft for more than nine years at the time of the accident. Beyond being quite short of recent experience, he wasn't rated for instrument flight when he elected to take his Piper Cherokee, N8523W, off the ground at Faulkton, South Dakota. His last biennial flight review had occurred in October 1996, and his last recorded flight had been in December of that same year.

His last flight had begun with an uneventful takeoff from Osceola, Wisconsin, en route to Gettysburg, South Dakota. The pilot had elected to land in Faulkton to pick up a little fuel.

At about ten minutes past two o'clock that morning (oh, yeah—did I forget to mention that it was a *night* flight?), a sheriff's dispatcher reported that the pilot had called the sheriff's office asking about fuel for his 235-horsepower Cherokee. The dispatcher arranged for a fuel truck to meet the Cherokee at the field and to fuel the plane from the truck.

When the driver arrived at the field, he asked why the pilot was flying on such a ratty night. Visibility was down to about two city blocks, here on the ground, and it certainly didn't look much better in the air, what with all the fog rolling around the local countryside. The pilot had replied that "It wasn't bad, once he got up in the air."

Although the Cherokee's powerful engine required 100-low-lead (LL) aviation fuel, the driver explained that the best he could do for the pilot was to pump him some automobile gas. While the pilot had been informed that 100-LL was available at the nearby bulk plant, that would require a trip laden with some five-gallon gas cans. The pilot didn't want to involve himself in that much work, apparently, and elected to take the automobile gas. At that point, the gas truck driver proceeded to pump about 22.1 gallons of the low-octane, high-lead, undesirable fuel into one of the Cherokee's wing tanks. That was a *definite* no-no!

Let's pause for a moment here. We have a pilot with almost no recent experience, flying without an instrument rating and clearly in instrument weather, and, to top it all off, loading his little Cherokee with no-no fuel.

Am I missing something, or is there a message in all this? And exactly how danged complacent can one get, anyway?

At any rate, our pilot paid his fuel bill at around three o'clock in the dark and foggy morning, boarded his little low-wing, high-performance airplane, strapped himself tightly down—and prepared to meet his Maker. Which he would do in less than one mile from where he then sat quietly, safely, and securely—and still wonderfully alive!—in the comfort of his warm, dry, parked, and motionless little airplane.

The fuel truck driver later stated that as he pulled away from the airport, he could see a little white light headed down the runway. We presume this was the Cherokee's aft navigation light.

While the aircraft departed Runway 13 (a magnetic heading of 130 degrees), the wreckage, found only 0.63 miles from the runway, indicated that the airplane was at the time of impact headed 250 degrees. One has to wonder why the pilot seemingly had turned the Cherokee about 120 degrees in only one-half mile after liftoff. He should have been in transition from takeoff to climb configuration about then, with close attention to flaps, air speed, power setting, and compass heading. Why roll into a turn at this critical point in the flight? Or, as one has to presume, had he already lost it by then?

If my own calculations are anywhere near correct, the pilot had begun the turn *almost as soon as the wheels had left the earth.*

For whatever it's worth, a toxicology report on the pilot's remains later showed quinine and amlopodipine in both his lungs and his liver.

***

Here's another one for you! A crash into the sea near Catalina Island off the shore of Southern California took the lives of both the pilot and the sole passenger. What's remarkable is that the pilot was licensed as an airline transport pilot (ATP) and was, at the time of the flight, a Federal Aviation Agency aviation safety inspector (operations). His passenger, who also held the coveted ATP rating, was also an FAA employee, this time a designated pilot examiner!

All we know of the accident is what can be culled from an eyewitness account. This report held that the aircraft was last seen in a thirty- to forty-five-degree nose-low attitude just before it impacted the ocean where, only ninety seconds later, it sank forever out of sight.

***

Too much of this aerial misfortune can only serve to both bore you and put you off flying. I don't mean to do that, and for this reason I'm going to include only one more really dumb stunt. This time, it's back to Alaska, where pilots really do know better.

Our Alaska pilot, holding a private pilot certification, had filed a VFR flight plan from Anchorage to Montague Island and return. The purpose of his flight was to locate a good beach landing area for his tricycle-geared Cessna 182, N21545.

The pilot was trying to find a suitable landing spot on the southwest side of the very mountainous island. The island itself is located at the northwest corner of Prince William Sound. Montague, popular because of its deer, elk, and brown bear populations, would be the location of a planned hunting trip for this pilot, if a good landing spot could be found.

He was hoping to land near a cabin located at San Juan Bay, and once he arrived at the island, the pilot began his scanning in earnest. He had flown for about fifteen or twenty minutes at an altitude of four hundred feet when he spotted what appeared to be a possible landing area. He configured the aircraft for a possible landing—or at least for a low-and-slow flyby for a closer look—when he decided that he was (oops!) low enough and applied a little power to stop his descent.

With full forty degrees of the big Cessna flaps hanging out in the breeze, the carburetor heat in the "On" position, and the airplane already trimmed comfortably for the descent, he was surprised when the added power didn't slow his descent even a little bit. The engine simply didn't respond.

On his way to the island a bit earlier, he had noticed a little engine roughness, accompanied by about a one-inch drop in manifold pressure. He also noticed that the carburetor heat gauge was showing minus thirty-five degrees Fahrenheit. When he applied carburetor heat, the best increase he could get raised the carburetor temperature to only about zero degrees Fahrenheit, but no further. He decreased engine power to idle, reapplied carburetor heat, and after about one minute, watched the carburetor temperature rise to about fifty-five degrees Fahrenheit, which resolved the engine roughness issue.

Now he was confronted with pretty much the same symptoms, but without the safety of altitude. Though he now alternately pushed and pulled the throttle control in and out, nothing seemed to be helping much.

The Cessna settled a bit more, and the wheels began to strike the low brush. Just as the wheels descended into the brush, engine power was restored, but by then it was too late. At this point, the Cessna simply settled to the ground and, predictably, nosed over. Both the wings and fuselage were damaged, though the pilot escaped without a scratch. Of course.

Had the pilot been flying a tail-dragger, such as a Cessna 180 or 185, he would simply have flown to the island, located the cabin, and landed on the first little six-hundred-foot stretch of beach that he came to.

While flying the outback with a tricycle-geared airplane isn't impossible, the pilot certainly has to choose his landing spots carefully. I suppose, too, that it might help if the pilot doesn't run into something while he's making his choice.

Chapter 20

Pilot Error

Stay clear of clouds. Reliable sources indicate that mountains sometimes hide out in there.

Most of us have done something while pooping around up there with our little flying machines that we later regretted. Maybe poor judgment put us just a bit behind the power curve. Perhaps even led to a precautionary landing or—even worse—an *emergency* landing.

Some pilots, I'm sorry to say, didn't walk away from the results of their poor judgment. Worse, some fliers even took innocent passengers with them when they went west. That's largely unforgivable, as far as I'm concerned. If you insist on sticking your own neck out, I suppose that's your own business. If you're going to do something that carries the potential to endanger the lives of your passengers, then you're walking on my shady side.

The NTSB, that entity primarily responsible for the investigation of aviation accidents and incidents, keeps pretty good records, all in all. Their list of accident reports provides a wealth of information for those who would profit from it. Word of all aircraft incidents and accidents does not reach them, of course, and for that reason many of them do not receive NTSB attention, nor benefit from NTSB's investigations. This is especially true of aircraft mishaps in Alaska, where I'd venture to say that *most* light aircraft incidents and accidents go unreported. Insurance concerns are probably at the heart of this silence. Comprehensive and collision (hull damage) insurance coverage is hard enough to acquire in the first place, when off-airport operations are going to be involved. It's also quite expensive. So, if nothing more than damage to the airplane is involved, many pilots would just as soon cover the repair costs out of pocket, avoiding any contact with their insurance carriers.

Among those that are reported—perhaps because most of these happened in front of witnesses or near population centers—are many that will raise eyebrows. And while their causes vary from one end of the spectrum to the other, almost all point to "pilot error" at the center of it all.

A few, admittedly, are simply mechanical failure and cannot be laid at the door of the pilot. And while we would like to attribute still others to low visibility or gusty winds, these generally fall into the category of the pilot's lack of good judgment. Hence, they will also be viewed as pilot error. Here are a few that should stir your coffee for you.

It was about five o'clock in the early evening of June 16, 1968, when the forty-eight-year-old pilot cranked up his Cessna 170, N2660V, and prepared to depart Alexander Lake. With 138 flying hours under his belt, and only 38 hours in this aircraft type, our pilot had loaded three passengers into the four-place airplane and proceeded to light out, probably for Anchorage, only twenty minutes away.

The weather may have been a little shabby, though we don't have any indication of that. What we do know is that the pilot began the takeoff with full flaps—that's 40 percent on the Cessna's huge barn-door flaps! While such a takeoff is possible, it certainly isn't recommended. Half that—20 percent—is the recommended maximum flap setting for the takeoff phase in most of Cessna's single-engine aircraft.

We might presume the pilot was a little nervous, too, since he attempted the takeoff with the carburetor heat control in the "On" position.

So, with lots of parasite drag hanging out there on account of the full flap position, and with an engine trying its best to develop full power under the impossible condition of burning warm air on account of the full carburetor heat, the pilot wisely decided finally to get rid of the carb heat. Which he then did.

During initial climb from the short airstrip at Alexander, and either in haste or on account of nervousness about the whole thing at this point, the pilot decided to try the carb heat again, but this time he pulled back on the red knob instead of the black or silver one. Those of you who fly will recognize this red control knob as the *mixture* control! You guessed it: the pilot starved out the engine when he inadvertently closed down its fuel supply. Of course the nice little Cessna almost immediately crash-landed. The plane was substantially damaged. Fortunately, no one aboard was killed.

On that same day, but much farther north, another pilot was about to get into trouble with his own four-place Cessna. This time, though, it would be a Cessna 180, that 230-horsepower workhorse that so many of us love.

This thirty-four-year-old pilot, on the ground at Anaktuvuk Pass, loaded three passengers into the Cessna and prepared to depart. With only 210 total flying hours to his credit, and less than 24 in the Cessna 180, he might have been a little concerned about the short runway ahead of him.

At any rate, he elected to try a downwind departure, having decided that the five-mile-per-hour tailwind wouldn't be much of a factor during the takeoff. In fact, even a nonpilot could quickly figure out that if an airplane needs fifty miles-per-hour airspeed to lift off, then a five-mile-per-hour headwind means he only has to go forty-five miles per hour across the ground to get his needed fifty-miles-per-hour air speed. Conversely, a five-mile-per-hour tailwind means he'll have to reach a fifty-five-mile-per-hour ground speed to achieve the required fifty-mile-per-hour air speed. Maybe of lesser importance on a long, hard-surfaced runway, but in the Alaska bush?

So, if for no other reason in the world, why decide to go ten miles per hour faster over the ground than is necessary? Especially since airplanes aren't primarily designed for ground operations, but rather for their performance in the air.

Anyhow, the airplane was loaded—perhaps even overloaded—and now headed downwind for the takeoff. It was at this point that the pilot lost directional control of his airplane. He ground-looped the great little aircraft, which, as a predictable result, was substantially damaged. Neither the pilot nor his passengers were seriously hurt, thankfully.

***

Even the "Good Guys" screw it up from time to time. Take the Alaska Fish & Wildlife Protection officer who blew a landing about fifty-eight miles southwest of McGrath. And on a perfectly good runway, too. After all, it was 1,500 feet long and gravel surfaced. What more could a Super Cub driver ask for, anyway? It wasn't like landing in the muskeg or a beach or along some windy mountain ridge.

The trooper later stated that during the landing roll, he applied the tundra-tire-equipped Cub's brakes and moved the control stick *forward*, the latter move made in an attempt to "soften" the effects of the rough gravel surface.

With those huge doughnut tires hanging out just below him—and those big things pumped up to only four or five pounds of air pressure—one wouldn't think that "softening" the landing would be all that high on the pilot's list of important considerations. The little Cub, probably pretty lightly loaded, too, just pitched up on its nose—and then went right on over. I admit that I've encountered this same surprise maneuver on a couple of occasions, so I know that it's not difficult to do. But it's *always* pilot error, isn't it?

The Cub came to rest upside down, with the surprised and cursing trooper suddenly hanging ignominiously inverted from his seat belt. I suppose that, for just a moment there, he was wondering why his sunglasses had suddenly flopped up against the bill of his brown baseball cap. And no doubt worrying about whether or not his big service revolver was going to fall from its now upside-down holster.

Smashed the tail feathers on the state's little Super Cub, of course, and damaged the right wing a bit. Cubs are tough, though, and a little rebuilding would have later put it right back into the air. Of course, all the bits and pieces, plus the required fix-it-up mechanics, would have to be flown in from McGrath, with some parts from as far away as Anchorage or Fairbanks, most likely. I really have to work pretty hard to develop any genuine sympathy for the pilot who chooses this goofy application of brakes and a *forward* stick after touchdown. Unless a tough downwind landing is really necessary on account of a one-way strip, it kinda makes the immediate future pretty easy to predict. In a moderate to serious tailwind condition, when landing or taxiing, a control stick pressed forward is sometimes the only way to keep the tail on the ground in the first place. And it should *always* be kept planted firmly on the ground once the landing has been accomplished.

***

And, here's another one for you! Only this time, it was a *mechanic's* error. There aren't many of these, but those that do occur can be really serious. It might be said that, in this case, it is nonetheless a pilot error, since the pilot might have caught this particular item if he had only taken a careful look at the mechanic's work. Still, it's a bit like pinning the blame on a layman for the mistakes of a doctor who has finished a rather complex medical procedure. So, I guess maybe I should just go ahead and hang this one on the mechanic.

On August 17, 2007, a Maule, M-7-235 (registration N56568) sustained substantial damage when it nosed over during a takeoff from Chena Marina Airport at Fairbanks. The commercial pilot and his one passenger sustained only minor injuries, but it could have been much, much worse.

Immediately after the incident—and even before either occupant had been transported to the hospital—rescue personnel had asked the pilot what had happened to make the Maule flop over on its back during the takeoff roll. The pilot told them that as he pulled back on the control yoke to begin the takeoff rotation, the plane had simply nosed over and pitched itself upside down on the runway.

An FAA inspector reported that a postaccident investigation showed the elevator cables to have been connected *backward*! When the takeoff pilot had pulled back on the control yoke, the airplane was being told to nose down rather than up, and, like a good little airplane, it did just exactly as it was told. The little Maule sustained major damage to its vertical stabilizer, the wings, and both wing lift struts. Somebody was looking at relatively big bucks to cover the subsequent repair. For my own part, I still think the pilot should have caught the mechanic's error.

Something else about this whole thing bothers me, too: why was this airplane carrying a passenger in what must surely have been the first flight after some serious maintenance work? Shouldn't a "test flight" have been performed somewhere along the line?

***

The following accident didn't turn out quite as well as the Maule mishap noted above did.

The pilot, his son, and a third passenger, a friend of the pilot, flew a Maule M-5-180C, registered as N5660F, from Gustavus to Fairbanks, Alaska. The flight occurred back on August 13, 2007. The little group was all set to hunt for the elusive Dall Sheep, that pure white big game trophy that ranks so very high on the list of things a good sheep hunter just has to do. Sheep season was just about to open, and the group wanted to scout out a good hunting area and then construct their tent camp and get comfortable before opening day. They had arrived in Fairbanks on August 11.

On August 13, after a day of rest and last-minute shopping, they flew from Fairbanks to a little gravel strip near Arctic Village. From here, they would pursue the incredibly keen-eyed white sheep. It's been said that the wild sheep has vision that's eight times better than a human's, the equivalent sight of a man using binoculars with eight times magnification. I can believe that, having spotted the big rams from more than a mile away through my own binoculars, only to discover the sheep just lying there in the sun, watching me and chewing their cuds like cows. Sheep, like cows, have four-chambered stomachs, you see. Anyway . . .

After two days of serious hunting, the party had still not seen a sheep, neither ram, nor lamb, nor ewe. More than a little discouraged now, the pilot, with an airline transport pilot certificate, the Holy Grail of the flying fraternity, loaded his friend aboard, and they lit out in the little Maule to scout out some more productive country. The pilot's son remained in camp. His father had said that a lightly loaded airplane would be better for the scouting work and that they would be back within thirty minutes at any rate.

Two days later, the boy flagged down a passing airplane and reported his father's missing airplane. Searchers soon located the Maule, which had crashed at the four-thousand-foot level in a canyon just a few air miles from the camp. The canyon was pretty narrow, and the sides were awfully steep. It must have been a great area to fly *over*, but clearly it was not a good area to fly around *in*. And it was one helluva bad way to end what should have been a great hunting experience for the pilot's son.

***

I don't want to appear critical of all these "pilot errors" you read about here. Over the years, I've been guilty of a few of them myself. And I will be the first to admit that the environment with which these Alaska outback pilots contend is nothing less than a severely harsh and unforgiving one. Still, they *are* pilot errors, however large or small. Almost all of them could have been avoided. Even the one you will read about just below . . .

Beach landings are considered by many of us to be our favorites. The air above the beach is almost always cool and stable. That is to say, almost no heat rises from Alaska beaches, and thermal bumps on short final—or during the touchdown itself—are almost unheard of. There may be some crosswinds, of course, but during the daylight hours these almost always arrive from over the water. And that usually means that there are no "bumps" in them. Offshore winds, though, are another kettle of fish. An offshore wind can crawl up under the onshore wing and try to flip the airplane over into the water, only a very few feet away.

There is the problem of landing on a beach when the tides are in, too, if the tides that day are a bit on the high side. If the waterside wheel should happen to drift into the water, it tends to immediately slow that side of the airplane, and to do so with truly dramatic effect. Without instant attention, this becomes a serious ground loop in a matter of milliseconds. Witness our next pilot.

As many of you may know, Alaska's "fly-out fishing trips" are a tremendously popular tourist attraction. Many wilderness lodges, and no small number of big city air taxi operators, feature these popular one-day excursions. Simply put, the pilot will fly a bush-equipped plane full of hopeful fishermen and women to remote fishing sites that are inaccessible by road. There, real no-one-else-around fishing can be had for truly reasonable prices. In some cases, camps and even boats with motors are provided, and in almost all cases, fishing equipment can be furnished to those who haven't brought their own. These fly-out trips are also a feature of many of Alaska's excellent wilderness lodges, and I can recommend them as truly memorable experiences. For the most part . . .

On August 10, 2007, a Cessna 185 (registered as N3306R) was approaching for a beach landing about forty miles southeast of Pedro Bay, where its owners operated a top-notch Alaska fishing lodge known far and wide as the Rainbow Bay Resort. The pilot, holding a commercial pilot certificate, was flying five fishermen on a fly-out fishing trip. With him that day were four passengers in the wheel-equipped, high-performance bush plane. Given the date of this flight, and the destination apparent from the location of the accident site itself, I'd hazard the guess that it was to be a day of incredible silver salmon fishing. At least, they were going to the right place for that.

It was a beautiful sunny day, something of a rarity at that date and in that area. The pilot had chosen a remote stretch of beach along the west side of notorious Cook Inlet, no doubt near the mouth of one of the many pristine and crystal-clear streams that feed into Cook Inlet and are known for their annual silver salmon spawning runs. I presume the pilot was landing toward the south, with the waters of Cook Inlet immediately off his left wingtip.

I presume that because after a good approach and a nearly flawless landing touchdown, the airplane decided to drift leftward down the sloping beach toward the cold and unfriendly waters of the huge inlet. The pilot's response to this potentially dangerous drift appears to have been a bit too little and a tad too late. The airplane immediately ground-looped sharply to its left, which must have placed one or both of the main wheels in or very near to the water. The obvious result, of course, was a collapsed right main gear and substantial damage to the right wing.

The usual technique for dealing with this drifting-downhill-and-toward-the-open-water problem is the application of moderate uphill rudder, with cautious light downhill braking to overcome the effects of the uphill rudder deflection and to aid in slowing the landing roll. It's not difficult, but it is a bit of a balancing act. In this particular case, however, the pilot later stated that he suspected the tail wheel had simply malfunctioned! Well, could be. At any rate, the marvelous Cessna was several times covered by Alaska's incredible tides before it could be extracted. The waters that covered it were salt waters, of course. Just about the worst thing that can happen to an airplane, except possibly for fire.

***

This next little tale reiterates clearly that "An ounce of prevention is worth a pound of cure." I trust it taught the pilot that taking care of the little things can erase most of the pilot's concerns over the bigger things.

This particular little boo-boo involved a Cessna 180, the airplane I consider to be the best overall flying machine that God ever invented. Anyway, here comes our pilot and his quiet little Cessna, descending smoothly on short final to the Skwentna Airport. The strip at Skwentna (I guess most of us still refer to these out-of-the-way airports as "strips") is a staggering 3,400 feet long and about 75 feet wide. Gravel, last time I was on it, and so danged long for most of us that we find ourselves taxiing even to get to midfield after landing. The driver of the Cessna 180 that just landed should have been able to make almost seven takeoffs and landings in that 3,400-foot length.

Instead, though, he landed just once, and as he approached the far end of the gravel runway, he attempted to make the 180-degree turn that would face the aircraft back down the runway. Didn't happen that way, though.

On previous flights, he had noticed that he had to "pump up" the left brake on account of a leak in the brake master cylinder, he later claimed. Probably just needed a new neoprene O-ring or something. Rather than pooping around with this minor brake repair, which could have involved as much work as bleeding the lines, master cylinder tear-down, parts replacement, reassembly, adding hydraulic brake fluid, bleeding the brakes again, and then replacing safety pins or cotter keys to safety the whole brake pedal system, our pilot had continued to pump the left brake on his landings as he flew closer and ever closer to this particular little disaster.

The ground loop that followed resulted in structural damage to one wing and its supporting lift strut. After that little escapade, our unhappy pilot would have plenty of spare time—only now, he would no doubt have precious little flying fun upon which to spend it.

***

So that you don't think "pilot error" applies only to fliers, consider those who operate powerboats. Here in Florida, where I now live, everyone and his dog seems to own a watercraft of one sort or another. And most of these operators appear too drunk to either operate a boat safely or to walk without incident. Consider the next tale, one that points out the small but historically intense civil war between aircraft and watercraft. Some of these battles occur in Alaska, too, though on a much smaller scale. This is, no doubt, because Alaska is so thinly populated.

It was on May 24, 2007, that Cessna N45WT, a C-206 floatplane, had completed its warmup and preflight checks at the Bayou Fourchon Seaplane Base near Leeville, Louisiana. The airplane, with the pilot and two passengers aboard, was owned by Chevron, USA, of Picayune, Mississippi. The airplane would fly again, but the small boat would never float again.

As the Stationair floatplane began its takeoff run, the powerboat emerged from a nearby channel and crossed in front of the Cessna's path. By now, the Cessna was pretty much committed to the takeoff. Still, the pilot attempted to avoid the boat and its operator, a gentleman who was clearly unaware that he wasn't the only living soul on the water that early afternoon.

Before completing the crossing, though, the daydreaming boat operator decided to make a last-minute U-turn in front of the speeding Cessna, which was now clocking more than forty miles per hour and certainly looking for about fifty-five, at which time he would begin to rotate for liftoff. The scene didn't allow for that, though, and the two-ton seaplane hit the fiberglass boat at about fifty miles per hour. None of us will ever know whether or not the boat operator even saw the floatplane roaring down on him. What we do know is that just as quickly as the floats hit the boat, the floatplane nosed over into the water. The pilot and his two passengers certainly got wet.

The boat operator didn't know that either, since he died at impact. Helluva way to end a nice day, isn't it?

***

And here's a crazy one for you. One of those once-in-a-lifetime accidents that is so unusual as to be almost unbelievable. But it's true.

On June 12, 2005, the pilot of a Cessna 206 wheel-equipped airplane, N51205, was cruising along near Skwentna, Alaska, when his sensitive nose detected smoke. Now, fire in the air may be the pilot's most serious problem, barring, of course, the loss of a wing or two during cruise flight.

At the time, the Cessna was carrying an external load of lumber—not unusual in and of itself. The lumber rack that had been installed beneath the airplane's belly, however, had never been FAA approved. The aircraft didn't have a "Restricted" approval for the carrying of external loads, either. Definitely unusual, since it seems clear that it had been the pilot's intention to drag more such external loads around Alaska's pristine skies and outback scenery. Otherwise, why build such a rack in the first place?

The pilot, cruising at about 1,500 feet when he first smelled the smoke, quickly scanned his instruments for a clue as to the smoke's point of origin, then he may have felt his feet growing warmer. With that clue planted in his head, he selected the first suitable gravel bar and made a quick approach to it. He was hoping for a safe landing, after which he planned to exit the airplane in a hurry, lest his boots actually begin to smolder while still on his feet.

Given the small distraction, though, one can't blame the pilot for blowing the landing. Once the wheels had found the gravel bar, our driver saw his next compelling maneuver to be one of instantly bailing out and removing his trembling physiology from the proximity of the still-moving aircraft. You shouldn't be surprised to learn that the Cessna then impacted a log. Still moving at a pretty good clip, the airplane flipped over, load and all.

The lumber, now burning with a vengeance, issued a smoke signal that was spotted by a helicopter pilot who happened to be flying nearby. Landing on the same gravel bar, the chopper pilot found the Cessna pilot pretty well banged up after his dramatic leap from the moving Cessna. In true Alaska fashion, the helicopter pilot aborted his own mission of the hour and transported the seriously injured pilot to the nearest hospital. Those of you who are familiar with the Cessna 206 Stationair will remember the location of its huge exhaust stack on the underside of the plane, a spot guaranteed to superheat the pile of lumber that the unhappy pilot had secured beneath the airplane's belly.

***

There are some pilot errors that absolutely boggle the mind. Take the example of the certified flight instructor (CFI) who had been scheduled to provide some instrument training to his private pilot student. This happened in Florida, a place filled with pilots who could benefit from a dab of Alaska flight instruction.

The instructor pilot had scheduled the following flight sequence: From Naples, Florida, to Miami, to Opa Locka, to Vero Beach, and then return to Naples. Got a map of Florida handy? That's quite a lot of flying.

The aircraft, by the way, was the very popular Cessna 152, this one carrying the registration number N625PA. This particular airplane, according to its owner, held a maximum of twenty-four gallons of avgas, not all of it usable, of course.

The aircraft had climbed to about five thousand feet en route to Miami. As they got closer to that big city, they were vectored around some thunderstorm activity, not at all unusual at that place and time. Once clear of the storms, they continued on up the Florida coast to Vero Beach, where they performed their first instrument approach of the day, a full VOR approach. After completing that approach, the aircraft was vectored for fifteen or twenty minutes before it was cleared to proceed to Ft. Myers, on the west coast and all the way across the state of Florida.

At Ft. Myers, the pilot requested an instrument landing system (ILS) approach, but the approach was later cancelled at the pilot's request, and the airplane then headed for Naples, farther south along Florida's Gulf Coast. At Naples, they requested vectors to the final for the Naples nondirectional beacon approach. A few minutes after being handed off to the Naples Tower for the landing, they reported "some engine trouble." The CFI assumed control of the aircraft and attempted an emergency landing, finally coming to earth in a field about seven miles northeast of the airport.

Later investigation at the site revealed that (a) there had been no damage to either of the airplane's wing tanks, (b) the left tank showed about one eighth inch of fuel in the bottom of the tank, and (c) the right tank showed about a half inch of fuel in the right tank. Hardly enough to maintain engine operation.

While these things do happen, each time I read about such an emergency, I have to ask myself: how in the world does someone run out of fuel in an airplane? Every pilot knows how long he has been in the air, how much fuel the airplane carried at takeoff, and how many gallons of fuel the airplane burns with each hour of cruise flight.

And I have to say it one more time: do not rely upon the plane's fuel gauges! Ever.

***

Every once in a while, the matter of "pilot error" is really a matter of "FAA controller error." Take the June 20, 2005, flight of Cessna 182, registration number N53538.

The flight departed the Naples, Florida, airport on a VFR flight to Key West, at the far south end of the Florida peninsula. After departure, the pilot—the plane's only occupant—contacted Fort Myers Approach Control, which issued a flight altitude of five thousand feet and instructions to contact Miami Approach for further instructions.

The Miami controller transmitted alerts for thunderstorm activity along the pilot's route and cleared the pilot to descend to and maintain an altitude of four thousand feet. He also provided the pilot with the Key West altimeter setting, a value that the pilot needed to guarantee that his airplane's altimeter reading was accurate. At this point, the controller committed the error that would soon cost the dependent pilot his life. He did not advise the pilot of available convective intensity level information. That is to say, he didn't tell the pilot how damned bad the thunderstorm activity really was. The pilot requested clearance for a flight path that was direct to Key West from his present position, and that was approved. The controller told the pilot that he was free to deviate slightly, if necessary, to avoid thunderstorm activity in his path. The pilot answered that he was sure he could stay clear of warning areas. His voice was never heard again.

A review of radar data revealed that the airplane vanished approximately eighteen miles south of Marco Island. During the subsequent search for the missing airplane and its pilot, aircraft debris was found. This consisted mainly of a passenger briefing card, one wheel assembly, a seat back, and one oxygen bottle. The main wreckage has never been found. Neither, of course, has the pilot's body. I find it interesting that the NTSB determined that this was clearly a case of "pilot error," since the pilot "continued flight into known thunderstorm activity that resulted in the loss of control and the subsequent collision with the water." It does admit that "a factor was the controller's failure to provide the pilot with convective intensity." Yes, that would have been a factor. And remember, FAA Order 7110.65, "Air Traffic Control," states: "Issue the level of echo intensity when that information is available."

***

The flight of N6886Y, a Piper PA-23 Cherokee, involved pretty much the same situation. This flight, with three aboard, departed Treasure Cay International Airport at Abaco Island, Bahamas, en route to Ft. Pierce, along the central Florida Atlantic Coast.

The pilot had requested, and was granted, an IFR Flight Plan. The Miami Air Route Traffic Control Center (ZMA) issued the clearance to Ft. Pierce via direct to Freeport, direct to Ft. Pierce, at an altitude of ten thousand feet. What they didn't tell the pilot was the known intensity of rain and thunderstorm activity along this route of flight.

Radar data shows the fated airplane passing through—or at least into—intense weather containing thunderstorms and heavy rains, with intense updrafts and downdrafts, at least moderate and probably heavy turbulence, all accompanied by strong horizontal wind gusts. Certainly the conditions were hard-instrument flying conditions. This plane, along with its three inhabitants, disappeared from both the radar returns and the earth that afternoon.

Pilot error? Well, yes, but still—it's difficult to think that the FAA hadn't helped this little error along just a bit, isn't it?

At the end of July 2005, a private pilot loaded his Cessna 180 at Fairbanks, Alaska, to—well, maybe just a little beyond—its load limits. Included in the load were six five-gallon cans of diesel fuel (a violation of the FARs in the first place!), a 150-pound iron stove, his mechanic's tools, several bags of groceries, and a large ice chest. This latter usually formed the front seat on the passenger's side. It's probable that our pilot used this Cessna for freight hauls to his remote lodge so frequently that it had become a pain in the neck for him to keep removing and replacing that seat to accommodate whatever load he was carrying at the time. The pilot's lodge, by the way, was located some forty-five or fifty miles from Fairbanks, just a short jaunt, really.

The pilot had also filled the Cessna's wing tanks with 80-octane aviation fuel and, in addition, had loaded aboard the mechanic. This passenger, a heavy equipment mechanic, was about to be lifted off for the last flight of his life.

With the Cessna loaded to an estimated gross weight of around 2,840 pounds, the whole ball of wax was just a shade under three hundred pounds overloaded. In reality, this sort of overload isn't usually a cause for much concern to many Alaska pilots. While flying overloaded airplanes is surely not recommended—and admittedly can prove to be very dangerous—Alaska pilots have been flying these loads since the first Alaska flights back in about 1926.

In this case, though, the pilot, his airplane, and indeed his passenger, went missing for the next six days. On that last day, the wreckage was found in tree-covered terrain. A postcrash fire had incinerated the Cessna and all it carried aboard. Both the pilot and his innocent passenger had died in the crash.

It may be of some significance to note that the pilot had undergone open heart surgery about three months before the accident. His medical certificate was not current, of course. And a later toxicological examination of the pilot's body revealed the presence of fluoxetine (Prozac), a prescription drug used as an antidepressant. Its use, by the way, is prohibited by the FAA.

I suppose we can list this accident as the result of "pilot error," though in my own mind it closer resembles a murder/suicide matter. In my estimation, that pilot had absolutely no right to be in the air as a pilot in command. In fact, he shouldn't even have been around the airport, as far as I'm concerned.

***

This next tale is a bit of a mystery to me. Why it resulted in a crash, with the loss of one life, is beyond me. Read on and see what you make of it.

On July 20, 2005, in a Maule M-7-235 (N5661J), a lodge owner and pilot was en route to glacier-fed coastal lake near Seward, Alaska, with four passengers aboard. We can consider this at least a full plane load, especially for a float-equipped aircraft with a 235-horsepower engine.

Both the flight and the approach to the lake were later reported by the commercially licensed pilot as routine in every way. The pilot later said that when the aircraft was somewhere between twenty-five and fifty feet above the surface of the lake, though, "It just quit flying!" With no excessive winds reported at that time, one can only presume that the pilot had allowed the airplane to slow to its stall speed before he had intended. At any rate, the plane dropped like a stone, hitting the water pretty much in a flat attitude.

The impact was sufficiently hard to collapse the float fittings and allow the floats to spread apart. The airplane's wings settled atop the damaged floats and sank to the point that only the tops of the wings and cabin were above water.

The lake, to no one's surprise, was thick with icebergs, a condition that has to lead to the assumption that the water was pretty damned cold. Still, the pilot and all the passengers were able to get out of the stricken airplane and climb atop the wings. That wasn't the end of the matter for them, since staying where they were would eventually prove to be an exercise in futility. They needed to get to dry ground as quickly as possible. Wet and shivering with cold, none would have lasted more than a few hours at most. With no other choice, they all left the aircraft and swam to one of the larger ice blocks and climbed up to assess their situation. Unfortunately, one of the passengers—the only one who hadn't climbed into his floatation device—was overcome by the cold water. His blood no doubt began to thicken, putting a strain on his heart, and his cold and water-soaked clothing was getting too heavy to manage. This unfortunate soul perished in the cold, clear water. Fortunately, the others were soon rescued and, except for being cold, wet, and suffering from mild shock, were in relatively good shape.

It may have been that the winds were dead calm, leading to a condition known as "glassy water" to floatplane pilots. In this situation, the pilot cannot determine, to any degree of accuracy, his exact height above the surface of the water. The answer to this is usually to try landing near a shoreline, where nearby features give a sense of scale and help with depth perception. On the other hand, it is usually a matter of using the same landing techniques as when landing in the dark: descend and land by controlling rate of descent through the use of power only. And under no circumstances should the pilot try to outguess things and rely upon the elevators during such landings. Without power, however, this technique is lost to the pilot, placing him pretty far behind the power curve. If he finds himself very close to the shoreline, he might be a bit more successful in a full-stall landing if his long experience will safely allow it. But with an airplane that had dropped out from under him, the altitude needed for recovery had to be somewhere beyond three hundred vertical feet. Such is the nature of a full stall, which must have been the case here, where the plane just "quit flying," as the pilot later stated.

Since the engine in the Maule was still operating, one simply has to lay this accident at the pilot's door, a thing that none of us really wants to do.

***

Some pilots—and in this case I'm using that word loosely—seem never to have learned any respect whatsoever for the world of flying. That's certainly the case here. In this instance, the pilot was dashing aloft in his Titan Tornado, an unregistered home-built craft that sported only a two-cylinder engine up front. Still, it was a ship designed to fly, and our pilot intended to do just that on June 23, 2005. The scene was outside Bath, Pennsylvania, showing that Alaska pilots aren't the only ones to get into trouble.

Our pilot pushed the throttle control forward, and his little home-built roared down the runway, looking for an air speed that would allow him to escape the surly bonds of earth, as they say. Successful at that phase, the small airplane began something of a troubled climbout, with the engine beginning to burble at about four hundred feet of altitude.

The little ship appeared to wobble a bit about both the horizontal and forward axes. As ground-pounders might say, the airplane appeared to "rock a little" in the pitch and roll axes. At any rate, only ten or twelve seconds were burned up in this flapping around before the aircraft fell off on the left wing, descending in an almost vertical attitude until it finally hit the hard earth below. The pilot, of course, was killed. Later investigation of the wreckage would reveal that it was providential that the plane carried no passengers.

As you probably know, the cylinders of an aircraft engine have two spark plugs each. Hence two magnetos, sort of a dual system designed to promote safety. In this little home-built, the forward spark plug of the rear cylinder was completely free of the threaded hole in which it was supposed to reside and was held inside the cowling with only its spark plug "lead" wire.

The spark plug itself was completely intact. Examination of the corresponding cast-aluminum spark plug hole, though, revealed stripped threads. In fact, the spark plug could be inserted, with no twisting, into the hole and then wobbled from side to side. I guess you and I would both have to consider that pretty much a loose fit! In this instance, our pilot was trying to fly a one-cylinder airplane. It didn't work out for him.

A further look into the pilot's qualifications revealed that, although he held a private pilot license rated for single-engine land operations, his last application for the required medical certificate had been denied. And that had been sixteen years before this accident! When that medical denial had been handed to him, it was on account of "administrative or legal" reasons, whatever those might have been. And at that time, sixteen years previous to this accident, the pilot had logged a total of 110 flying hours. It's too bad that he hadn't developed, somewhere along the way, enough respect for the flying world to have checked his engine and airframe operation prior to his last flight. It's hard to imagine that the loose spark plug condition actually slipped his attention.

***

And here's another puzzler for you. It happened at just past noon on a relatively clear day about sixty miles west of Arctic Village, Alaska. The plane, a Piper PA-12, stalwart old taildragger that it is, was being driven by a pilot carrying the rating of an airline pilot, no less.

The pilot later stated that he had landed at this same spot at least once before, when he had prepared a better landing area by clearing a swath of brush from a flat spot about nine hundred feet long and forty feet wide. More than enough for the PA-12, usually. In the hands of a skilled backcountry pilot, that nine hundred feet would have been enough for about three landings and takeoffs, even with a driver lacking the impressive ATP rating.

Anyhow, here comes our airline pilot, banging along in N78481, with a hunting companion occupying the back seat of this popular two-place Piper.

The flight had departed the Galbraith Lake Airport shortly before the accident and had proceeded directly to the pilot's little secret landing spot. It was here that the pilot decided on an approach that would align the aircraft for a landing toward the east. The pilot later said that the airplane quickly reached the end of his strip's nine hundred feet, at which point he applied heavy braking. It must have been pretty heavy at that, since the loaded airplane simply pitched over onto its back. Though neither the pilot nor his passenger received anything more than very light bumping and bruising, the little PA-12 received structural damage to its left wing, the vertical stabilizer, and the right wing lift struts. The pilot told the NTSB investigator that he had noticed that the wind-indicating flagging he had earlier tied to the brush at both ends of the strip indicated a change of wind direction. If he *had* noticed the wind change before landing, I wonder why he didn't abort the intended landing and approach from the opposite direction for a safer, into-the-wind landing? Of course, I wasn't there, so I shouldn't assume more than I really know, should I?

***

This next series of events leads me to remember the old country axiom that "Ya can buy 'em books, ya can send 'em to school, but ya can't make 'em learn!" This seems to have been the case with one pilot who flew with a group of ten airplanes that departed Washington State to visit the great expanse of Alaska. Or at least some small part of that great expanse.

Flying a Beechcraft Bonanza V35B, number N912DB, this pilot and his passenger had joined the rest of the group on a trip to Denali National Park, that park that includes mighty Mt. McKinley. The trip to the mountain—in fact, into the mountains anywhere near the big guy itself—is a thrill for any pilot, including those who make the trip every day. Or even several times a day, as do the serious bush fliers living in Talkeetna, Alaska, drop-off place for all Mt. McKinley climbing teams.

Before this group of "outside" pilots (those who come from the Lower 48) began their insertion into the Alaska Range to get up close and personal with the big mountains, they were briefed by both their group's leader—an experienced Alaska mountain flier—and an FAA inspector about the hazards of serious mountain flying. And plunging into mountains that rise almost directly from sea level to heights above nineteen thousand or even twenty thousand feet certainly constitutes serious mountain flying.

The team leader laid out a suggested route and safe altitude through this awesome mountainous terrain, with instructions about their next airport landing where they would all meet and hangar fly about the experience for a while. The group of airplanes and their pilots and passengers then departed in small groups at close intervals.

The accident pilot, along with two other pilots and their ships, elected to fly up a canyon parallel to the one being flown by the rest of the group. At this point, and with around twenty thousand hours in these mountains, I gotta tell you that this was an error so large as to be quite beyond my poor powers to fathom. Apparently, the plan was for this small splinter group of three to meet with the rest of the group somewhere on down the line.

One of the pilots flying behind the accident airplane noticed sharply rising terrain ahead at the end of the canyon they had chosen and began his climb almost right away. The accident pilot, obviously enjoying his intimate views with his nap-of-the-earth flying, was a little too little and a little too late with his decision to get the hell up there where he belonged. His Bonanza impacted a rock face about five hundred feet below the five-thousand-foot saddle he needed to cross. What can I tell ya? Ya buy 'em books, ya send 'em to school, but ya can't make 'em learn.

***

Like the pilot who was checking on a party of hikers in the Girdwood, Alaska, neck of the woods. The accident site was about eight or nine miles north of that small community and in an area with some pretty awesome scenery. Most of it, though, is rather vertical. It happened on the third of May 2007, and it went something like this. . . .

A group of mountaineering club folks were on Eagle Glacier during an outback, cross-country ski trip. The pilot of the Bellanca 8KCAB, registered as N5038K, was checking on the party's progress. He first made a low pass over the party. Someone in that party later commented that the little airplane was about eight feet above the snow-and-ice-covered glacier.

The pilot then turned to make a second pass over the party and proceeded to bang into the glacier about 150 yards beyond the party of hikers. Upon impact, the Bellanca flopped over onto its back, which must have demanded the immediate attention of the small group that had watched it.

They pulled the injured pilot from the airplane and then called for rescue. Alaska is used to outback rescue operations, and they get plenty of practice at it. While they waited for the rescue helicopter, the ski group members rendered what medical aid they could, which appears to have been sufficient. The pilot, banged up and a little on the unhappy side, recovered fully. The little airplane did not.

It is interesting to note that the weather at the time was reported as about eight hundred feet overcast—and hazy! Doesn't sound to me like the kind of weather that encourages glacier flying, but what do I know? Except that I've never plopped one upside down on a glacier.

***

There are times, too, when the pilot can't seem to get his story straight. Take the pilot who dropped his Piper PA-22 floatplane onto the tundra near Cooper Landing, Alaska, on September 19, 2007. Since this is around hunting season time, one presumes his problem may have had to do with a heavy load of camp gear or meat and horns.

At any rate, the pilot reported that the floatplane was slow in getting up onto the step and into the planing configuration during its takeoff run. Although he lays this problem to the winds, which were gusting to around thirty knots, and to the heavy chop of the water. My own experience has been that a thirty-knot wind would help get an airplane off the earth in a very short time, but what do I know?

The pilot reported that the little Piper did get off the water, but only to settle back down on the rough surface. And while there is a singular technique recommended for "rough water takeoffs," we don't know whether or not this pilot used that technique. Or, in fact, if he was even familiar with it.

Having settled back down onto the rough water surface, I reckon the pilot, now somewhat committed to the takeoff—but not at all confident of a really sterling success—simply elected to keep on keeping on.

The airplane finally did get airborne and was enjoying its short period in ground effect, though the flight from that point would be decidedly short. In fact, it would be measured in only seconds.

The pilot later reported that, though he lowered the airplane's nose in order to pick up a little much-needed air speed, the airplane only climbed to about one hundred feet above the earth. At which point, of course, the loaded Piper floatplane decided just to quit the effort and rush downward to land in the small trees ahead. The pilot did say that he was able to dodge some of the large trees directly in his path, but that didn't help much. Once he had rolled the wings out of level, the stall speed would have increased, and he was already remarkably short of seriously needed air speed.

The floats collapsed, of course, since the airplane was loaded at least to its rated capacity. The right wing then struck the ground, which didn't do it much good, either. Oh, and the fuselage and horizontal stabilizer were structurally damaged, too. A pretty costly takeoff, especially considering that it wasn't successful anyway. All in all, the pilot and his passenger weren't having a really good day, up to that point.

You'll remember that the pilot noted that the airplane was slow to come up on the step due to the rough chop. That chop was caused by the sobering winds, which were gusting to thirty knots. In reality, the winds, coupled with the choppy water surface, should have helped him break free of the water at a relatively early point. One has to presume, then, that the airplane was truly loaded to at least its gross certificated takeoff weight. Most likely, since this was a hunting trip, the plane was a bit on the overloaded side and likely was outside its gravity envelope at that.

The pilot did say later that he "should have reevaluated the conditions after the airplane settled into the water following the first liftoff." I certainly have to agree with that. Neither the pilot nor his passenger was injured in the incident, I'm happy to report.

***

Another clearly overloaded aircraft did much the same thing near McGrath, Alaska, on September 10, 2007. This time, though, it was a Cessna 185, clearly a true "bush plane" in every sense of the word. This one carried the pilot and three passengers, along with the "baggage," which very likely included either hunting or fishing gear.

The plane was located on a rough and uneven little gravel airstrip, this one measuring about 960 feet long and 40 feet wide. Normally, this is considered quite suitable for something like the Cessna 185. Powered by a Continental-Teledyne engine rated at 310 horsepower for takeoff, the nominal 300-horsepower engine is a capable and dependable power source. Since this incident actually occurred somewhere outside McGrath, I don't know the strip's elevation above sea level, but this could have played an important role in airplane performance. The Cessna 206, for instance—at sea level atmospheric pressure and at seventy degrees Fahrenheit—requires a takeoff run of only 600 feet. To clear a 50-foot obstacle (e.g., tall trees) at the far end, this takeoff run is increased to 1,180 feet. Since the Cessna 206 is slightly wider, and a tad heavier, than the Cessna 185, I'm going to interpolate these numbers and suggest that the Cessna 185 can do at least this well. Given its mechanical flaps (over the slower-to-operate electrical flaps of the C-206), there are some pilot techniques that can reduce these takeoff distances dramatically. All this is to say that the 960-foot strip related to this incident may have been either more than enough or not quite enough, depending upon the surrounding terrain. At any rate . . .

At the moment this takeoff began, the pilot had set the big Cessna flaps to ten degrees. Somewhere along the takeoff run, he pulled the floor-mounted flap handle to lower the flaps to twenty degrees in order to lower the stall speed slightly, thus promoting an earlier liftoff. That didn't seem to work for him, and as the Cessna neared the end of the airstrip, the pilot aborted the flight. Simply shutting down the throttle control didn't help him, and he then applied the brakes. In fact, he applied "heavy braking," according to his later statement. Too little and too late, as they say, and the Cessna charged ahead and off the end of the airstrip. The landing gear collided with a gravel bar, and both main landing gears collapsed. The result of all this noise and dust was serious structural damage to the landing gear, to both wings, to the fuselage, and to the rear empennage. No one aboard was injured. It will be a long time, though, before the pilot stops going over and over this takeoff in his mind. Or nontakeoff, if you like.

***

It doesn't matter much to whom you talk—the response is always the same: that Super Cub is one helluva flying machine! Because it is. It has remained virtually unchanged since the first one rolled out of the factory. Oh, the engine is now a little larger, and the airframe has been beefed up a bit. Two more wing ribs have been added to each wing, too. But by and large it's the same little airplane that hit the skies quite a few decades ago. Almost anyone can fly one, though not many can fly it to its performance limits. My own favorite, N1858A, was an agricultural model that began life with only a 125-horsepower Lycoming engine hanging out front. With its later 150-horsepower engine—and even though it was full IFR, right down to the glide slope and marker beacons—the little flat-back model could easily escape the earth in ninety feet. Many of Alaska's bush-modified Cubs can take off in less than fifty feet, and some at around thirty-five. Staggering, isn't it? And it is said that, while there isn't much you can do to hurt a Super Cub wing, there isn't really much you can do to improve it, either. And I've found that to be true. Extended wings, droop tips, and flap seal kits may improve the Super Cub's performance a little, but the improvements come at the cost of lowered performance in windy conditions, especially at lower air speeds. Besides, almost no one really needs more than the Super Cub can provide in its factory production mode. And the vast majority of those who have added all these "improvements" to their little Cubs aren't skillful enough to fly to the airplane's performance limits anyway!

One of the problems about this little bomb of a bush plane is that younger or less experienced pilots sometimes can't resist the impulse to yank the little dude off the ground and immediately begin a high-angle-of-bank steep turn and alarming nose-high climb configuration. And while this little airplane will often suffer through this nonsense, there are pilots who just can't wait to show off a little, beginning this risky business much too close to the ground. This hotshot exercise is frequently interrupted when one wingtip strikes a nearby tree and ends with the little fabric-covered flying machine precariously parked some fifty feet or so above solid ground.

I guess that maybe the best rule you can carry with you as you fly—from your very beginnings as a fledgling pilot through your years as a very experienced flier—is this: "Maintain thy air speed, lest the ground rise up and smite thee!" Almost all the other "rules" boil down to that one simple maxim.

One of Alaska's Fish & Wildlife Protection officers (a part of the Alaska State Troopers) let that slip from his mind, it appears, on September 3, 2007, when lifting off a remote bush site in a high-performance Piper Super Cub. The trooper, by the way, carried a commercial pilot certificate. It's probably a minimum requirement for troopers who fly as a part of their duties. Anyway . . .

About twenty-five or so miles from Valdez, Alaska, our trooper belted himself into his little big-foot Cub, did an engine run-up, checked to make sure that the controls were all working—and that the control surfaces moved in response to control displacement—and looked downfield through the curved Plexiglas windshield. He might even have glanced upward through the Cub's "greenhouse" window above, just to remind himself of the condition of the sky up above.

Then he pushed the window ledge–mounted throttle knob forward against its stop and prepared himself for the thrill of leaving behind the limits of the ground-bound. You know—slipping the surly bonds of earth.

Didn't work that way, though. Whether the little Cub was seriously overloaded (or he was taking off with the carburetor heat control to "On"?), or the little 150-horsepower Lycoming engine was already carrying a load of carburetor ice, I'm sure we'll never know. What we do know is that the trooper later reported that the Super Cub did slip free of the earth and did manage to climb above ground effect. That's when the fit hit the shan, as they say, and the airplane immediately lost lift and descended, without ceremony, to flop back onto the earth it had only seconds before so gleefully departed.

"Maintain thy air speed, lest the ground rise up and smite thee!"

Well, it certainly smote the trooper that afternoon. Smote the little Super Cub, too, which now just lay there with structural damage to its wings and fuselage.

***

Perhaps one of the saddest bush aircraft accidents in my mind occurred back in the early sixties, again in Alaska. In this case, the pilot had been ferrying men to and from a rough camp in the remote Alaska outback. The operation required the use of a four-place floatplane, and the pilot was using an older model. Still, it was more than sufficient for the task, and the pilot and his plane had made several successful trips prior to the flight that would end in tragedy.

Having picked up three passengers at the remote lake, the pilot had advised everyone to get strapped in and prepare for the takeoff. With the engine temperature already warm, the preflight didn't require the usual taxiing to perform an engine warmup. So, after making sure his passengers were safely belted down, the pilot turned into the wind, pressed the throttle control forward, and brought the control yoke back into his lap. He held it there until the air speed had built to the point that he could pitch the airplane over onto the step and begin the acceleration that would bring the craft and its load up to takeoff air speed. In almost no time at all, the airplane seemed to lift itself off the water, looking for the altitude that would make it happy.

The pilot, though, thought he needed to change direction before beginning the climbout and rolled into a steep left turn only seconds after leaving the disturbed surface of the remote lake. It was at this point that the left wingtip struck a tree, and the airplane turned more quickly to head back out over the water. But it had lost its flying speed and stalled, allowing the nose to "come through," as they say, and point itself at the water. It was in that nose-down configuration that the four-place impacted the surface of the lake, instantly pitching over onto its back and beginning to sink.

The pilot and his three passengers were able somehow to climb from the cabin and, in short order, were all perched atop the floats like so many birds on a wire. Colder than the birds, though, and soaked all the way through. I suppose it's not necessary to tell you that there isn't much warm water lying around in the Alaska outback. And if there were even one little puddle of it, this small lake wasn't it.

Phil, a diminutive carpenter and part-time trapper, was among the three inconvenienced passengers. He'd been a friend of mine for a number of years, and it seemed that I'd stumble across him every year or two when I was somewhere around Cooper Landing down there on the Kenai Peninsula. He was usually a pretty laid-back soul, but as he relayed this story to me, he was far from his normally cheerful self.

The airplane was slowly sinking deeper and deeper into the frigid waters as the decision was made to swim to shore and get a fire going. The shoreline was less than fifty yards away, and, as one of them had noted, the brisk and chilling wind would at least be at their backs during the breathtaking swim. One of the passengers, though, had to beg off. He couldn't swim a lick and was absolutely petrified at the thought of leaving the seeming safety of the float upon which he stood shivering in concert with his partners. Promising the nonswimmer that they would build a raft and get him off that danged float in right short order, the pilot and the other two passengers slipped into the shockingly cold water and began thrashing their way toward the narrow dab of rocky beach at the shoreline. In no time, the three of them were standing on the shore, dripping and shivering like a pack of wet hounds, and promising again that they'd get their partner off that float and to dry land right quick.

With that, Phil, the smallest and certainly in the best physical condition of the lot, took off, wet clothes and all, at a dead run toward a camp that he knew to be about two miles away. He couldn't have been more than about a half-mile away when a quavering voice came across the water from the slowly sinking airplane to the stricken man's amigos on shore.

"Boys," the voice said above the wind, "She's sinking. Ya gotta hurry here."

"He'll be right back," came the reply from the beach. "We're gonna lash up a raft and get you off there right away."

The two on solid ground began to gather up what brush and limbs they could find close by. One of them thought of how different things looked from varying perspectives. For instance, from where he stood, he could note that the aircraft was still slowly sinking in the lake. He knew that his partner, glued to the top of that float hull, could only see the water as slowly rising.

"Boys, ya gotta hurry up, here. This thing's still a-sinkin'," he called out several times.

For a time, they all wondered why the airplane wasn't drifting a little closer to the shore, but then they came to the conclusion that the nose and prop were probably stuck in the mud at the bottom of the shallow lake and that only the tail end was slowly settling into the water. It would do that until the inverted stabilizer also touched the bottom, but it looked as though that wasn't going to happen in time to help very much.

It was just over an hour when Phil arrived, almost on his last legs, carrying several lengths of rope of different diameters. Lengths of parachute shroud line—popular in Alaska but not really worth a helluva lot in the bush, especially around water—were mixed in with quarter-inch laid hemp line and a healthy length of half-inch braided nylon. Enough, they all thought, that they could safely tie together some sort of floating platform to reach their stricken friend and bring him to safety.

By this time, the water had risen to the stranded man's belt. He was getting light enough in the water now that he had to be very careful that his feet didn't slip off the float. If they did, he knew he'd never again have that purchase. Surely he'd just drown. He was so cold now, though, that his circulation had slowed and his thought processes had begun to shut down. He no longer felt the cold water, except when he swept his hands through the water in an aid to holding his position on the float.

"You boys gotta do somethin', now," he called in a voice that had lost all but the last of its strength. He knew this bad situation was coming to its end . . . one way or another. And at this point, he wasn't sure he cared all that much. He was damned tired, now, his emotions almost completely drained, and his strength all but gone.

The three on the beach had lashed together a crude raft of sorts, but when they dragged it into the water, it simply submerged itself about halfway. Working on a quick fix, they lightened it somewhat and pushed it out a bit against the chop and onshore wind. It was only then that they realized that someone would have to swim behind the raft, pushing it against the wind for the hundred yards or so to the inverted floatplane. One of them actually tried that, but he didn't get more than eight or ten feet in spite of all his struggles.

Phil, probably their best swimmer, was too flagged out to even make the attempt. He knew, as well as did his partners, that to try would be to seal his own fate in this cold, remote lake.

"Boys, ya gotta help me. I ain't got much time!"

Up to his chin now, and in spite of his waterlogged clothes and boots, he had become too light in the water to maintain a solid footing on the irregular float bottom. Besides, he had already about slipped off several times. He knew he couldn't balance himself on the sharp float keel for much longer.

"Boys, ya gotta hurry. . . ."

And that was the end of it. He lost his footing for the last time and disappeared below the choppy surface of the cold, remote, and unnamed lake somewhere in the unforgiving Alaska outback. A tough, tough way to go.

***

On March 14, 2008, a *Palm Beach Post* headline proclaimed in bold print: "MARTIN PLANE CRASH KILLS 4." The Martin County crash site is only a few miles from our Palm Beach County, Florida, home. I can see no reason other than gross pilot error for the mishap that killed all aboard this gentle, easy to fly, and most forgiving four-place Cessna model, its C-172 Skylane.

The plane was registered to Kemper Aviation, based at Palm Beach County's Lantana Airport, known as South County Airport by FAA designation. (It was from here that I had formerly done quite a bit of banner-tow flying, enjoying the required slow-flight along South Florida's golden beaches.) The plane, N284SP, was piloted by Kemper Aviation's managing partner and chief instructor, a chap by the name of Jeff Rozelle. I can tell you that his instructors thought quite highly of him. His remaining instructors, that is. He lost a handful of them recently. The FAA is already investigating two earlier fatal crashes involving Kemper aircraft, and several of his former instructors had bailed out on him.

Along with Mr. Rozelle (age thirty-six) that morning was graduate student Damion Marx (thirty-five years old) of Boca Raton, Florida. He was a student at Florida Atlantic University (FAU), studying integrated biology. Phil Heidemann (forty-three) was also aboard that morning. Phil was working on his master's degree in biological sciences at FAU. It was said that he was also assisting Damion that morning. The last passenger aboard, Gareth Akermann (also thirty-six) was from Halifax, Nova Scotia. Gareth was on a six-month contract with the university in its efforts to study the habits of migratory birds, mostly waterfowl, it was said. The Cessna had departed Lantana Airport but had stopped at Okeechobee, some distance to the northwest, to board the last passenger before beginning the bird-watching phase of the flight. Most probably, this third passenger was Gareth. It is believed that this was to have been the final flight of this year's contract. Well, it was. . . .

This was to be a typical flight, in that the university had a deal going with Kemper Aviation. Once every several weeks, on a planned schedule, a Kemper aircraft would lift off for another investigative flight into Martin County's bird country, so to speak. Always, the flights were low level and at reduced air speeds. By low level, it is known that the flights routinely operated at two hundred to three hundred feet above the ground. That's a comfortable altitude range for Alaska bush pilots, who may not fly above those elevations for months on end. For the average stateside pilot, however, these low altitudes are normally seen only when the pilot climbs through on his way up or descends through during his descent. Or when he is crop-dusting or towing advertising banners.

Routine or not, though, low altitudes are nothing to be casual about. Especially at slow air speeds! "Slow flight," as it is called, is a very special flying technique. Every pilot should master it, and most believe that they have. In fact, very few have, and I have to think that easily 98 percent of those who have are Alaska pilots. A pilot who is comfortable and capable on the ragged edge of real slow flight is a good pilot, and I'll fly with him any day! They really are rare.

Slow flight, at its very best, is a flight configuration wherein the airplane, in a wings level and straight-ahead mode, is operated very near the airplane's (at its present gross load) stall speed—the air speed at which the airplane's various flight surfaces will no longer support flight. Though the full "stall" may happen in a helluva hurry, the surfaces actually stall separately: the rudder stalls first, the elevators stall second, and the wings stall last. Truly, all this is sort of academic, since the airplane has just quit flying, period.

These stalls will occur at higher air speeds as the airplane becomes more and more out of a "straight-and-level" flight configuration. Stall speeds vary with load conditions, too, so that a usually docile airplane, flying empty, straight and level, and with power off, will stall at maybe thirty-five miles an hour, may just as easily stall at ninety or one hundred miles an hour if it is carrying a full load, flying in a steep bank, and under climb power.

The fall hunting seasons in Alaska see quite a bit of this sort of thing. Two guys in a light airplane out looking for moose provide the usual scenario. A moose is spotted, the plane descends to probably two hundred feet or so—if the plane wasn't already down there, that is—and then begins to circle the moose. This act is usually done for any one of several reasons, and it's usually done by hunters who are even then skirting on the very edge of game law violations. At other times, it might be a low-time pilot "buzzing" his own home, or the home or farm of friends or relatives. In any case, it's always the result of an ill-advised, low-altitude maneuver during which the passenger, if there is one, is gawking at something on the ground, and so, unfortunately, is the pilot.

At any rate, both the pilot and his passenger in this little two-place Piper—or Citabria or whatever—are now focusing intently on the moose (or whatever else may have attracted their attention). The pilot has already committed the ultimate sin: flying the airplane is no longer his primary objective. He has allowed himself to become an observer. He may see that the moose is really a pretty good one and now thinks it deserves an even closer look.

While the pilot's a little distracted, the high wing seems to want to come on over the top, but a little rudder pressure on that side will take care of that. And it does for a moment. Oops, slightly more top rudder now, as the pilot's nose is nearly pressed against the side window in his effort to get a closer look at the moose. And then—*wham!*

The low wing has suddenly stalled and the high wing *does* come on over the top. *Instantly!* By now, the nose has fallen through to point at the ground (actually, the tail has raised itself to give the pilot and his passenger this view of things), and the airplane will have to lose between five hundred and seven hundred feet of altitude before the pilot can stop the spin and the resulting dive that has so quickly developed. But the pilot has only two hundred feet! And another avoidable pilot error has made the local newspapers.

And so it very likely was with Cessna 2845-Sierra-Poppa from Kemper Aviation. Observers in the area reported that the Cessna was seen to be flying low and slow while making turns close to the ground. And if the Cessna really did enter into that low wing stall and spin scenario, no intervening miracle could have saved the group once that high wing began its short trip over the top.

The Cessna's nose and propeller impacted first, of course. The Cessna immediately flopped over onto its back. From initial impact point to final resting place, the aircraft seems to have slid only about forty or fifty feet. And now for the worst part . . .

That accident occurred in a field so large that the airplane could have safely landed after a routine approach from any direction of the compass.

I make that point because my appraisal as written above may be completely wrong. What is absolutely clear to me is the fact that the airplane crashed while in a stalled configuration. I can't believe Kemper's co-owner and chief flight instructor would stall the Cessna on a simple, straight-in landing, even a dead-stick, engine-out emergency landing! I can't believe, either, that the engine might have quit, forcing the pilot to make this unsuccessful landing. If that had been the case, why would the aircraft impact the earth in a near vertical attitude? After all, a full stall is required for *every* landing, otherwise the airplane will just keep right on flying, right? It has to quit flying in order to land and stop. Nope, pilot error, that's my appraisal of it, no matter how many lawsuits may eventually be filed against the manufacturer of perhaps the world's safest four-place airplane.

Chapter 21

The Usual Problems

A GOOD LANDING IS ONE FROM WHICH YOU CAN WALK AWAY.
A GREAT ONE IS ONE AFTER WHICH THE PLANE
CAN BE USED AGAIN.

In April of 1965, a series of small inconveniences began. I say "began" because they seemed to continue for a short time, too. They may have been little things, but they seemed to plague me whenever I strapped myself into the driver's seat. Let me give you a little insight into the life of a single-engine, outback pilot's everyday puzzlements.

I had flown Cessna 180 N3140C from South Lake Tahoe to Pacific Airmotive, a maintenance facility located at the Burbank Airport in Los Angeles. This trip was my first look at Los Angeles from the driver's seat, though I had been there several times previously as a passenger on one of the big iron flying machines. My approach past Edwards Air Force Base (AFB), Fox Field in the high desert country at Palmdale, and finally over the Los Angeles Hills had been made as part of a night VFR flight through California's Owens Valley. That wide, flat valley had led me past Mono Lake and Mt. Whitney, the highest point in the continental United States.

As I passed the Los Angeles Hills, I marveled at the sea of lights ahead and below me. Why, I wondered, would so damned many people all crowd together in one small valley to live in such cramped conditions? There must have been a gazillion lights down there!

When I contacted LAX (Los Angeles) Approach, they directed me to another frequency for Burbank Approach, who in turn asked me to "report the four stacks."

"Say again?" I asked, obviously confused.

"The four stacks—the four stacks. Report the four stacks!"

"I'm out of Alaska, partner. I'm a stranger down here. I'm short on grub, and I'm not too long on sleep. You gotta make more sense for me than that."

"First time in the big city, is it? Just raise your left wing, four-zero-Charlie," came the tower's reply. "See the Constellation out there?"

"Yeah, Roger—four-zero-Charlie has the Connie."

"Follow the Connie, four-zero-Charlie."

"Roger—follow the Connie for four-zero-Charlie," I came back.

Soon I saw these four huge, red-and-white–striped chimney towers looming out of the darkness, slightly off to the left of the Cessna's nose. The Connie was still ahead and a bit higher but clearly descending now. I reported the four stacks.

I was given another frequency change, and a very nice female voice from the Burbank Tower brought me to the pattern, where I flew a nonstandard right traffic, settled to the dark runway, and began to look for the Pacific Airmotive ramp, where I would tie the little Cessna down for the night.

The guys at Pacific Airmotive were really helpful. When I told them the airplane would be flying through the Canadian outback directly to Alaska, they understood the need for attentive maintenance. I thought. . .

Among other things, I had asked for new 8.50x6.00 tires and tubes to replace the original 6.00s mounted on the little four-place Cessna. I was told that no such animals as 8.50s were available because no size like that was even being made. Since I had been flying those oversized tires and tubes for many years, I certainly knew better than that. I asked someone to call Akron, Ohio, and run a check on it. So—I eventually got my 8.50x6.00 tires and tubes.

I also told the mechanics that I wanted the voltage regulator replaced. Be sure, I told them, to install a *new* one, and *for Pete's sake, don't just file the points on the old one!* The mechanic said he understood and that a new regulator would be installed on the firewall, replacing the original.

The ship was ready in two days, and late in the evening of April 19, 1965, I climbed aboard, fired 'er up, and lit out to the north. I would be flying past Edwards AFB again, this time in the opposite direction, and then on up the valley and into Lake Tahoe. The mountains ahead would force me above twelve thousand feet, a thin-air altitude that causes most Alaska pilots to develop nosebleeds and to become a little dizzy from the height. We are much more comfortable down there somewhere between twenty feet and two hundred feet!

The first thing maintenance had done was to remove the battery and place it on a trickle charger. It's a routine courtesy, and all pilots appreciate it, I'm sure. I did. Until later, that is.

As it turned out, the mechanic had removed the old voltage regulator, had taken a close look at it, and had then decided to touch it up with a point file instead of replacing it. He had then simply reinstalled the original regulator, against my specific instructions and against our earlier agreement. I suppose this gesture was his way of helping hold down the costs of my requested maintenance. But for a seven-dollar voltage regulator? Anyway, by the time I had passed the hills north of Burbank, the old points had stuck once again, and I could no longer transmit. By the time I passed Edwards AFB, only a few minutes later, I couldn't receive on any of the radios, either. So much for the helpful battery charging.

I landed at Lone Pine to see about buying a new voltage regulator but was told I would have to wait for morning when someone would have to drive someplace else to buy one. I hadn't shut down the big Continental engine, since I knew I'd probably have to try to hand-prop the 230-horsepower beast back to life if I did. Which I wouldn't have been able to do anyway, most likely. I had no recourse other than to just climb back aboard, taxi to the runway, and take off again, climbing out northward once more.

I continued the climb to twelve thousand, then leveled off to set up my cruise. In a few more minutes, the red instrument lights dimmed and went out. I was pretty sure the battery was then on its last legs. I turned off all lights, including the navigation lights and anticollision beacon, and cruised smoothly on through the dark night toward Lake Tahoe. I was hoping to save the battery's last gasp for one more engine start the following morning, when I planned to fly to Reno, Nevada, for a new voltage regulator.

There was no activity at the South Lake Tahoe airport, and I didn't bother with the radios. A night landing on the 6,300-foot runway was no problem, and I soon had the little Cessna tucked away for the night.

The following morning, I lit out for Reno, just thirty minutes away. I had already called to make sure that they had the regulator I needed.

The battery had come up a bit overnight, and I was able to talk to Reno's tower. I had telephoned them earlier, arranging an arrival time and advising them that I might be without radios. They just asked that I enter the pattern with a standard entry to the active runway and go through the old wing-wag about receiving their light signals. Everything seemed to be going my way for a change. I decided to leave the radios on, just to be on the safe side. They wouldn't take much power, and I thought the battery might last at least that much longer after its overnight rest. As it turned out, though, this whole flight would last only a few minutes anyway.

I made a power landing—that is to say, one of those really glass-smooth landings that sees the main gear touching down softly while the tail is still up there off the ground, the best and smoothest of landings when carrying passengers—but the moment the wheels touched the blacktop, the left tire blew out!

I'm one of those guys who never relaxes on the controls until the engine has been switched off and the prop has stopped turning. Comes from years of flying taildraggers and floatplanes, I suppose. It was just as well, that morning. The flat didn't give me a really serious problem, but it did keep me busy for a moment or two, riding the brake on one side and the rudder on the other.

When I finally had the little airplane settled down, we were stuck smack dab in the middle of Reno's active runway. The tower called me to suggest that, if I really wanted to park the thing, wouldn't it be better to first taxi it off the active?

I explained my little problem, and the tower guys arranged for a tow cart, which dragged my sorry little backside to the maintenance facility where I could get both the new regulator and a repaired left main tube. When Pacific Airmotive had stuffed the floppy new tube inside the big 8.50 tires, they had pinched the left one between the tire's thick rubber rim and the metal wheel hub. As it turned out, I was becoming less than thrilled with the work they had done for me. Still, no harm—no foul, I suppose.

On May 4, three of us left South Lake Tahoe for Alaska and a spring bear hunting and fishing trip. One of these passengers was a California hunter and Lake Tahoe resident named Jay. The other was Basil C. Bradbury, who would later become one of my Alaska assistant guides and, ultimately, the man with more world-record big game animals than any other. The trip would be a disaster!

Not long after leaving Tahoe, I found the cylinder head temperature wasn't where it should have been. The EGT showed the exhaust gas temperature right on the money—with the engine properly leaned out, that is—so I suspected a faulty gauge or thermocouple, one or the other.

I landed in Troudale, Oregon, just upriver from Portland, and one of their fine mechanics ran a check of things, replacing the thermocouple for us. We were off the ground again in no time at all, and the rest of the trip was pretty much without incident. Until we reached Gulkana, Alaska, that is.

We had departed Whitehorse, Yukon Territory, and had cruised smoothly into Northway, Alaska, where we cleared U.S. Customs. And, after the usual pie and coffee, we were off again, this time on the nonstop leg to Anchorage. Scabby weather forced us to land at Gulkana, and it later cleared barely enough that we were allowed a zone clearance for departure. The word was that we shouldn't try to come back right away: the weather was "measured two hundred feet sky obscured in show showers." If the truth were known, that's really my kind of weather. Long trips on sunny days bore the wits out of me. Still, it was well below minimums, and Gulkana wouldn't let me back in until it got much, much better.

One hour and twenty-three minutes later, we landed at Anchorage's Merrill Field, twenty-three hours and four minutes flying time since we had departed South Lake Tahoe, back on the civilized California/Nevada border and high in the Sierra Nevada Mountains.

Well, the entire trip was one great big wash. The weather remained terrible, and we weren't able to satisfy the request by a fishing tackle manufacturer that we get some pictures of his gear and, in the same frame, a photo of a fishing brown bear. We were calendar early for that, but with a little better weather, it might have been possible. Anyway, no deal.

On June 6, we lifted off Anchorage's Merrill Field again, this time southbound. First stop: Northway, about two hours out again, for the usual excellent pie and a last cup of that great Alaska coffee. And to clear U.S. Customs on the way out, of course, though that wasn't really a requirement when leaving the country.

After Northway, it was another two-plus-twelve to Whitehorse, Yukon Territory, for Canadian Customs and avgas for the Cessna. We were looking for Ft. St. John later the same day, for a total of 1,271 air miles before dinner and a good night's sleep. This leg of the trip wouldn't be as routine as we might have expected.

First of all, we were about forty air miles south of Whitehorse, after the customs and avgas thing, and were climbing out of nine thousand for ten when, without any sort of warning at all, the engine quit as dead as a stone. That may have been the loudest silence I have ever heard. Seconds later, the engine came back to life with neither a gurgle nor an apology, and it has never balked again, as far as I know. Smooth day, all engine instruments in the green, and no apparent reason at all for the shut-down. Ah, well—another of life's little mysteries. But, it surely was quiet there for a minute!

We made Watson Lake one hour and fifty minutes later. Topping the tanks, hitting the little boys' room, and stretching our legs took only a short time, and, with no little trepidation, we were on the road again.

The "little trepidation" was on account of a lousy weather forecast for our en route pleasure. The lousy forecast turned out to be true. My logs for that leg of the flight read: "Measured 200 ft., sky obscured in light rain and fog."

Now, this route isn't flatland flying. Usually, it's made with altitudes of up to ten thousand feet where Very High Frequency (VHF) communications are decent, Visual Omnirange Receiver (VOR) reception is fair to good, Automatic Direction Finder (ADF) tracking is close to excellent, and the views are out of this world. This leg, though, would be a whole 'nother matter.

About halfway along the route, I heard Ft. St. John trying to raise us on the VHF Comm radio, but we were flying much too low to transmit to them. In fact, we were following the ADF needle around one small hill after another, trying to keep to the valleys and still make forward progress. Often, we would be flying ninety degrees or more away from our intended course.

Okanagan Helicopters had readied a search for us, as none of my many transmissions was getting through to them. We weren't lost, and we weren't down in the Canadian wilds of British Columbia. We were simply flapping along up there as best we could, just at too low an altitude for successful radio transmissions. St. John and the helicopters would just have to wait for us to pop in on them, I guessed.

At about the halfway point, we crossed the little private strip at Jedney. I gave them a call on their published low frequency, and the guy was quick to tell me that his field was closed due to its wet and muddy condition. I was flying at about one hundred feet at that time and had looked the strip over as we passed above it. I replied to the guy that, if the weather got much worse and we had to turn back, it might be a good idea to avoid standing in the middle of his muddy little strip. Closed or not, his private airport might be our best chance to take a break without bending the airplane in the trees and brush somewhere else along the way.

When we finally found Ft. St. John, two hours and forty-five minutes after leaving Watson Lake, we could see the big search helicopters still on the runway. With instructions to overfly the field, do a 180-degree turn at the southern end, and fly a standard left-hand pattern to the landing, we were almost there.

Except that, once I passed overhead and began the turn, I thought I'd lost St. John again. The visibility really *wasn't* all that good, I guess, and it took me another few moments to find the field, even though I knew it was just outside the left window and straight down below the overloaded Cessna.

The rest of the trip to South Lake Tahoe was pretty routine, though at Redmond, Oregon, we elected to land on a taxiway rather than on a runway. The crosswinds there were pretty brisk. Our ground speed in the heavily loaded Cessna 180 had been 174 knots, really zipping along for that bird, and I knew it would be much easier just to go with the flow, so to speak. We had been traveling in winds of about 50 knots. The Flight Service Station (FSS) guy didn't want to hear about any sort of departure from standard procedures, so I decided not to bore him with any more reports. When we dropped in to check the weather ahead—after having landed on his taxiway, I admit—we just allowed as how, yeah, it was a little breezy out there. Clearly, he wasn't a pilot himself!

On June 12 of that year, I was at Lake Tahoe when I received a telephone call from a guy who identified himself as John Robinson. John had purchased a Cessna 180, even though he hadn't logged a single flying hour in his life. He said he had heard that I was familiar with the Cessna and wondered if I would fly him to a place or two in it. He would ride the right seat and observe. Later, he would get his own flying license. I agreed, and later that day I met John and had a look at his new purchase.

The Cessna, registered as N2956C, was mounted on what is called "crosswind" gear. This kind of landing gear was supposed to allow the wheels to swivel slightly, reducing the airplane's handling anomalies when landing in a crosswind. It didn't take more than one glance to tell me that these would be a real problem on beach landings, but John certainly wouldn't be making any of those. I just told him that they looked pretty neat and let it go at that.

He first wanted to fly from Lake Tahoe to San Diego, which we did on June 13, returning to Tahoe the same day.

On June 29, he had planned a trip to Placerville, so we made that flight, too. A complete electrical systems failure made that flight a little goofy but caused no real problems. A few days later, though, would produce a flight that certainly had its white-knuckle moments.

On the Fourth of July, John wanted to visit his family in Vancouver, Washington, just across the Columbia River from Portland, Oregon. The grass strip there was about twenty-one hundred feet long and fifty feet wide, so it was plenty big enough for the loaded Cessna taildragger. I checked it out in the *Airguide Publications Flight Guide*, an airport and frequency manual that belongs in every light aircraft, I believe. I learned that there were power lines crossing at the west end. We would probably be landing from east to west, since there was also a pretty good bridge beyond the west end of the strip.

I had told John that we would have to be airborne before 4:00 PM on the Fourth of July in order to make the landing in any sort of daylight. He understood that, but he diddled and dawdled until 6:00, setting us up for a nighttime approach and landing. I guess I wasn't particularly bothered by that, since I had plenty of experience in both nighttime flying and nighttime landings, even at unlighted strips. After we were all strapped in, we taxied out and lifted off from the South Lake Tahoe airport and, once we were west of the Sierras, turned northward and took up a course for Lakeview, Nevada, where we would have to stop and top off the tanks. More time lost, of course, and as we later approached Portland in the dark, I called to get a frequency for the little field at Vancouver. I was told that Vancouver had no voice communications but that Portland Approach Control could give me whatever assistance I might need.

Since I had never been to Vancouver, Washington, before—nor to Portland, Oregon, either, for that matter—I had no idea what the airport environment really looked like. One of the reasons, of course, that I would have preferred to arrive during the daylight hours. I did know that Portland had a departure corridor for the big boys and that I had to avoid that airspace at all costs.

Portland Approach told me that the grass strip at Vancouver lay at the west end, and just downstream from a row of boat storage and repair facility buildings that would appear to me as World War II Quonset huts. Having descended below the departure corridor at Portland's big airport, I was low over the river and westbound when the first of the waterside buildings appeared ahead of us. Farther along, I could also make out the bridge that spanned the river, and I knew the grass strip would appear before I reached that bridge. Still, it was a pitch-black night, and if I hadn't had so much dark-of-night Alaska bush flying behind me, I wouldn't have been trying to find that little, unlighted field in the inky, pitch-black night.

I was flying almost level, using power and two notches of the big Cessna flaps, when I passed the last of the boat facilities. Dead ahead, and not more than about forty feet below us, I could see the dark area that would be the little grass strip beside the river. Portland had told me that I might be able to spot the strip because there were some fireworks scheduled "near there somewhere." I had eased in forty degrees of the big flaps by then and had slowed for the touchdown, now only seconds away.

Just as the main gear touched the soft grass, all hell broke loose! Damned if the fireworks were scheduled for *somewhere near* the strip . . . they were being held *on* the strip! The whole view through the windshield seemed to explode at once, and rockets were blasting off with alarming regularity and no pauses between the launchings!

Dead ahead I could see a fire truck scurrying to get out of our path, and several scores of people were likewise racing for the edge of the strip, hoping I wouldn't mow them down before they got there, I'm sure. I don't doubt that I had scared them nearly as much as they had scared me. An airplane is made to fly, and dashing ahead with a loaded airplane on a little grass strip in absolute darkness—and remembering the airplane's teeny-weeny little brakes—is a little shy of a really soothing and relaxing landing.

I had shut down the power and was holding the control yoke forward, both to see ahead better and to ease the tail down to get that third roller down gently on the grass. I was also braking, as best I could. I didn't want to yank back on the yoke and jam on the brakes, since that would put the big engine cowling in front of the windshield, and I wouldn't be able to see a damned thing straight ahead of us. And I certainly didn't want to brake so hard that the nose pitched down to bury the spinning prop in the turf. It was truly a juggling act for a moment there, but the Cessna behaved itself well, and we were soon at a speed that allowed me to stop the plane and look around for the best place to get the hell out of everyone else's way. I couldn't leave the plane parked on the runway, of course, and I was looking for a spot to tie it down for the night. I finally found an area that would allow this, and, after taxiing very slowly to the spot and anchoring the Cessna to the earth, we all piled in with John's family, who had come down to meet us, and drove to their home for dinner and a good night's sleep. We would all stay in Vancouver that night, returning by way of Redmond, California, the next day.

Speak of pilot error—this was a situation where the pilot's confidence slipped into overconfidence. Since I didn't know the lay of the land around there and had no clear idea of exactly how far ahead that bridge might be, I had committed to a one-way landing with no options. And I'd been at this flying stuff long enough to know that the pilot is a fool who allows his options to dwindle down to nearly nothing.

***

During the first quarter of 1967, I had been asked by Bill Heinkel, manager for the Washington, D.C., partnership of Daniel, Mann, Johnson & Mendenhall, architects and engineers, to fly him and one of his engineers around that area in their search for likely looking COMSAT sites. Flying a Mooney Super 21 was a lot of fun for me. I'd been flying high-wing taildraggers for some time, and the slick little low-wing retractable with its sexy, swept-forward tail was kinda neat. I could use the plane for my own personal flights, too, during off time, so I happily arranged one day to fly my wife and small daughter to North Philadelphia to visit one of my wife's beautiful sisters and her sister's family there. We had planned to make the short flight on April 3.

It was a gorgeous spring day when I checked out the Mooney and then made sure we were all properly belted down. I started the comfortable little four-place, received a taxi clearance from Washington's Dulles Airport Ground Control, and taxied to the active runway for the run-up. With everything in the green, and the little Mooney chomping at the bit to get on with it, I took the active and advanced the throttle to takeoff power. Smooth as silk, the little craft surged ahead, eager to take its place in the clear, blue sky.

In short order, I had the wheels tucked away in their wells, had turned on course for Philadelphia, and had reached our cruising altitude of two thousand feet. It was then that my wife decided to hang her purse on the door latch. When she did, the door popped open, the loud rush of air invaded our little world, and she let out a little screech. And I began worrying about the airflow across the vertical stabilizer!

I found I was unable to latch the door again from the inside. Without risking tearing the door handle off its mounting screws, at any rate. I called Dulles Tower, told them of our predicament, and requested a clearance to land on the nearest runway.

The tower asked if we needed trucks, emergency vehicles, or foam, to all of which I replied heck no. We only needed to land again and secure the danged door! We weren't an accident looking for a place to happen, for cryin' out loud.

As I reduced power and reentered the traffic pattern, though, the gear alarm switch suddenly came to life, screaming its little lungs out. That scared the hell out of my wife, of course, who was already unnerved by the roar of wind rushing around the unlatched door.

I thought I might have reduced the manifold pressure a bit too far without having lowered the landing gear, but that wasn't the case. The gear was already down and locked. I added just a bit of power to see what that would do, and the alarm quit its screeching at once. The minute I reduced power again, though, back it came, seeming even louder than before.

"Horse feathers," I thought. "We've got a short somewhere in the gear switch alarm system. What the hell is next?"

After landing and turning off onto the assigned taxiway, we returned to the maintenance shop, where the guys put a quick end to the electrical short and its shrieking alarm. With gentle instructions to my wife that she might want to avoid hanging her purse on the door latch again, we once more lit out for Philadelphia. This time, things went more smoothly. Though I haven't flown a Mooney in the many years since then, I'll always have a very soft spot in my heart for that economical, fast-flying, and attractive little airplane. It's the only flying machine I know that can still get one mile an hour cruise speed for each rated horsepower of its engine.

Of course there will always be a few problems that come up when operating any piece of machinery. Airplanes included. Most of you have already had your share of them, I reckon. But, don't despair—you'll no doubt encounter a few more before you're done.

Chapter 22

Bad Weather

Helicopters don't really fly. They're just so ugly that the earth repels them.

On December 14, 2006, Andrew "Andy" Simonds departed Port Heiden, Alaska, way down there on the Alaska Peninsula, with Aniakchak Crater (a long extinct volcano) lying about fifteen miles off his right wing. He was bound for his home base at King Salmon, about one hour north. Andy lifted off at around ten minutes past six in the evening and, five minutes later, used his radio to report to his company operations in King Salmon that he was airborne, with an estimated time en route of one hour.

It was full dark around Port Heiden, just as it was all over Alaska at that time of day, but Andy had flown this route many times, in spite of his young age. Andy was only twenty-five years old.

The low-wing Piper Cherokee, registration number N8361Q, was one of the Peninsula Airways (PenAir) fleet of aircraft, at that time stationed at King Salmon. The ship was utilized primarily for local flights into several areas of the Bristol Bay region. On this flight, the aircraft carried only one passenger, Ms. Renee Matson, forty-five years of age.

The weather in this neck of the woods is sometimes a little discouraging, with low ceilings, fog, and moderate to high winds being commonplace. This night was no different, with winds from 290 degrees at sixteen knots, gusting to more than twenty-four knots. The Port Heiden station reported that the wind was just about directly onshore from the waters of Bristol Bay and blowing toward the Aleutian Range, of which Aniakchak Crater is a part. It wouldn't have been too turbulent, however, since these winds were generally coming in off the cold waters of Bristol Bay. Visibility was down to four miles, but occasional transient snow squalls added to the weather mix no doubt reduced that visibility to a mile or less from time to time.

Clouds were reported at six hundred feet, but with almost flat, lake-filled tundra between Port Heiden and King Salmon, that is usually considered by experienced pilots to be more than sufficient. There is only one three-hundred-foot-high hill between the two towns, as I recall it, and the Bristol Bay beach lay just off Andy's left wing that night. He knew that he could always use that beach for an emergency landing field if things really went south for him at some point along the way.

I've flown that route—both ways—in much worse weather than Andy was confronted with that night. And I admit that I was once within eight or ten seconds from aborting the flight, too, opting instead for a nighttime beach landing. Just as I rolled the wings out of level to begin the turn that night, I saw the glow of the King Salmon USAF station's radome dead ahead through the nighttime mist. Surely a most welcome sight, since I wasn't all that thrilled at the notion of a beach landing in the pitch black night, even in the taildragger four-place Cessna that I was driving at the time. Andy wasn't so lucky, though, and one hour after his earlier notice of departure from Port Heiden, his flight operations still hadn't heard another peep from him.

An air search by other company aircraft was initiated at half past seven that evening, and, only seven minutes later, Andy's flight was officially logged by the FAA as missing.

An ELT signal was detected about fifteen miles northeast of Port Heiden (only eight or ten minutes' flying time that night for Andy). A ground search was initiated from Heiden, but rough terrain put a quick stop to that.

At about ten o'clock that same night, a Coast Guard HH-60 helicopter out of Kodiak Island spotted the wreckage in flat, snow-covered terrain. Indications were that Andy may have tried to abort the flight, since the wreckage was widely scattered along a heading of about 130 degrees magnetic, just about opposite the direction he should have been headed. The wreckage track, about one hundred yards long, would seem to indicate that Andy had either turned or was in the act of turning back toward Port Heiden when the Cherokee impacted the snow-covered tundra, and the plane may have been in almost level flight.

Thus ended PenAir Flight 842, scheduled to depart Port Heiden at 2:45 in the afternoon but delayed on account of scabby weather until Andy's later departure at just past 6:00 that evening. Sadly, neither Andy nor Renee survived the accident.

***

PenAir had been haunted by bad weather several years before this tragic accident, that time in October 2001. It was again in the Bristol Bay area, though this time the problem occurred at the town of Dillingham.

One of Dillingham's claims to fame may be its herring industry, which, for a short time each year, sees a whirlwind of activity centered around the harvesting of herring eggs deposited just offshore. There are occasionally upwards of nearly a dozen Super Cubs and other high-performance light aircraft flying within a one-mile diameter here, spotting the schools of incoming herring for the waiting fishing fleet. As far as I'm concerned, this is the world's most dangerous flying, and I've only done it once. There just isn't enough money to entice me into doing that again! Too much of a pilot's safety depends upon the flying of others.

PenAir was operating a Cessna 208 Caravan, registered with the FAA as N9530F, as its Flight 350, which was that morning scheduled to carry nine passengers from Dillingham to King Salmon, sort of the next town over, so to speak. The weather was good, though a bit chilly at twenty degrees Fahrenheit. Alaskans know this temperature as above discomfort, though below freezing. A little later in the winter, it could get as much as sixty or seventy degrees colder in this neck of the woods.

The previous day had been one filled with typical area weather: rain and mist or thin fog, for the most part. The rain had turned to light snow with mist beginning about 10:15 the night before the flight. N9530F had been tied down outside, exposed to the weather overnight, which was also usual at Dillingham. What with continuous light rain until the thermometer dropped below freezing, one could pretty much expect ice on the wings, windshield, tail surfaces, propeller, and other exposed aircraft parts. No doubt this would have been smooth ice, too, heavy and hard to see, especially if it were later covered with snow or frost. When the light snow did begin to fall, it could be expected that this snow, if it continued for more than an hour or so, would cover any trace of the hard ice that may have formed when the temperatures had dropped. Clearly, deicing procedures were going to be required.

The pilot for this flight was properly licensed and had logged about 3,100 flying hours as pilot in command. He had both a single-engine and multiengine commercial pilot certificate with instrument rating. He also held an airframe and powerplant mechanic (A&E) certificate. His logbook showed that he had accrued about 74 hours in the Cessna CE-208 model that he would be flying that day. All in all, not a staggering flight record, but certainly one that qualified him to act as the pilot in command for this flight.

It was not until the pilot reached the field at around eight o'clock that morning that he learned from the flight coordinator that he would be flying the Cessna 208 to King Salmon with nine passengers aboard. This was no surprise, one would suppose, since flights between Dillingham and King Salmon were almost run-of-the-mill occurrences. Besides, it was one of those flights that could be made in some pretty scabby weather, since there was literally no high ground between the two airports. Aeronautical charts show the highest ground out there as somewhere around three hundred feet above sea level, actually less than pattern altitude of the airport on either end of this trip. At any rate, this flight was doomed to be a short one indeed. It would end just short of three-quarters of a mile from the departure end of the Dillingham runway. This is a tad less than twenty seconds of flight, at ninety miles an hour. No, sir, not a long flight at all.

Another pilot that morning reported clear ice on his own airplane and had said that the ice was between one-quarter and one-half inch thick. He said the ice was about as tough as epoxy. And another PenAir pilot reported airframe icing with a snow or frost covering.

Just after eight thirty that morning, a pilot from another company on the field saw the PenAir pilot performing his preflight walk-around and inspection. He noticed that the big Cessna hadn't yet been deiced. Just before nine o'clock, the Caravan pilot asked the ramp supervisor to fuel the Cessna with sixty gallons of Jet A fuel. This ramp supervisor then reminded the pilot that the aircraft would require deicing prior to departure.

The Caravan pilot continued on into the flight operations area, where he asked his supervisor about deicing procedures for the Caravan at the Dillingham field. This wouldn't have been unusual, either, since the pilot was relatively new to the Dillingham area and perhaps to the PenAir way of doing things. The procedures were described to the pilot, and he was reminded that he should be sure that the aircraft was thoroughly deiced that morning.

It's interesting that the PenAir ramp employee who fueled the Cessna that morning noted that he had trouble removing the fuel tank filler caps on account of the hard ice and in fact had been forced to use a tool of some sort in order to get the caps off. One presumes that by "tool" the employee meant a screwdriver.

After fueling, the ramp supervisor sprayed deicing fluid on the airplane. This supervisor observed that there was about one-eighth of an inch of snow or frost on the wings before they were deiced. He did not physically touch the wing surfaces after the deicing, since they then appeared clear of snow and frost. It is very likely that this was the point at which fate stepped in to arrange the tragic events that followed.

Though there was at least one ladder at Dillingham's PenAir operations, no one claimed to have observed the pilot climb up to inspect the upper wing surfaces subsequent to the deicing process. Another PenAir check pilot, however, said that the wings *looked* clear from where he stood, which was a short distance behind the Caravan, a place from which the upper wing surfaces could certainly be seen. Surprisingly, no one seems to have checked to verify that the fuel caps were secure, either. This last fact baffles me as much as anything. A missing fuel cap can be expected to quickly produce a disaster of one sort or another. At best, only the very shortest of flights without a fuel cap will be possible. Without a fuel cap, flight time on the capless tank can usually be measured in minutes, rather than hours. The Venturi effect of fast-moving air across the filler necks will quickly siphon away into the atmosphere just about all the tank's contents. And I *have* been there!

Eyewitnesses seem to recall differently the series of events that followed the Caravan's apparently normal takeoff. What we do know is that the aircraft, at an altitude of around one thousand feet above ground level (AGL), appeared to pitch up suddenly and then perform a half-roll to begin a rapid nose-down descent. It struck the frozen earth, nose first, at about a forty-five-degree angle.

Believe it or not, one passenger actually survived the impact. This passenger was quickly transported to hospital facilities in Anchorage but died the following day.

It is interesting to note that PenAir's FAA-approved deicing and anti-icing program required that the deicing mixture should contain 50 percent glycol, which has a freeze point of minus thirty-three degrees Fahrenheit, or about minus twenty-eight degrees Celsius. Tests of the deicing mixture used on the

Cessna Caravan that morning showed its glycol percentage at slightly below 30 percent. This translates into a mixture with a freeze point of about five degrees Fahrenheit, or around minus fifteen degrees Celsius. From a practical standpoint, this might seem sufficient for the temperatures at Dillingham that morning. The industry standard is for the freeze point of deicing fluid to be at least eighteen degrees Fahrenheit below the outside temperature, which in this case would have meant a free air temperature of about seven degrees Fahrenheit. The free air temperature at Dillingham that morning, remember, was standing firm at around twenty-five degrees Fahrenheit.

It is perhaps more interesting still to note that PenAir's deicing/anti-icing program *didn't require that the critical surfaces of their aircraft be inspected after deicing had taken place*. On the other hand, it was shown that the upper wing surfaces of the Cessna 208 were visible from a position behind the airplane and from a distance of only fifteen to eighteen feet. Further, we know that the wings were at least casually observed by another pilot that morning.

The trouble with all this is that clear ice is terribly hard to see. The best indicator of its presence is the human hand, and it appears that no one made that sort of aircraft inspection that morning. Moreover, clear ice is heavy ice. Not only does it destroy an airplane wing's flying characteristics, it can add a phenomenal amount of weight to an airplane. Pilots know that this combination leads, without question, to higher stall speeds. In some cases, wing stalls can occur even before on-board stall warning systems are triggered to operate.

In all fairness, the pilot probably *thought* that the wings were clear of ice. In reality, they very likely were not. Ten lives were lost that morning on account of this senseless oversight. Familiarity had bred contempt in this pilot for the last time. Ever.

***

I understand that it's easy for a pilot to substitute logbooks full of experience for common sense and long-ago training. I've been as guilty as the next guy, from time to time. I had a rule, though: no passengers aboard when I was stretching the envelope. Never. Some pilots don't bother with this distinction, as was the case in this next fatal flight.

The little Cessna 150, FAA registration number N2932J, was being flown by a private pilot with no instrument rating. Still, he was banging around up there in some pretty sobering IMC weather. In the old days, this was known as IFR weather, the IFR standing for instrument flight rules. Nowadays, it's known as IMC, for instrument meteorological conditions. Probably makes more sense, but I still find it hard to get used to. But, back to this very disarming story . . .

The flight had originated with a takeoff from Smith Mountain Lake Airport at Monetna, Virginia. The pilot had gone wheels-up there at about 11:15 that morning, September 4, 2006. He and his passenger were headed for Florence Regional Airport at Florence, South Carolina. At 11:20, just a few minutes later, the pilot contacted Roanoke Approach Control and asked for VFR flight following services. The flight was radar identified at about two nautical miles south of the Smith Mountain Lake Airport. Ten minutes later, the pilot issued the sort of radio transmission that none of us ever wants to hear.

"Roanoke Approach, Cessna 32-Juliet requesting radar vectors."

When the controller asked about the request, the pilot replied, "We're kinda lost in some fog up here."

Asked to state his present heading, the pilot said, "I can't tell you. I think we're upside down." Are you kiddin' me? Upside down?

The controller instructed the pilot to turn right, and eighteen seconds later—or the equivalent of about fifty-five degrees of turn—advised the pilot to stop the turn.

During that time, the aircraft appeared to have completed a *left* turn and was at that time heading generally northeast. Radar had the plane's altitude at between 4,500 and 4,700 feet AGL.

Ten seconds later, or about twelve minutes after his first radio contact, the pilot's voice was again heard. This time, however, he didn't seem as confident as he had during his first transmission.

"We can't see, we can't see, we can't see!" And, a few seconds later, the pilot made one more transmission, garbled beyond recognition. Those were the last sounds the world ever heard from him.

The controller stayed with him, advising him to stay calm and to neither climb nor descend, and that he was now painting an altitude of 4,500 feet.

It would appear that the little Cessna was indeed inverted, since the pilot no doubt earlier input control pressures to initiate a *right* turn, in response to the controller's request, but the aircraft had actually turned *left*. I think this is very likely substantiated since the next thing anyone knew for sure of the little Cessna, it was seen to be falling to the earth—*in pieces!*

A bystander saw most of the airplane hurtle to the ground in the nearby woods, but the wings just sort of "floated" down behind it, according to this witness.

Another witness said she heard the airplane, saying it sounded as though it were landing in her backyard. She saw the wings "twirling in the air" as they descended, clearly not still attached to the airplane.

The pilot had earned his private pilot license only two and a half months before he elected to take off into weather he knew he couldn't handle even before he had started the engine that morning.

***

I've written elsewhere about Alaska's Shellabarger and Mystic Passes. Neither is particularly friendly. At times, neither are Anderson, Gunsight, Peters, Simpson, Rainy, or Ptarmigan Passes. Lots of Alaska's pilots will fly through none of them, and I sure don't blame them for that. Once a pilot enters any of those passes, he's in it up to his ears. And not a one of them is a "maybe" pass. They're simply "go" or "no-go," no two ways about it.

On September 15, 2006, a float-mounted De Havilland DHC-2 Beaver had departed Galena, Alaska, headed for Lake Hood, the world's largest seaplane base. Aboard the Beaver were the pilot and a single passenger. The pilot was rated as a private pilot, something Alaska doesn't see very often. That is, most Beaver pilots seem to have at least a commercial pilot rating. That isn't to say that this private pilot wasn't qualified to fly the Beaver. He very likely was. It's his common sense and judgment that come into question here, as far as I'm concerned.

The flight had departed Galena at around two o'clock in the afternoon. By a quarter past four that same afternoon, one of the pilot's friends contacted the Anchorage Alaska Rescue Coordination Center (ARCC), successor to the former 10th Air Sea Rescue bunch, reporting the aircraft as overdue. He further stated that the missing Beaver had been a flight of two and that the two aircraft had become separated near the narrowest part of Mystic Pass while trying to push their way through. The second airplane had aborted the flight and landed at Farewell Lake to wait for better weather, but the first had flown on ahead—and had just quietly vanished.

The pilot of the trailing aircraft later reported that the two airplanes were in constant radio contact and that the lead ship was about one-half mile ahead of his own. He stated that as the weather deteriorated to the point that three-dimensional vision had been reduced to two dimensions, he had been able to turn around and scoot back out to Farewell Lake.

Before turning around, the trailing pilot had informed the lead flier that he was uncomfortable with the lack of visibility and was aborting the flight. The lead pilot's final radio response reportedly was, in part, "Turn around if you can . . . I'm not able to."

The chilling last words of a pilot whose options were then down to one: try to push on through, all the while hoping and praying for something good to happen. It sometimes doesn't. . .

The Alaska Wing of the Civil Air Patrol (CAP) and members of the Alaska Air National Guard began a concentrated search the next day, and the wreckage was spotted at the 3,700-foot level in Mystic Pass at about three o'clock that afternoon. Rescue personnel from the Alaska Air National Guard's 210th Rescue Squadron reported no survivors when they reached the site at around five o'clock that same day. Impact appears to have been at near cruise speeds for the Beaver, and a postimpact fire had consumed what little was left.

One has to think how easy it would have been for this pilot to have simply elected to turn around before the pass choked his route down to a single, unacceptable option. He could have enjoyed a good dinner and a warm night's sleep. As it turned out, tomorrow never came for him. Nor for his innocent passenger, either.

***

Kodiak Island is perhaps best known for the famous—some would say "infamous"—Alaska brown bear. Certainly the largest of bears aren't known to live on the island, but a helluva lot of the species do live there. What many don't know is that the U.S. Coast Guard has a large facility there. In my estimation, it is Kodiak's Coast Guard helicopter rescue pilots who are perhaps the greatest fliers in the entire world. They have been known to perform successful air rescue missions above seas running to eighty feet and in winds clocked above one hundred miles an hour. It is these men who operate under the proviso, "We have to go out—we don't have to come back!" Now, that's damned scary!

Kodiak can also claim bragging rights to some pretty lousy weather, from time to time. An example of that, which included heavy rain showers and relatively high winds, might be the afternoon of September 21, 2006.

It was that day, at about a quarter past one in the afternoon, that a De Havilland Beaver, registered as N5154G, was returning from a narrow fishing stream about seventy-five miles north of Kodiak to its headquarters lodge at Igiugig, Alaska. That's where DES, LLC, the plane's registered owner, owned and operated Alaska Sportsman's Lodge. The lodge is located at the lower end of Lake Iliamna, where the cold, clear lake waters pour out to form the Kvichak River, a truly great rainbow trout and salmon fishing stream.

Aboard the Beaver that day were the pilot, licensed as an airline transport pilot (ATP), and five passengers. This isn't really a crowd aboard the husky, load-carrying Beaver, though it is at least a moderate load. The Beaver can certainly handle that sort of load, though, and then some. At any rate, the Beaver and its load of fishing clients had departed Iguigig earlier in the day and had flown to Kodiak Island and the narrow fishing stream northwest of the town itself.

The fishing was pretty good, but steadily deteriorating weather finally caused the pilot to announce that they would have to fold up, climb aboard, and light out for home before the weather got much worse. By that time, rain showers had reached the point that they could only be called "heavy," and the east wind had picked up to somewhere between twenty and thirty knots. That's pretty crappy weather in anyone's book.

Once the party was all aboard the heavy floatplane, the pilot took care of his preflight chores and then started his takeoff run to the east, or directly into the wind. The story of subsequent events seems to vary a bit, depending upon which of the survivors one is speaking with.

The pilot's version is that he took off into the prevailing east wind, and after having established a positive rate of climb, he turned left to avoid obstacles. He further stated that after another half-mile or so of this crosswind flight, he turned from the north toward the west, which would have placed him at that point in low-level flight with an appreciable tail wind. It was at this point that "a strong downdraft from the mountain behind the plane threw the plane to the ground."

Surviving passengers seem to agree, though, that the pilot rolled into a pretty steep left turn almost immediately after having left the water and about 150 feet above the earth. It was at this point, they agree, that the Beaver began to shudder and buffet. Almost immediately it then descended, nose low, into the swampy ground.

All survived except the passenger who had occupied the right seat next to the main cabin door. At impact, this soul was partially ejected and was pinned beneath the fuselage as the stricken plane rolled over on its right side. About three feet of cold swamp water then poured into the cabin, and the partially ejected passenger remained pinned beneath it. Whether this passenger received fatal injuries on account of his being partially ejected or was drowned after being pinned under water is sort of academic at this point.

The surviving passengers all seem to agree on one point: the airplane was placed into a "steep turn" shortly after takeoff. I'm confused by that, since every student pilot learns, very early on, that only the shallowest of turns are made in really windy conditions. And every student practices these turns until he or she can perform them in a manner that is completely satisfactory to the instructor.

The Beaver's pilot appears to have logged a total of 4,770 hours as pilot in command. His logbooks also show that he had flown the left seat in the Beaver for at least 1,860 hours. Succinctly put, the pilot was certainly qualified to fly the Beaver.

When Alaska State Troopers later asked the pilot to provide a urine sample for a routine test, he stated that he was unable at that time to do so. Over the next five hours, he consumed a large quantity of water but said he was still unable to provide the sample. He finally did, however, submit to having a blood sample drawn. The trooper sent this sample directly to the Federal Aviation Administration Civil Aero Medical Institute (CAMI), located in Oklahoma City, Oklahoma.

On November 22, CAMI's toxicological examination of that sample revealed the presence of tetrahydrocannabinol carboxylic acid (marijuana). Heavy rains, high winds, and pot? I believe that I shouldn't have any comment about that.

Chapter 23

Malibu Meridian at Sitka

THERE ARE OLD PILOTS AND THERE ARE BOLD PILOTS, BUT THERE ARE NO OLD, BOLD PILOTS.

The Piper Malibu Meridian is pretty much at the top of America's contemporary single-engine airplanes. At nearly a million bucks a copy, I guess it's pretty safe to say it's just about out of the financial reach of most of us, too. Maybe you can afford to buy one, but I sure can't. Of course, it wouldn't work for me anyway, what with its low wing and little bitty wheels.

The Meridian is a major aircraft program from New Piper Aircraft, Inc. It was first rolled out of Piper's Vero Beach, Florida, plant on August 13, 1998. The first customer delivery was made on November 7, 2000. The most obvious difference between the Meridian and its predecessor, the original Malibu, is the increase in power over the original powerplant. The Meridian originally boasted a 350-horsepower engine out front. The new Malibu pokes an engine out there that develops more than 550 horsepower! But, more than that, the turboprop model has a thermodynamic rating of 1209 hp. The streamlined plane can operate at max power way up there at thirty thousand feet and streak along at a staggering 262 knots. In short, it's one whopping piece of airplane!

It was just such an aircraft, owned by Hendrickson Aviation of Lewes, Delaware, that departed New Jersey early in the first week of August 2007. It had made stops in Scottsdale, Arizona; North Las Vegas, Nevada; and once again in Victoria, British Columbia. When the Meridian departed Victoria, it carried Robert Hendrickson (forty-five), presumed to be the pilot, along with his fiancée, Linda Kundair (thirty-four), and Robert's two daughters, Julianne (fourteen) and her younger sister, Emily (only nine). The flight was scheduled to land in Sitka, Alaska. And it did.

The weather at Sitka that afternoon—it was just after lunch time when the folks at Sitka heard the Meridian approach the city of about nine thousand permanent residents—was a little on the low side, actually. That's probably why the witnesses heard the airplane quite a while before they actually saw it. And take it from me, Alaskans are keenly aware of aircraft sounds and speeds. They live with low-flying airplanes all day, every day.

According to those who were later interviewed, the Meridian apparently circled overhead several times before finally emerging—at an unusually high speed—from the bottom of the low-lying clouds. Some witnesses said that the airplane's engine sounded pretty loud, though others appear to have made no such observation. There are those who noted that the aircraft appeared to circle the town several times before finally appearing, leading to the speculation that it was attempting to land at the Sitka airport.

Whatever the pilot was trying to do in those last few moments, it is clear that the Meridian clipped a tree at about the same time that it appeared out of the ragged cloud deck. This great airplane, which had begun its trip far away back in New Jersey several days before, was just about to complete its last flight.

Immediately after plunging through the bottom of the low clouds, it struck the home of Tess Heyburn at 285 Kogwanton/Back Street. Tess was, at that time, sitting in a nearby restaurant enjoying a midday break and a snack. The plane instantly burst into flames, and there was some genuine concern that nearby propane tanks might get hot enough to explode. This meant that it was too dangerous to approach the plane to render any possible assistance, though it was clear that there would be no survivors.

The crash site was only one block from crowds of cruise ship tourists who, up until that moment, had been enjoying the many pleasant fruits of the vacation trips that steam through the Inside Passage from the Lower 48 states to various points in Alaska. In fact, there were 2,800 of them from two different cruise ships docked in Sitka at the time. It's certainly true that the pilot wasn't familiar with Alaska in general, nor with Sitka in particular. One has to think he was carrying the proper approach plates for the published Sitka instrument approaches and departures, though. An unfamiliar pilot might get a little nervous about the nearby mountains, but if he stayed where he belonged, there was certainly nothing that should unnerve him to the point of losing his cool over it. My own guess is that he might have put off studying Sitka's Approach Plates until the Meridian was already in the air for this leg of the trip.

If that's true, one could presume that flying the high-performance Meridian on solid instruments doesn't provide the very best environment for studying Sitka's plates. That's conjecture, though, and is certainly a bit unfair. I only know for sure that the Meridian crashed at Sitka, killing all aboard.

It might be unfair, too, for me to admit that I have a feeling of trepidation when I read of stateside pilots who are flying to Alaska to do a little sightseeing. Or "flightseeing," as we call it. I have no doubt that many of these stateside pilots are much better fliers than I'll probably ever be. On the other hand, this is my country, and it took several decades of flying for me to learn as much about it as I have. And *one* of the things I have learned is to avoid "shortcuts." It boggles my mind to observe, year after year, that visiting pilots tend to take lightly the advice of Alaska's mossback pilots. And, further, that so many think it clever to take an apparent "shortcut." If there ever is a shortcut between here and there, the old Alaska pilot would long ago have told them about it. And if he didn't tell them of a shortcut, well there just ain't one! Period.

The author with his Cessna Floatplane, N756VR, on Shadow Lake in the Talkeetna Mountains.
Photo by John Erskine, Anchorage, Alaska

Chapter 24

The Long Last Flight

In the ongoing war between high-speed aluminum and fixed earth, the earth has yet to lose a battle.

Maybe the worst flight I have ever made started on the last day of August, back in 1981. My wife's birthday, by the way. I had flown to a small—and very, *very* private—airstrip near our home in West Palm Beach. In another week or so, I would fly this beautiful airplane to St. Cloud, Minnesota, where I would sell it. At a stunning loss, by the way. It would break my heart.

I had flown to the small field—well, certainly not very small by Alaska bush standards—to visit friends. After a smooth landing on the steel-mat-and-grass strip, I had almost come to a halt in my landing roll in order to turn left off the runway and toward the clubhouse when things went south for me. The right main gear collapsed, leaving me with something of a conundrum. I was right smack dab in the middle of a very private, but very busy, little airstrip.

I shut down all the systems and starved the big engine into silence. And then I climbed down to see what I could find out about this new and disturbing situation. I always carried a small automobile jack in the right float locker of this ship. With amphibious gear that was both electrical and hydraulic, one could never tell when jacking the plane up to lower the gear would be necessary. This was one of those times, for sure.

After raising the right float free off the ground by about six inches, I climbed aboard again, and—using the small panel-mounted plunger designed for this purpose—I mechanically lowered the right gear until I felt it lock into place again. With the master switch in the "On" position, I now got all four of the gear down-and-locked green lights. Then I climbed down to stick my nose into the forward float compartment.

I could tell almost immediately that the hydraulic system had blown an O-ring seal, since red hydraulic fluid covered the bottom of this float compartment. Ah, well, a trip to Palm Beach International Airport (PBIA) and one of its shops there should provide the necessary fix.

After taxiing to the clubhouse, I tied the airplane down and called my wife, asking her to meet me with the car at the airfield. Soon, we were both back home, where I headed to my airplane library upstairs to dig up the Wipline maintenance and parts manuals for the big amphibious gear. It didn't take long to find the part number and size of the ruptured O-ring, and I was soon off to PBIA for the part. And for some more hydraulic fluid, of course.

The next day, I put the landing gear back into operation and cycled the gear several times to make sure it was all right. It was, and I turned my attention to the trip to St. Cloud, Minnesota, where I would sell off one of my very best friends, the turbocharged Cessna N9975Z.

On September 13, I climbed aboard, settled in, preflighted the marvelous six-place airplane, and cranked 'er up for the long flight to St. Cloud. All told, the flight would mean fifteen hours and eighteen minutes in the air. All the air wouldn't be smooth, either, I was certain. Neither would it be dry and sunny. It would be something of an adventure, though it wouldn't really be a pleasant trip. I didn't want to get rid of this ship, but finances at that time made it necessary. And we always do the necessary things first, right?

The weather was almost severe clear when I filed VFR to Jacksonville, Florida, requesting flight following for traffic separation and any new en route developments that might crop up. Two hours and six minutes later, I was letting down into Jacksonville to top the tanks and check the weather ahead. The last time I had landed in Jacksonville, it was in the dark of night after Peggy and I had plowed through the front of Hurricane Kate, back on November 21, 1985. A very slow and very, *very* bumpy flight, I can tell you that!

From Jacksonville, I filed three-plus-thirty to Dublin, Georgia, which is located between Savannah and Macon. This leg actually took exactly three hours and thirty minutes. After topping the ninety-gallon tanks, I checked the weather again. This time, the flight path ahead didn't look so good.

A line of severe thunderstorms along a swath about forty-five degrees to my flight path was approaching from the west. I calculated the speed of the approaching squall line, estimated my arrival time at Wood County Airport in Williamstown, West Virginia, just across the Ohio River from Marietta, Ohio, where I had grown up, and figured I would be landing there just barely ahead of the storm's arrival. It wasn't a sure thing, and I knew it would be close, but I thought I might have a pretty good chance of beating the storm. It was reported to be a dandy, and while I have every respect for thunderstorms, I nevertheless piled in, strapped down, and lit out for the hills of West Virginia and Ohio.

This leg was going to be in the neighborhood of 450 miles, and I figured it would take me about three and a half hours to complete. Actually, it took three hours and thirty-six minutes. The last fifteen minutes of it saw me in the most ferocious turbulence, lightning, and heavy rain that I've ever encountered. And that's over a span of more than thirty flying years.

I had long ago air-filed an instrument flight plan, leaving the VFR environment behind. By the time I had passed abeam of Parkersburg, West Virginia, my personal pot was boiling over, and I was up to my chin in some really lousy weather. All I could see of the outside environment was the flat-black disc of the spinning propeller.

The addition of floats to a light aircraft tends to smooth out the wrinkles in the air, usually making for a rather smooth flight. Moderate turbulence can seem almost mild. All the bumps seem softer and seem to hit the airplane much more slowly. Not so during this flight!

I called ahead and requested the ILS Approach to Runway 5 at Wood County and almost immediately received the clearance. I had all I could do to physically hold the turbocharged Cessna on course. I was beginning to feel that I was lucky just to keep the big bucking, pitching, and rolling thing in the air at all. Lightning seemed to come from everywhere at once, and though I was still wearing my brown-lens sunglasses, this lightning was dazzlingly bright! Only the thundering rain and severe turbulence were giving me a break from the tuck-in-your-tail-and-run lightning! It was the worst few moments of my entire flying life. Maybe only Wiplinger's heavy amphibious floats saved the airplane's structure that day, who knows? I can tell you that the turbulence was more than severe. So, stay away from thunderstorms!

I broke out of the heavy clouds just inside the outer marker, reported the environment in sight, and canceled the IFR flight plan. Then I turned forty-five degrees to the left and almost dove down to the Ohio River nearby. This is where I had intended to land in the first place. What pilot with floats would pass up a nice river in favor of a danged old blacktop runway?

After landing and tying down behind the LaFayette Hotel in Marietta, a place familiar to me from my childhood of four decades earlier, I booked into the hotel. I didn't mention that I had an airplane tied up at their back door, since that would only have led to confusion in the small town of Marietta. Then I telephoned a longtime friend and former classmate, Dave Finch. I would meet Dave and his wife, Shirley, for drinks and dinner later in the evening.

The next morning saw the frequently serious Ohio River fog right down on the deck, so I took the opportunity to walk the familiar old streets of my hometown. Marietta had been founded in 1787, which really did make it pretty old, I guess. Certainly it had a grand history, with which I won't bore you here.

After walking the streets, and stopping to stare for a while at my former childhood home, I realized that the fog wasn't going to burn off anytime soon. I checked out of the hotel, preflighted the heavy amphibian, and then cast off to set us adrift in the Ohio River current.

I energized the electrical system, hit the boost pump and pushed the throttle in to get the proper fuel flow, retarded the throttle again, and then hit the starter. The big engine turned over right away, and I dropped the oversized water rudders for directional control. I taxied slowly upstream in the thick Ohio River fog using the directional gyrocompass until it suddenly got very dark inside the cockpit. I knew that I had just taxied under the Ohio River Bridge that connected Marietta with Williamstown, West Virginia. That gave me all the positional reference I needed. By that time, the engine had warmed sufficiently, so I ran the magneto checks and then set the trim wheels and flaps.

That done, I verified that the fuel selector was on the fuller tank and that the cowl flaps were open for the takeoff. And then I just turned in a tight little circle on the water, picked up the proper compass heading again on the directional gyro, raised the water rudders, and advanced the throttle to takeoff power.

There wouldn't be any boat traffic on the foggy Ohio River in that particular place, so I wasn't worried about running over anyone. When the big ship lifted free of the river, I began the climbing right turn that would avoid Harmar Hill, which I knew was almost dead ahead, and then picked up the heading that would take me past Columbus and Cincinnati, with my next intended landing to be at Ft. Wayne, Indiana. This leg would be slightly over two hours.

I had left the river fog behind me and was flying in clear and sunny weather by the time I had passed Zanesville, Ohio, en route to Columbus. Zanesville, by the way, was the former home of the famous Zane Gray, prolific writer of old Western cowboy tales.

I had by now left the smooth air behind, too, and was then banging along in turbulence that was again somewhere between moderate and severe. While the heavy floats hanging below me tended to soften the bumps, I was still encountering thermals that would reach two thousand feet per minute in both updrafts and downdrafts. Sometimes I just don't like sunny weather! I had filed a VFR of two-thousand-feet, holding a transponder setting of 1200. Columbus Approach Control reminded me of my filed altitude and my failure to maintain it.

"Cessna Seven Five Zulu, you're now at 2,500 feet. Didn't you file for 2,000?"

"Yessir, I did. But when I started, I was flying a Cessna Stationair amphibian. Right now I'm riding along in an Otis Elevator!" I responded.

"Roger that. Keep a handle on it," came the reply.

The landing at Ft. Wayne went without incident, and after topping the tanks once again, I lifted off with a heading that would take me to Rochester, Minnesota, southeast of Minneapolis–St. Paul. A line of terrible weather required me to alter my course for this leg, and it took three hours and twenty minutes before I could slide the heavy amphibian onto the runway at Rochester. It was here that I found a motel for the night, I guess in an attempt to put off the final leg into St. Cloud, Minnesota, where I would say goodbye to a very faithful airplane. N9975Z had served me well in Alaska and Canada, had performed almost perfectly in the Bahama Islands, throughout the Gulf of Mexico, and in the countries of Mexico and Belize. I was trying to delay my last flight in this wonderful airplane. We had become good friends over the past years. It was going to be very hard to part company with her.

The following morning, September 15, found fog down to the ground in Rochester. I needed an early start, though, so I took a taxi to the airport right away. The ship had been fueled, and I took my time with the preflight. Soon, that chore was behind me, and I had no choice but to file my flight plan and move on.

Because of the ground-hugging stratus, I had to file an instrument flight plan, and I knew I was destined for a zero-zero takeoff. When I walked through the terminal to the tiedown area, I could see the commercial airline passengers lined up against the huge windows, wondering when the fog would lift enough for them to board their outgoing flights. Since I was flying under Part 91 of the Federal Aviation Regulations, I didn't need the higher weather minimums that were required of the airliners, so this down-on-the-deck fog wouldn't delay my own takeoff. I could legally fly in weather much worse than could the airlines. Strange, but true. When I walked from the terminal toward the parked amphibian, I'm sure those passengers wondered what the hell I thought I was doing. When I taxied away, I was sure of it.

The winds were calm, and ground control helped me find the runway. When my clearance was delivered, I repeated it for departure control and was then cleared for the departure.

Locked on the runway heading and with the faint centerline stripe only vaguely visible beneath the propeller spinner, I slowly advanced the throttle to takeoff power and then pulled the throttle back so as not to overspool the turbocharger on this first-of-the-day takeoff. A zero-zero instrument takeoff means that the pilot dare not allow the nose of the airplane to drift even one degree on either side of the runway heading. It takes a helluva lot of faith in both the airplane's instruments and in your own ability to follow them unerringly. If you tend to sometimes be a white-knuckle pilot, don't even *think* about it!

With no heavy load behind me, and taking off from a hard, dry runway (of which this airplane had seen precious few!), it was only moments before I rotated the nose and lifted off the unseen world. With instructions for a climbing right turn from the field, I found myself clear of clouds and flying in bright sunlight as I climbed up through nine hundred feet.

I locked onto the correct heading, cancelled my IFR flight plan, and proceeded VFR over-the-top to St. Cloud. It was bright, sunny, and smooth all the way that morning. I sort of longed for the usual Alaska weather of rain, clouds, and turbulence. It seemed somehow wrong to be flying this ship in such good weather for its swan song flight.

The turbocharged Cessna Stationair, mounted on Wipline 3730 amphibious floats, had carried me safely—and damned comfortably—from the Arctic Circle to Central America and the Bahama Islands. It had carried me in temperatures above one hundred degrees and below minus fifty degrees Fahrenheit. It had followed my instructions and inputs through rain, hail, snow, airframe icing, no end of mountain turbulence, and scorching sun. It had never balked, and it had never failed. Each time I asked the great ship to do something the performance charts said it couldn't do, or certainly *shouldn't* do, the faithful ship had done it for me anyway. Until this last flight, I'm not sure I ever began a flying day with less than an overload in this Cessna. The very first flight I had made in her was with more than six hundred pounds above the allowable limit. I admit that this isn't the way flying is supposed to be done. It's just the way we did it in Alaska. And N9975Z did it with the very best of them.

She hauled my sorry carcass out of one mess after another, it sometimes seemed. And she did it with dignity, charm, and a sophisticated ease that made anything seem possible. I came to think that it was. She was so capable that she sometimes seemed completely disdainful of negative factors. She could even be aggressive, when that was required.

I guess I'll forever miss her.

Chapter 25

The Future of Bush Flying

If all you can see is the earth going round and round, and all you can hear are loud noises from the passenger compartment behind, then all is not as it should be.

Though Alaska has been in a development mode for several decades, you can still stand in downtown Anchorage and just about see it all. Ten years ago, you could stand across the street from the stunning Captain Cook Hotel, look across Knik Arm toward Point McKenzie—not more than three miles away—and know that, if you wanted to walk there, it would take you months and months and months. Recently, a new road has been constructed, changing all that. That road will take you fifty miles north, whip you around 180 degrees, and then lead you fifty miles south to arrive at Point McKenzie. Still only about three miles from where you started. Anchorage's residents call that real progress, and it is. It's in the neighborhood of only three hours by automobile to Point McKenzie now, and it has opened a whole lot of land to local development—mostly for the construction of personal homes and cabins.

On the other hand, you can look to the south, across Turnagain Arm, and see Point Possession. The waters between Anchorage and Point Possession—and indeed between Anchorage and Point McKenzie—enjoy twice-daily tides that can reach thirty-nine feet at certain times of the year.

A floatplane leaving Lake Hood can pass Point McKenzie in less than two minutes! From Merrill Field, the trip is a little longer, since the pilot must avoid flying over the city itself. That trip could take as much as three or four minutes. And from Anchorage International Airport, less than one minute, if the pilot departs the north runway!

It's still not possible to drive to the state capital at Juneau, which is accessible only by water or air. And, to make a point, a bank robber would be easily foiled in any attempt to reach the Lower 48 states by road, since a single Alaska State Trooper can close the whole state if he just parks his cruiser along Alaska's only land access, the Alaska Highway, at someplace like Northway or Tok Junction. He could wile away his time by enjoying some good pie and coffee at Northway or one of those big, good, full meals at Tok Junction. With one additional trooper at each of the two main airports, Anchorage and Fairbanks, a total of three troopers can close the whole state, an area two and a half times the size of Texas!

The oil and gas development at Prudhoe Bay was accomplished through the expenditure of thousands and thousands of flying hours. It was only later that the infamous "Haul Road" was constructed.

Dillingham, accessible only by sea or by air, had only seven miles of streets and roads the last time I was there. Still, there were eight cars and trucks driving around in that community. The town is a hub of activity during the salmon and herring seasons, but no road or railroad access is available. Nor will such access be available in the near future, I'm quite sure. By the near future, I mean maybe as much as fifty, seventy-five, or one hundred years!

Why? Well, first of all, some pretty serious mountain ranges lie between any "civilization" and Dillingham. And while modern technology can certainly punch a road through them, what for? Private enterprise can't afford it, and the government has no reason to expend either the effort or the zillions of dollars such an undertaking would require.

King Salmon, Pilot Point, Port Heiden, all down there on the Alaska Peninsula? Forget it! Dutch Harbor or Cold Bay? Never happen!

Alaska is really, *really* spread out over huge distances. Flying from coast to coast in Alaska is a longer trip than flying coast to coast in the continental United States, I'll tell you. And between any "here" and "there" will be found almost nothing but a terribly reluctant and ruggedly imposing wilderness. As Robert W. Service once penned, "It's a land where the mountains are nameless, and the rivers all run God knows where."

Towns and villages boast only the most meager of populations. Such population centers as Seward, for example, could brag of only 1,600 residents the last time I looked. One-half of the entire population of the huge state of Alaska resides in Anchorage. At this time, all these more remote communities, and many more like them, are satisfactorily served by the several good, safe, and dependable airlines that are headquartered within the state.

Alaska has precious little power. The major cities have enough power generation to serve the static population with almost nothing to spare. During the late afternoon of almost any midwinter day, at a time when the "big city" of Anchorage is enjoying real darkness, residents are used to "brownouts," when all the lights, including street lights, dim and almost go out. This is when the heaviest electrical demand is made, of course, what with heating, cooking, and lighting demands as people prepare for dinner. Coal-generated electrical power is transmitted across maybe sixty miles or more of truly open wilderness and then has to pass beneath silty Knik Arm, with its dramatic tides, to reach the city. I will give it this, though: Anchorage is almost never stricken with power outages, even during winds in excess of one hundred knots. Florida sure as hell can't make that claim, I'll tell you.

But, unlike the Lower 48, there are no provisions in Alaska for transmitting power from one grid to another. Florida can share power with California, for example. Just doesn't happen in Alaska. That's the primary reason that Alaska has little or no industry of any consequence. Without sufficient power, no manufacturing is in the cards for Alaska in the near future, either. Given that, what is to encourage expansion and high population growth for Alaska? Not much!

A few years ago, the government asked that all businesses turn down their heating systems and turn off their office lights during the nighttime in an effort to conserve electricity. Though Alaskans did that, it was really just an exercise in futility for them, since power conservation does no practical good up there. They cannot share their saved power with anyone else, and it's generated and available to Alaskans, whether it's used or not.

There was at one time—back in the late seventies—a big plan being laid for a series of two dams in the Upper Susitna Valley, near Devil Canyon. The upstream dam would have been an earthen dam designed to allow the Susitna River's high silt content to settle out in order to protect the generating equipment that was to be placed at the second dam, a few miles downstream. This second dam would have spanned Devil Canyon itself, a very narrow and very deep canyon that would have required only a short-span concrete dam. The Sierra Club and other protectors of the environment shot those plans down in a hurry. Too bad for Alaska that most of the noise came from the other states. The vast majority of these complainers, by the way, had never seen the area to begin with and hadn't the foggiest notion what they were talking about. Still . . .

Their claim was that it would spoil the spawning grounds of several species of Pacific salmon. The truth is, however, that no salmon has *ever* navigated the impossible Class VI waters of Devil Canyon in the first place. Every last one of them has stopped at Portage Creek, at the lower end of the canyon itself. Still, the project was abandoned, even after much seismic work had already been done. That dam would have provided power along the entire rail belt, a distance of more than five hundred miles. And that, in turn, would have opened the possibility for both manufacturing and land development. But without it, that sort of progress virtually came to a dead halt. As far as I know, Anchorage still relies upon coal-fired generators for most of its power. I have to wonder how long that nonrenewable fuel source can hold out.

Without local industry to support it, construction of roads to remote towns and cities will have a long wait. While there is admittedly some airport expansion, which puts a few of Alaska's more remote towns along the route for local scheduled airlines, there will be no roads and no railroad spurs to these remote spots for decades. More likely, for generations to come. Such development takes huge quantities of money, and Alaska's small population—still something not much more than a half million people—doesn't present a sufficient tax base for the funds needed for the huge undertaking required. It just isn't in the cards. From where I sit, the Alaska bush pilot will be in business for a long, long while yet.

The majority of Alaska's bush pilots provide their unique services to smaller villages, hunting and fishing lodges, individual homesteaders, and the odd miner or trapper living way out there somewhere in the bush. These folks don't want outsiders in their neck of the woods anyway, and any attempt to punch roads through to them would meet with particularly stiff resistance. In many cases, this would very likely mean resistance up to and including live fire from folks who truly do know how to shoot straight and who are not very timid about protecting what they clearly see as their own little domains. And I can't help but agree with them.

Perhaps the biggest problem the bush pilot will soon face, in my estimation, will be the matter of equipment. Those few active outback pilots do not really make much of a demand upon airplane manufacturers, in the overall scheme of things. Witness the hiatus in the manufacture of Piper's Super Cub and of Cessna's 180 and 185 lines. Not just every general aviation pilot in the contiguous forty-eight states is enamored of flying taildraggers, those almost ancient light aircraft designs having their nose wheels stuck back there under the tails. There are many places in Alaska, though, to which its bush pilots ply their critical trade and at which an airplane with its tiny nose wheel cannot safely operate. With a minimum number of taildragging aircraft rolling off a manufacturer's assembly line, the costs simply have to increase. This means that the cost of owning and operating such a plane must rise, too. In fact, it already has. Sort of a cat-and-rat farm, if you will.

Those who live in the remote outback districts of this huge state don't, as a rule, enjoy much in the way of steady incomes. There will be a definite limit to the dollars they can set aside for the costs of buying and flying in their needed supplies and necessaries.

The pilots, of course, have an answer to most of this. The airframe and powerplant mechanic. That cadre of hard-working and experienced airplane mechanics who keep the older models safely flying. That profession, too, though, is staring at some shortcomings. One example is the shortage of those who are skilled in working with fabric-covered airplanes. This includes the Super Cub and a half dozen "improvement model airplanes" based upon the earlier and certainly proven Super Cub design. It's just not everyone who can re-cover a fabric-covered airplane. And there are a whole lot of those airplanes still flying the backcountry today. That includes many that are already fifty or even sixty years old. And are still flying. Goodness! They're still flying Curtiss Robins, Stinson Reliants, Gull Wing Stinsons, Stearmans, and Wacos up there!

It was a 1929 Curtiss Robin that extracted me from the bush site of my first—and only, thank goodness—aircraft loss back in 1958, when the Curtiss was already around thirty years old. It was the Curtiss Robin, too, that set an endurance record of 653 hours and 34 minutes, back in 1935. And it was a $900 Curtiss Robin that took Douglas "Wrong Way Corrigan" from New York to Dublin, Ireland, back in July of 1938.

Corrigan, whose pilot license was suspended for five days on account of this untoward flight, received a bigger ticker tape parade in New York City upon his return than did Charles "Slim" Lindbergh after his earlier nonstop, trans-Atlantic flight in the *Spirit of St. Louis*.

My last Super Cub was a 125-horsepower 1952 agricultural model. I had that airplane completely rebuilt, including the installation of a new 150-horsepower engine, and for all practical purposes it was a brand-new aircraft. It had been flying for more than thirty-two years by the time I traded it in 1984. There may be a limit, though, to the number of times a single airplane and its structure can undergo a complete rebuild. And it's not cheap to accomplish, either.

It can be said that newer airplanes will soon come along to step in where the Pipers and Cessnas may have finally left a vacuum. Maybe. But technology seems these days to be leaning toward small, private jets. Two- and four-place, high-speed, low-wing models are even now available to the relatively few pilots who can afford them.

The problem is that a jet engine doesn't develop its rated power with any appreciable speed. Bush flying requires instant response to power applications, whether during approaches and landings or during takeoffs. I just don't foresee a small jet that will operate from three or four hundred feet of soggy tundra, and a Super Cub certainly will do that. Moreover, a jet wouldn't be happy working off sandy beaches or gravel bars: their engines tend to eat sand and swallow small gravel, and they will do neither with very pleasing results.

More than that, most of these new hot rods have low wings, a definite no-no in a lot of Alaska's outback. High wings keep those airfoils above the weeds, tundra, and small willows. Low wings take a severe beating, even when successfully used in such airplanes as the Piper Cherokee line.

You have to understand, too, that many of the bush pilot's clients are accessible only by water, which means a float-equipped airplane, or perhaps an amphibian. I know of no jet that can be float-mounted. The first time one of those jet engines ingested water thrown up by the floats' spray rails would be just about the last breath it ever took.

From the emails I still receive from readers of *Flying the Alaska Wild*, I believe there are sufficient numbers of young pilots who are bold enough to step into the hip boots of retiring bush pilots. The problem with that is that not all of the newcomers will find flying jobs in cities like Anchorage or Fairbanks. Some will have to gravitate to outlying communities or sportsmen's lodges. And not all pilots who have young families will want to live in those environments. Especially during the cold and dark winter months when temperatures can drop to sixty or even seventy degrees below zero. Some can, of course, but many simply cannot. Besides, the lodges mostly close for business during the winter months, and most of the other flying demand seems to die down, too.

The impediments to future bush pilots are many, and by degree are not trivial. Still, perhaps there will be enough pilots to fill the need. The problem will eventually boil down to the equipment. Very likely, a few more new Alaska aircraft builders will spring up to respond to this need. Several already have, but their manufacturing will have to undergo large expansions in order to answer the call, I would think. And perhaps they, too, will come to the scratch line in time.

It is sufficient to guess that the bush pilot will continue to be with us for decades to come. But the profession will become harder and harder, rather than easier. And the backcountry will always remain unforgiving.

There seems always to be a sufficient number of commercial pilots standing in line for summer flying jobs with several of Alaska's fixed base operators, wilderness lodges, and air charter services to fill the seasonal needs for the large number of tourists who travel to Alaska in the warmer months. Hunters, fishermen, camera bugs, hikers, and just plain vacationers. But this, too, has its downside.

Many of these pilots, most of whom are younger men, are, for the most part, lacking in real outback flying experience. That's not to say that they are not qualified for the licenses they hold. It does say, however, that many are unfamiliar with the huge Alaska wilderness over which they must fly. It takes a powerful lot of flying to become familiar with all the mountain passes, rivers, and lakes that present themselves to the outback pilot. Almost without limit are the tales of visitors who climb into a bush plane headed for some remote lake, river, or lodge, only to find that their pilot isn't familiar with the routes and has succeeded in getting himself lost. The client still must pay for the flying time, even though the pilot is at fault in such cases.

Perhaps it will just be the raw and unforgiving wilderness challenges that prove to be the lure that will keep the bush pilots flying in the years ahead. Certainly it won't be the huge monetary rewards!